THE POLITICS OF
BUREAUCRACY

COMPARATIVE STUDIES OF POLITICAL LIFE

SERIES EDITOR: MARTIN O. HEISLER

THE POLITICS OF BUREAUCRACY
A Comparative Perspective

B. Guy Peters
University of Delaware

Longman
New York and London

FOR SHERYN

THE POLITICS OF BUREAUCRACY:
A Comparative Perspective

Longman Inc., New York
Associated companies, branches, and representatives
throughout the world.

Developmental Editor: Edward Artinian
Editorial and Design Supervisor: Nicole Benevento
Design: Pencils Portfolio, Inc.
Manufacturing and Production Supervisor: Donald W. Strauss
Composition: Fuller Typesetting of Lancaster
Printing and Binding: The Maple Press Company

Library of Congress Cataloging in Publication Data

Peters, B Guy
      The politics of bureaucracy.

      (Comparative studies of political life)
      Includes bibliographical references and index.
      1. Public administration.   2. Bureaucracy.
3. Comparative government.   I. Title.
JF1501.P43   350   77–24584
ISBN 0-582-28001-X
ISBN 0-582-28000-1 pbk

Manufactured in the United States of America

ACKNOWLEDGMENTS

There are a number of people to whom I owe a debt of gratitude for assistance and encouragement in this project. First among these is my teacher and friend, John Collins, who first stimulated my interest in the politics of administration. This was to have been a joint venture, but that unfortunately was not to be. In any case, if there is anything of merit in this book, it owes a great deal to his help and encouragement.

In addition other faculty members at Michigan State University and a number of colleagues at Emory University, the University of Delaware, and the University of Strathclyde have all provided useful suggestions and criticisms. These include among others Keith Baker, Phillip Morgan, Christopher Dunleavy, and Brian Hogwood. The United States–United Kingdom Educational Commission and Richard Rose provided an extremely stimulating year in Scotland.

A special debt of gratitude also goes to Martin Heisler who, as editor and friend, was very supportive of this project and provided many useful suggestions. In addition Sam Postbrief and Warren Ilchman as reviewers helped to substantially improve the manuscript. Finally, Edward Artinian has been a patient and understanding editor.

And last but certainly not least a very special thanks goes to my wife, Sheryn, who had to put up with many evenings with me absent, and with typing the final version of the manuscript.

Of course, despite all the help, there are probably errors, and for those I have only myself to thank.

CONTENTS

1 INTRODUCTION

Government is increasingly a part of the daily life of the average citizen. Once relegated to the rather basic tasks of delivering the mail, policing the streets, and defending the nation in time of war, the modern government provides a host of goods and services too large to enumerate here. Moreover, governments now regulate a large number of actions that once were left to the whim of the individual and the free market. Many activities that were virtually unknown thirty years ago are today the subjects of extensive governmental regulation, if not outright governmental ownership and management. Television, atomic energy, and large-scale commercial aviation are only three of a number of possible examples.

This increase in the government's workload does not mean that government is more popular. If anything, the public image of government is more negative—especially in industrial countries—than it has ever been. Almost paradoxically, the more government does, the more negatively it is regarded. The sheer bulk of government and the associated taxation, combined with the publicity given its failures, have reduced the faith and possibly even the allegiance of citizens.

Before dealing with the failures and problems of government, let us first ask a more basic question: how does government manage this expanded workload? The best answer is that it is largely done by public administration, by those mythical bureaucrats generally blamed for most of government's failures. Administration and bureaucracy are apparently almost as old as government, but they have become an increasingly significant part of the governing apparatus of virtually every country in the world.[1] Despite this apparent importance, we probably have less systematic information concerning this aspect of government than any other. Elections, political parties, legislatures, and the courts—the glamorous parts of the political system—have been analyzed extensively. These parts of government provide a vast quantity of readily usable data for the researcher. Administration, on

1

the other hand, is far from glamorous, has been generally considered nonpolitical in most Western societies, and has appeared to defy adequate quantification and theoretical analysis.[2]

If our knowledge of administration in any one country is inadequate, then our lack of knowledge of the comparative dimensions of administration is appalling. We still apparently lack the conceptual and operational basis to make sense of scattered and disparate findings.[3] This volume seeks to provide one relatively well integrated viewpoint that will be useful in the development of a more adequate knowledge of comparative public administration.

THE IDEA OF PUBLIC ADMINISTRATION

At the outset, we should present some idea of what we mean by public administration, and particularly we should try to differentiate the commonly employed "bureaucracy" from the more general term of public administration. Most public administrative agencies are indeed bureaucratic, but the correspondence is by no means complete even in those agencies that do display bureaucratic tendencies.

In the main, we shall be thinking of public administration as:

1. In functional terms the process of rule-application. That is to say, the process through which general social rules are converted into specific decisions for individual cases.[4]
2. The structure of government whose primary function is to perform the functions outlined in (1).

The functions outlined are somewhat restricted. We are not much concerned with rule making or with deciding who the rule makers should be. At the same time, we are interested in the political and economic functions of administrative agencies even when they are not performing strictly administrative functions. For example, the political interactions of administrative bodies in the budgetary process are only tangentially related to the direct application of rules, but they are directly related to the survival and maintenance of the organizations that perform the administrative functions.[5] Thus the study and analysis of public administration have come to mean a good deal more than what is strictly considered "administrative." Further, either through necessity or abdication by other candidates, administrative agencies have become major rule-making bodies in both developed and underdeveloped societies.[6] They also perform a number of functions that might ordinarily be considered judicial. We shall be concerned with these, but mainly to the degree to which they elucidate the structural and functional aspects of the principal administrative roles.

Here we should further differentiate traditional bureaucratic notions concerning administration from this somewhat looser definition.[7] The meaning of bureaucracy has been broadened in popular parlance, and in some scholarly writing, to include any administrative organization. We shall use bureaucracy somewhat more strictly, to mean

> organizations with a pyramidal structure of authority, which utilize the enforcement of universal and impersonal rules to maintain that structure of authority, and which emphasize the non-discretionary aspects of administration.[8]

Several scholars have gone to some length in detailing the various components of Weber's conception of the ideal-type of bureaucracy, showing that the components are not of necessity interrelated in actual organizations.[9] We shall largely accept these analyses and therefore adopt a conception of bureaucracy much less stringent than either Weber's or the commentators on Weber.[10] At the same time, however, not every public organization should be considered bureaucratic. Some have adopted very loose organizational structures and have tended to relax the use of hierarchical authority. Nevertheless, the vast majority of public organizations have a number of bureaucratic elements that tend to structure their performance. In dealing with the social and cultural aspects of administration, we shall point out how certain value systems and systems of social organization contribute to the effectiveness of the hierarchical forms of authority, while others tend to cause a reexamination of that type of management.

COMPARATIVE ADMINISTRATION AND COMPARATIVE POLITICS

The first major point to be made here is that we conceive of public administration as an integral part of the political system. Therefore, the analysis of public administration is amenable to much the same type of analysis as comparative politics in general. As such, we shall be examining Easton's "authoritative allocation of values" but be looking at it as performed in bureaucratic structures rather than in legislative, executive, or judicial structures.[11] The process of decision making is perhaps better hidden in bureaucracies, but decisions are made there. We shall be seeking to ferret out the manner in which they are made and the effects of those decisions on the political and social systems.

This equating of public administration with politics may appear quite logically to some readers as common sense. Still, a long intellectual and governmental tradition in most Western societies attempts to separate the two functions. For example, Woodrow Wilson wrote:

> Administration lies outside the proper sphere of politics. Administrative questions are not political questions. Although politics sets the tasks for administration, it should not be suffered to manipulate its offices. The field of administration is a field of business. It is removed from the hurry and strife of politics; it at most points stands apart even from the debatable ground of constitutional study. It is a part of political life only as the methods of the counting-house are a part of the life of society; only as machinery is part of the manufactured product. But it is, at the same time, raised very far above the full level of mere technical detail by the fact that through its greater principles it is directly connected with the lasting maxims of political wisdom, the permanent truths of political progress.[12]

As long as it was assumed that administration was a simple nondiscretionary action, it was useless to think of administration in the more general context of the political system.

Fortunately for our understanding of the political process, the artificial dichotomy between politics and administration has been eroded in both the scholarly and the popular literature. As the workload of government increased, more and more decisions were of necessity made outside the "political" branches of government and in the administrative branches. It became increasingly apparent that government decisions were not all made in the hallowed halls of the legislature; rather, a good number of them were made in the less impressive but more numerous halls of administrative office buildings.[13] Likewise, in the scholarly literature, the increasing use of systems theory and structural functional analysis tended to emphasize the interconnectedness of politics and administration rather than their separation. Unfortunately, this literature also tended to make assumptions concerning the dominance of inputs over governmental characteristics in the determination of policy.[14]

Still, there needs to be a further integration of the study of comparative public administration and the general study of comparative politics. Both the emphasis on systems analysis and the emphasis on the politics of development in comparative politics make it imperative that we develop a more complete understanding of administration.[15] In the first place, the systems approach by its very nature emphasizes that all parts of the political system are interrelated. We cannot afford to exclude the administration of laws made, perhaps, in legislatures from this general examination of how the political system governs. Moreover, the basic idea that structures are multifunctional while functions are multistructural draws attention to the fact that many decisions are made in bureaucratic structures of government. A careful analysis will reveal, furthermore, that more decisions are made in the bureaucracy than are made elsewhere. Also, decisions made in the "political" structures tend to be structured, if not determined, by information gathered and disseminated by administrative agencies.[16]

The study of political development has also helped emphasize the need for a more complete knowledge of administration and the political effects of administration. Although the West was somewhat dubious that its rather peculiar governmental forms, such as parliamentary democracy, could be transplanted successfully to the underdeveloped world, they were much more confident of their ability to transplant bureaucratic administrative practices.[17] After all, administration was the simple (?) application of the rules to each case, not involving the judgment of the official in the slightest. The results of this attempted transplantation were less than encouraging and brought to light the need to understand the particular social, cultural, and economic patterns that allowed bureaucracy to operate. It was obvious that these factors greatly affected the manner in which administration was carried on, but the exact relationships were less than clear. It was found that not only did development have to be administered, but administration also had to be developed.[18] Thus our discussion can draw from the problems of development in the newer nations of the world. This will be both in terms of the particular administrative problems involved in attempting to bring about social change in a traditional society and also about the cultural and social effects on administration.

The third manner in which the study of administration can gain from the study of comparative politics generally is in the study of the "end of ideology" in the developed countries of Europe and North

America.[19] In the late 1950s the idea that ideologies were dead and that politics had become largely a matter of compromise and negotiation became popular. Events of the 1960s largely dispelled the more extreme interpretations of the thesis, but good empirical evidence still shows that ideologies and ideological styles of decision making in government have declined.[20] As government becomes less ideological, the role of administration is also likely to be enhanced. Administration tends to be the source and the repository of most of the information available to government. As the political system begins to become more concerned with what will work, as opposed to what is consistent with a certain ideological position, the more important that information becomes. The study of changes in ideological perspectives among the population can and should be coupled with some concern over the administrative implications of these changes. For example, is a growing acceptance of the political role of administration a cause or an effect of the "end of ideology"? And just what are likely to be the long-range effects of the politicalization of administration when associated with the depoliticalization of much of the rest of the government?[21] Finally, much of the literature on the deideologized, "postindustrial" state has emphasized the role of the individual and of a growing individualism in the future affairs of government in the developed country.[22] While this may be regarded as just as much an ideology as the more collective ideologies of the past, it presents a new set of challenges to administrators. They must not only provide a reasonably uniform set of services to individuals fitting certain social and economic categories (e.g., the poor, young, sick, taxpayers), but they must also be willing to adjust the rigidity of the bureaucratic rules and procedures to meet more individual cases. The effects of these demands on the structures and processes of administration can be an interesting and useful linkage between the study of comparative politics in developed societies and the study of comparative public administration.

We believe that the artificial separation once developed between politics and public administration has been eroded to some degree but has not entirely disappeared. We hope that the analysis of public administration and its comparative role in the formation of public policy will further help to erode that barrier. We shall be looking at administration as an integral part of the decision-making structure of government. Further, we shall be looking at the linkage developed between administration and those structures that we would normally think of as "political." We expect that this inquiry will show us that much of what appears to be administrative is actually political, with rather explicit political reasons for the making of administrative decisions.

ADMINISTRATION AS A SYSTEM

In line with this conception of public administration as an integral part of the political process is the conception of public administration in a systemic framework. Systems theory, or the systems approach, has become the closest thing to a paradigm that the social sciences have developed.[23] Although this approach is certainly open to a number of valid criticisms, it constitutes a useful manner of conceptualizing and organizing information about a process or an institution.[24] Moreover, by conceptualizing components of larger systems as systems themselves, e.g., the administrative system within the political system, we may be able to specify further the manner in which the total system functions.

Our conception of the public administrative aspects of government in a systemic framework is hardly innovative, but we hope to be able to work through the relationships among the concepts somewhat more thoroughly than has been done in the past.[25] In particular, we shall be concentrating on the relationship between environment and administration, the political relationships between administration and other political institutions, and the outputs of administration both to the remainder of the political system and to individuals who are the clients of administration.

A diagram of this systemic conception of administration is presented in figure 1.1. Several rather important things should be noted from this diagram. First, administration is regarded as a very important connection (*interface* in the usual language of systems analysis) between the society and the political system in general. Thus, not only do a good number of special demands for administrative services come to administrative structures for resolution, but also a good number of more general demands are initiated through administrative structures. Various pressure groups will make demands directly upon the administrators for the resolution of certain difficulties that in turn become the subject of more general political controversy. Likewise, the relationships between the administrative structures and individuals will lead to the formulation of general rules concerning governmental procedure and practice. One obvious example is the relationship between the police and the accused in criminal proceedings, which has been the subject of extensive legal and legislative action.

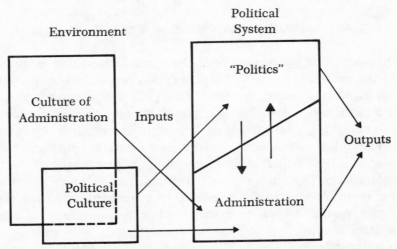

FIGURE 1.1 Public Administration in a Systems Perspective

Further, the accretion of a number of individual cases across time may lead the administrative bodies to attempt on their own to have a change made either legislatively, judicially, or by executive ordinance. As noted, an increasing proportion of new legislation in modern societies is emanating from administrative bodies. Some of this is because the "political" officers of government seek help in the drafting and justification of legislation, but another part of it is the result of the initiative of the administrative bodies. Having the expertise and the access to information, administrative offices can be valuable sources for new legislation in their particular areas of competence.

A second factor to note in figure 1.1 is the conception of the environment of administration. We conceive of this as being divided between one set of general constraints in the society at large, and another set of constraints that are due to this being *public* administration, not just administration. For example, when discussing the cultural constraints involved in administration we can speak of a certain set of general cultural values concerning administration. These include such things as the attitude toward interpersonal authority relationships, the general patterns of organization and management in the society, and the use of ascriptive versus achievement criteria for advancement within the stratification system. These types of values would be important for studying any type of formal organization, public or private. We shall also discuss a set of cultural and normative constraints that pertain only to *public* organizations. These include such things as the cultural norms concerning the acceptable scope of regulation and coercion by government, the conceptions of political and social equality, and patterns of political trust. These are largely irrelevant for private organizations but of crucial importance for public organizations.

A similar dual set of constraints exists from the social and economic environment. The fact that some nations have more economic and human resources than others can serve as an inhibiting factor for the development of both public and private organizations. It may be simply impossible for some societies to support any large-scale organizations of the type known in the "developed" world. At the same time, particular types of restraints may apply only to public organizations. If the taxation system is antiquated and inadequate, it may actually assist the development of private organizations, but it will certainly inhibit the growth of large-scale public organizations. We should not look at this only negatively. Just as the environment may put extra constraints on public organizations, it may also give them extra advantages, not the least of which is the ability to use either implied or actual coercion in order to gain needed resources. In either case, public administration operates in a dual environment because of its dual nature as a public body as well as a formal bureaucratic organization.

The third feature worthy of note in our graphic portrayal of the administrative system is the rather complex set of linkages developed with other political organizations in the government and the society. We have been arguing throughout this discussion that administration is a political function, and we hope that our discussion makes something of that linkage clear. We shall be arguing that administration is intimately involved with a variety of political actors and political acts. Moreover, these linkages are by no means unidirectional (the legislature "commanding" the administration to do something or not to do other things) but rather involve rather complex processes of bargaining and negotiation.[26] Thus we must conceive of the administrative structures of government as political not only because they make decisions affecting the "authoritative allocation of values." They are also political because the manner in which they go about affecting this allocation is "political" in most formal and common-sense meanings of the term. This is most obvious when agencies bargain for their growth and survival in the budgetary process, but it is also true in the day-to-

day decision making of organizations.[27] Public administration operates in a political arena and therefore must adopt political methods.
There is no room for Weber's bureaucratic robots in such an administrative conception. There is considerably more room for Downs',
Tullock's, and Williamson's rational actors seeking to maximize the
desired outcomes for the agency.[28]

In summary, we have a working conception of public administration
in a systemic framework. Although not novel in itself, the rather
strict attention to the comparative aspects of this systemic framework
constitutes something of advancement. Moreover, the use of this
framework provides us with a useful way of categorizing and discussing the major linkages involved in the administrative process. It
stresses the interrelationships that we believe are a crucial aspect of
administration and the more general political system.

ADMINISTRATION AND PUBLIC POLICY

A third major point is the relationship of public administration and
public policy. As noted, the intellectual history of the study of public
administration has tended to cloud this relationship severely. This has
been unfortunate because administration, like all aspects of government, is principally interesting and important because of what it
does for and to the people in the society. Government and politics can
be good clean (?) fun to observe and discuss, but ultimately we must
ask: so what? In this case, there is a ready answer to that potentially
devastating question. It is simply that the political system is involved
in making public policies that in turn advantage some people in the
society and disadvantage others.[29] Laws against murderers disadvantage people who enjoy violence and advantage people who want to
get home safely every day. Nevertheless, all laws are meaningless unless they are enforced, and this is where public administration comes
into the picture. The administrators—including the police—are
charged with putting the laws of the legislature or the ordinances of
an executive into effect.

In fact, one could reasonably argue that the manner in which the
laws are enforced gives them their true meaning. If laws are administered differentially for various segments of the society (e.g., ethnic
minorities, youths, lower-class individuals), then the application of
the law has given a different meaning to the piece of legislation than
was intended by its drafters.[30] This conversion by decision making on
the part of administrators of the legislative output of the nation to

actual operational rules is of interest when we examine administration. A good number of these operational rules will be written down as administrative ordinances and the like, but a number will also be simple traditional or habitual actions on the part of administrators. Thus the standard operating procedure of many police departments is to stop and question only certain types of individuals. This may be justified from their perspective by a certain probability of the occurrence of crimes by certain social groups, but it points out that the probability of being questioned by the authorities is not determined by laws concerning vagrancy, etc., but rather by the actions of individual administrators. This is certainly not true only of the police as administrative or enforcement personnel. Blau along with Lasswell and Almond have shown that it is also very likely to occur in social services where the receptionist and similar screening personnel determine who has the possibility of receiving aid.[31] Those people whom the "screeners" reject initially have no possibility of receiving aid, while those who get by this initial step have some relatively good possibility of receiving aid.

This brings us to another point we shall be making in discussing the role of the administrative apparatus in public policy. Often, the lowest echelons of the administration have the most to do with the outputs of administration. Thus it is often the cop on the beat, as opposed to the commissioners, chiefs of police, or other upper-level personnel, who determines what the operational policy is going to be. Or the receptionist at Blau's public-employment office makes many crucial decisions for the agency, as did the field agents in Blau's analysis of FBI agents. As a general rule, it is necessary to discuss and to understand the operations of the lowest level of administration in order fully to understand administration. Unfortunately, most of the literature on administration deals only with the upper echelon. This is understandable; according to the organizations' charts, these are the positions that exercise formal authority and control and formally make policy.[32] We believe that much of this emphasis is misplaced. The upper levels are certainly important to understand, but not to the exclusion of the soldiers in the field who daily confront the problems about which the upper officials make policy.

Following from this point is the assumption that the outputs of the political system will have two basic components. The first is an objective component, that is, what the political system actually provides the citizen in the way of gratifications and deprivations.[33] Thus we can examine the net sum of gains and losses that the individual receives from being a member or subject of a certain political system. There is also a subjective component. This concerns the style in which those gratifications and deprivations are delivered to the individual. Individual citizens will value services according to the amount of services that they receive and also according to the way in which they are treated in the delivery of those services. This has become most apparent recently in the delivery of social-welfare services in a number of societies. Despite the fact that most developed countries have rather extensive systems of social welfare, many clients and critics of these systems argue that although economic citizenship is granted to the individual, the demeaning manner in which the services are administered tends to deny the client his "social citizenship." [34] Basically, the receipt of social assistance sets the individual apart as a special type of person who is somehow less worthy than his peers. This holdover from the economic liberalism and social Darwinism of the nineteenth century has been most apparent in the United States but has also been manifested in a number of other societies with developed systems of social welfare.

Administration is extremely important in the development of the objective component of public policy. It is, however, most crucial in defining the subjective component of public policy. The administration, and especially the lower levels of that administration, actually deals with the clients. Thus, for most clients, what government is and does may be personified in the actions of lower-echelon administrators. Their style in handling clients, the courtesy and consideration they show, as well as their competence, can do a great deal toward defining the role and the respect of the political system in the society. Thus we believe that a great deal of emphasis must be placed on this admittedly vague matter of administration. Some limited interviewing studies of clients of public agencies have shown that there are substantial differences in the evaluations of services and the evaluation of the style of administrative personnel.[35] At present this evidence is unsystematic, but there is good reason to believe that this is a directly measurable phenomenon. In any case, we shall be concerned with the interpersonal side of administration in the delivery of services to clients. Just as we pointed out previously with respect to inputs from the society to the political system, the administration also serves as the major point of contact on the output side of government, and as such it is important in actually delivering services and in the interpersonal aspect of service delivery.

In summary, we find that administration and policy, instead of being discrete phenomena, are actually interrelated. In both an objective and a subjective manner the nature of the administrative system can influence the policy outputs of the political system. Administration does make policy, although these policies are not always written and promulgated in the same manner as the rules made by legislatures and executives. Moreover, the operational rules developed by administrators can be more telling for the actual outcomes for individuals than are the formally promulgated rules. Administrators are in addition the major personal contact between citizens and their government. As such they define not only a large percentage of the objective outcomes of the policy process. While the objective component of administration and policy is certainly important for the individual, the subjective component cannot be ignored and may actually be more important in developing attitudes of loyalty, commitment, and affection among the citizens for their government.

AN OVERVIEW

The remainder of this book is divided into seven chapters. Chapter 2 provides an overview of the increasing involvement of government in the lives of its citizens and demonstrates the increasing involvement of the administrative system in providing these services. This is supplemented with a discussion of the general sources of administrative power in dealing with the society and with the remainder of the political system. The third chapter deals explicitly with the cultural foundations of administration. The study of comparative administration obviously involves these differences, and we attempt to catalog some of the probable effects. As well as needing economic and cultural support, the public bureaucracy also needs personnel. The fourth chapter discusses the recruitment of personnel, especially in the light of models of representative bureaucracy. The fifth chapter reviews some classical questions of administrative organization and attempts to relate those questions to the policy choices of bureaucracy. The sixth and seventh chapters are a discussion of the interaction of political and administrative forces in the formulation of policy. The final chapter deals with the problem of administrative responsibility and the need to control the seemingly uncontrollable bureaucratic structures that characterize modern public administration. Various schemes have been tried and proposed for accomplishing this difficult task; we attempt to evaluate their effectiveness as well as their cultural transferability. At this point in time the conclusions we can reach are limited concerning the nature of administration across cultures. The evidence is limited. We mainly aspire to ask the right questions, with the possibility that some of the answers will be able to stand a more rigorous examination.

NOTES

1. S. N. Eisenstadt, *The Political Systems of Empires* (New York: Free Press, 1963).
2. See Nicholas Henry, *Public Administration and Public Affairs* (Englewood Cliffs, N.J.: Prentice-Hall, 1975), pp. 3–32.
3. Some notable attempts in that direction have been Ferrell Heady, *Public Administration: A Comparative Perspective* (Englewood Cliffs, N.J.: Prentice-Hall, 1966); Michel Crozier, *The Bureaucratic Phenomenon* (Chicago: University of Chicago Press, 1964); Mattei Dogan, *The Mandarins of Western Europe* (New York: Halsted, 1975).
4. See Gabriel A. Almond and G. Bingham Powell, *Comparative Politics: A Developmental Approach* (Boston: Little, Brown, 1966).
5. See chapter 6.
6. See chapter 2.
7. See Anthony Downs, *Inside Bureaucracy* (Boston: Little, Brown, 1976), pp. 24–31.
8. Max Weber, "Bureaucracy," in *From Max Weber,* ed. H. H. Gerth and C. Wright Mills (New York: Oxford University Press, 1946).
9. Stanley H. Udy, Jr., "Bureaucratic Elements in Organizations," *American Sociological Review* 23 (1958): 415–18; Helen Constas, "Max Weber's Two Conceptions of Bureaucracy," *American Journal of Sociology* 63 (1958): 400–409; Richard H. Hall, "The Concept of Bureaucracy: An Empirical Assessment," *American Journal of Sociology* 69 (1963): 32–40.
10. Thus we will be looking at any and all formal organizations involved in the implementation of public policy and the delivery of public service. See also Alfred Diamant, "The Bureaucratic Model," in *Papers in Comparative Public Administration,* ed. Ferrell Heady and Sybil L. Stokes (Ann Arbor: Institute of Public Administration, 1962), pp. 79–86.
11. David Easton, *The Political System* (New York: Knopf, 1956).
12. Woodrow Wilson, "The Study of Administration," *Political Science Quarterly* 2 (June 1887): 209–10.
13. Evidence on this point is given in Richard Rose, *The Problem of Party Government* (London: Macmillan, 1974).
14. See Martin O. Heisler with Robert B. Kvavik, "Patterns of European Politics: The 'European Polity' Model," in *Politics in Europe,* ed. Martin Heisler (New York: David McKay, 1974), pp. 27–89.
15. See Roy C. Macridis, "Comparative Politics and the Study of Government: The Search for Focus," *Comparative Politics* 1, no. 1 (October 1968): 79–90.
16. See chapter 7.
17. Joseph LaPalombara, "Bureaucracy and Political Development: Notes, Queries, and Dilemmas," in *Bureaucracy and Political Development,* ed. Joseph LaPalombara (Princeton: Princeton University Press, 1963), pp. 34–61.

18. Fred Riggs, "Bureaucrats and Political Development: A Paradoxical View," in LaPalombara, *Bureaucracy and Political Development.*

19. For a discussion of this literature, see Mostafa Rejai, *Decline of Ideology?* (Chicago and New York: Aldine/Atherton, 1971).

20. The literature of "postindustrial" society and politics is perhaps the best evidence of this trend. See Daniel Bell, *The Coming of Post-Industrial Society* (New York: Basic Books, 1973); Bertram M. Gross, "Planning in an Era of Social Revolution," *Public Administration Review* 31, no. 3 (May/June 1971): 259–96; Samuel P. Huntington, "Post-Industrial Politics—How Benign Will It Be?," *Comparative Politics* 6, no. 2 (January 1974): 163–91.

21. Timothy M. Hennessey and B. Guy Peters, "The Paradoxes of Postindustrialism," *Policy Studies Journal* 3, no. 3 (1975): 233–39.

22. Ronald Inglehart, "The Nature of Value Change in Postindustrial Societies," *Politics and the Future of Industrial Society*, ed. Leon N. Lindberg (New York: David McKay, 1976), pp. 57–99.

23. David Easton, *A Systems Analysis of Political Life* (New York: John Wiley, 1965).

24. Heisler, *Politics in Europe.*

25. R. Schlesinger, *A Systems Analysis of Public Administration* (Ann Arbor: Institute of Public Administration, 1963).

26. See chapter 7.

27. In the United States, the operation of the "Iron Triangle" of agency, pressure group, and congressional committees is a classic example of this interaction in policy.

28. Downs, *Inside Bureaucracy;* Gordon Tullock, *The Politics of Bureaucracy* (Washington, D.C.: Public Affairs Press, 1965); Oliver Williamson, "A Rational Theory of the Budgetary Process," *Papers in Non-Market Decision-Making* 2 (1967): 71–90.

29. Or, as Lasswell put it, politics (and administration) is a question of who gets what, when, and how.

30. This discrepancy has spawned an increasing concern with the politics of implementation. See Jeffrey D. Pressman and Aaron Wildavsky, *Implementation* (Berkeley: University of California Press, 1973).

31. Peter M. Blau, "Orientation Toward Clients in a Public Welfare Agency," *Administrative Science Quarterly* 5 (1960): 341–61; Gabriel A. Almond and Harold D. Lasswell, "Aggressive Behavior by Clients toward Public Relief Administrators," *American Political Science Review* 28 (1934): 643–55.

32. Thompson bases an important analysis of organizations on the increasing separation of authority and expertise, with authority remaining at the peak of the organizational pyramid, and expertise—and experience in the field—at the bottom. See Victor A. Thompson, *Modern Organizations* (New York: Knopf, 1961).

33. Karl deSchweintz, "On Measuring Political Performance," *Comparative Political Studies* 2 (1970): 503–11.

34. T. H. Marshall, "Citizenship and Social Class," in *Class, Citizenship and Social Development* (New York: Doubleday, 1965), pp. 89–126.

35. Lewis C. Bowman, Eleanor C. Main, and B. Guy Peters, "Clients in the Atlanta Model Cities Program" (Report, Emory University, 1971).

2
THE GROWTH OF GOVERNMENT AND ADMINISTRATION

We began our introductory chapter with the statement that government is a pervasive fact of everyday life, and further that public administration is an especially pervasive part of government. This chapter documents that generalization—if indeed any documentation is required—but more importantly it attempts to provide an explanation for the growth of government and the public bureaucracy. This explanation has several facets, only one of which is an assumption that bureaucracies are inherently acquisitive and seek to spread their influence into everyday life largely for personal and organizational reasons.[1] Another facet must be the nature of the tasks performed by government: their complexity, technological content, and volume. Finally, the weaknesses of political institutions presumed to be in competition with the bureaucracy for decision-making powers are increasingly apparent; it might be argued that rather than forcing its own expansion, the bureaucracy may be filling a void left by alternative institutions. Administrators may not be motivated entirely by altruism and a sense of the public good—indeed bureaucracies can be fruitfully analyzed as competitive institutions seeking to maximize their own budgets—but it is doubtful if they could have been so successful if other institutions were capable of meeting the challenge of policy making in the contemporary political era.[2]

THE DEVELOPMENT OF GOVERNMENTAL POWER

There have been a number of attempts to provide explanations for the growth of government.[3] Some have argued that this growth is a function of socioeconomic development; as a society grows more complex, there is a greater demand for public services.[4] Other explanations have focused on ideological and political pressures for expanded state benefits [5] and on pressures within political institutions for increased budgets.[6] In a discussion of the development of public policies, Rose developed a classification of public policy that also helps explain state expansion. Policies are classified into three categories: defining, resource mobilization, and social.[7] The defining functions of government are those without which the state would cease to exist, e.g., tax collection, administration of justice, defense, and foreign affairs. The resource-mobilization functions are those aiding specific economic structures within the society, such as industry, agriculture, and transportation. Social functions are, rather obviously, those that bestow direct personal benefits on citizens as citizens. In general, the development of state functions in Western societies has been evolutionary, going from the defining functions to the resource-mobilization functions to the social functions. Further, governments have tended not to drop functions once adopted, and this ratchet effect has produced significantly increased state involvement in most phases of human life.

Going from this rather broad discussion of the development of the state to a somewhat closer examination of more recent changes, perhaps the best indicator of the extension of the public domain is the growth of the public budget. This is the most common measure of the growth of government for the man in the street, perhaps since his taxes pay for most of it, and it does have considerable validity as a measure of the degree to which government is likely to have an impact on an individual's life.[8] Table 2.1 shows the proportion of the gross national product employed in the public sector in a number of countries. These figures begin in 1950 and continue through the early 1970s, and they show expenditures both with and without transfer payments (e.g., social security benefits). Transfer payments and industrial subsidies are part of total expenditures but represent money put back into the economy for private individuals or organizations to make final consumption decisions. The figure for public expenditures without transfer payments represents final consumption decisions by the public sector (e.g., for building bombers or hospitals or roads). Also, there are very complex transfers among levels of government; thus, money raised at one level may be spent at another. Some may be spent on consumption goods by the recipient, so we must be careful in determining where the funds go and how they are spent.

Two things are evident in table 2.1. First, levels of expenditure both with and without transfer payments have tended to increase over the time period reported. These increases have not been dramatic, but they have been consistent. The second thing to note is the marked difference in the level of expenditure by the developed and the un-

TABLE 2.1

Percentage of Gross National Product Going to Public Expenditure

Country	1950 [a]	1960	1970	1974
United States				
With transfers	24.6	30.0	34.1	37.9
Without transfers	13.3	19.8	22.5	22.7
Sweden				
With transfers	31.2	42.3	57.4	63.8
Without transfers	—	25.0	26.4	28.9
United Kingdom				
With transfers	34.1	32.8	43.6	59.0
Without transfers	—	20.1	28.5	38.0
Colombia				
With transfers	7.0	11.9	13.0	13.2
Without transfers	—	9.2	8.7	11.1
India				
With transfers	5.8	19.6	21.6	22.4
Without transfers	—	16.8	18.3	18.8
Kenya [b]				
With transfers	—	13.1	20.0	23.0
Without transfers	—	—	15.6	19.2

SOURCES: United Nations, *Statistical Yearbook*, 1975, 1962, 1954; United States, Bureau of the Census, *Statistical Abstract of the United States*, 1975; Sweden, Statistiska Centralbyran, *Statistiska Årsbok för Sverige*, 1975.

[a] These available United Nations statistics did not disaggregate expenditures by transfer and consumption categories in 1950. The U.S. data are derived from the U.S. *Statistical Abstract*.

[b] Kenya did not exist as a nation-state in 1950 and therefore had no meaningful public expenditure figures.

derdeveloped nations. It is difficult to argue that any nation is representative of any broader group of nations, but by most standards the countries in table 2.1 represent examples of both developed and underdeveloped countries. The data show substantial differences in the proportion of GNP devoted to the public sector between these sets of nations. Even the United States, which most authors characterize as having an underdeveloped public sector for an advanced industrial nation, has proportionately three times as much of its total economic

TABLE 2.2

Proportion of Gross National Product Coming
from Primary Sector (Agriculture, Forestry, and Fishing)

Country	1950	1960	1970	1974
United States	8	4	3	4
Colombia	38	34	26	27
India	50	47	44	41
Kenya	—	38	31	26
Sweden	9	7	4	5
United Kingdom	5	4	2	3

SOURCES: United Nations, *Statistical Yearbook,* 1975, 1962, 1954.

resources devoted to public consumption as does India or Colombia.[9] The contrast with the fully developed "welfare states" of Western Europe is even more striking.

Relying on the public budget to compare the importance or impact of government in developed and underdeveloped societies is perhaps unfair. Almost by definition, the economies of underdeveloped countries are more reliant on agriculture and extractive industries than are those of developed countries (see table 2.2). This means that not only is there an immense gap in the total wealth available for social action both public and private, but also that the resources that exist are more difficult for the government to extract from the economy. There are simply fewer "free-floating resources" that the government is capable of obtaining from the economy through taxation, and then of redirecting through public expenditure.[10] Thus, although governments may use a higher percentage of GNP in the developed countries, as related to that portion of the economy that is "modern" and therefore capable of ready extraction, the rate of usage may be more comparable with those of the underdeveloped world. The data in table 2.3, although somewhat mixed, show that the underdeveloped countries do tend to make rather substantial public expenditures when one considers the difficulty of resource extraction. Thus, in the terminology of Almond and Powell, the extractive capabilities of underdeveloped countries tend to be weak; as a consequence, so are their distributive capabilities.[11]

A second measure of the growth of government is the proportion of the total work force employed in the public sector, both including and

TABLE 2.3

Public Expenditure as a Percentage of Readily
Extractable (Secondary and Tertiary Sectors) GNP

Country	1950	1960	1970	1974
United States	26.7	31.3	35.2	39.5
Colombia	11.3	18.0	17.6	18.1
India	11.6	37.0	38.6	38.0
Kenya	—	21.1	28.9	31.1
Sweden	34.3	45.5	60.0	67.2
United Kingdom	35.9	34.2	44.5	60.8

SOURCES: As in tables 2.1 and 2.2.

excluding the armed forces. The conclusions reached with regard to
the level of public expenditure are applicable to the data on the level
of employment in public service, although here the distinction between developed and underdeveloped nations is not so sharp. The
civil services of seemingly all countries included in this "sample" have
grown at rather rapid rates since the end of World War II. The data
reported here are for central government employment; the increase
might have been even more dramatic if employment at the subnational level had been included.[12] Rather obviously, what this means
is that government is more likely now to have an influence on the lives
of individuals within the society. In the case of public employment,
this influence comes from increased probabilities of contact with an
employee of government—a welfare worker, an agricultural agent,
an air-pollution inspector, or the all-too-familiar tax collector. This is
also associated with an increased probability that the individual will
not only have contact with a representative of government, but more
importantly, that the behavior of the individual will be influenced or
regulated by such a contact. Both the growth of the budget and the
growth of public employment also mean that government activities
may also be more important in regulating indirectly the behavior of
the remaining private sector. Governments come to compete with
corporations for prospective employees; they enter the same capital
markets to borrow money; and they may compete for the same raw
materials to build roads or airplanes. In so doing, the government may
have an influence on the nature of the marketplace that was not
evident when government largely fulfilled the role of night watchman.

This is perhaps most evident in employment and in capital, where the unionization of public employees and rather massive borrowing by public bodies have put them into quite favorable positions vis-à-vis private concerns in attracting scarce resources.[13]

Components of Governmental Growth

Let us now proceed to disaggregate some of the broad patterns of growth in the public sector. This will enable us to understand more fully what the sources for growth are, and it will also go some distance in providing explanations for that growth. By examining the major areas of policy growth, we can begin to understand the pressures that have been placed on modern governments as well as something of their response.

An obvious place to begin a discussion of governmental growth is national defense. The growth of defense expenditures has been most noticeable in those nations engaged in the cold war, but it has also been evident in the newer nations who have sought a large defense establishment as a symbol of national prestige and as a means of ensuring the survival of the current regime in the face of internal threats.[14] Further, a number of smaller "cold wars" exist between nations of the Third World, so there have been added incentives for the development of significant military forces and expenditures.

The data reported in table 2.4 show a slowdown in the growth of military expenditures in developed countries, if not in absolute terms, at least as a proportion of the total government budget devoted to defense. For most nations this proportion has actually declined. There is at the same time a continued growth of military expenditures in less-developed countries. The major growth of military expenditures in the developed countries came during the 1950s when the tensions of the cold war and the need to develop a new technological infrastructure for defense interacted to produce rapid increases in expenditure. Some lessening of tensions between East and West, as well as popular pressures, has helped to slow down these increases. The underdeveloped countries, on the other hand, have continued increasing their defense expenditures. Some of this increase may be explained by the need to create a military infrastructure, which developed countries already possess, but some of it may also be attributed to popular pressures for socioeconomic changes, many of which could not be realistically fulfilled in the short run.[15] Therefore, in order to preserve their ruling positions, governments have relied on

TABLE 2.4

Percentage of Public Spending Going to Defense,
Social Services, and Transportation

Country	1950	1960	1970	1974
United States				
Defense	26.3	29.9	23.8	17.3
Social services	31.6	36.2	43.5	50.4
Transportation	5.3	4.7	5.6	6.1
Colombia				
Defense	13.7	12.9	11.1	8.9
Social services	15.2	18.0	34.2	31.3
Transportation [a]	1.0	2.0	2.0	1.5
India				
Defense	12.3	9.1	12.6	11.2
Social services	7.1	8.7	12.0	10.8
Transportation [a]	3.0	4.0	5.0	5.0
Kenya				
Defense	—	3.5	5.0	6.5
Social services	—	22.0	18.8	32.6
Transportation [a]	—	0.5	1.5	2.5
Sweden				
Defense	17.6	17.9	13.5	11.4
Social services	38.9	45.0	58.8	61.0
Transportation	5.2	3.6	2.3	3.1
United Kingdom				
Defense	18.8	19.5	11.3	10.2
Social services	29.4	33.1	37.6	45.2
Transportation	3.1	4.2	4.4	4.3

SOURCES: As in table 2.1.

[a] Transportation expenditures for Colombia, Kenya, and India are rough
estimates based on secondary sources.

the military to keep order, and in a large number of cases the military
itself has seized power. Paradoxically, the need to provide order and
stability—or at least the desire for the regime to maintain itself—has
diverted resources away from the very programs that in the long run
might provide the desired economic benefits.

If the liberal's bugaboo of defense expenditures cannot be made the
total villain for the growth of public expenditures—at least in the in-

dustrialized countries—the conservative's nemesis of social expenditures does not emerge blameless. In the industrialized nations, significant increases in the proportion of the total budget are being allocated to social purposes. The increases are less dramatic but still apparent in the less-developed countries. Thus, one major impetus for the growth of the public sector has indeed been the growing demand for programs designed to redistribute income, or at least to provide a certain amount of economic security.[16] It is important to note, however, that the majority of these expenditures are transfer payments; the actual consumption of goods and services in social programs is generally less than in defense programs or resource-mobilization programs. These monies simply pass through the public sector from individual to individual, or from time period to time period, but are essentially returned to the private sector for consumption decisions.

Two other categories of expenditure should be discussed. The first is the category of resource-mobilization expenditures discussed by Rose. This is a broad category, so let us concentrate on expenditures for transportation as one indicator of the general trend in this body of expenditures.[17] The data for the underdeveloped countries in this regard are rather weak, but those for the developed countries show few substantial increases over time. In modern societies the demands and needs for improved transportation have been important, but this growth has not been as rapid as would be expected, and the lack of apparent growth is in part a function of the replacement of mass transportation by highways. In general, what is true of transportation is also true of other resource-mobilization activities, as the state continues to support industry and commerce, but only in about the same proportion as it has for the last several decades. There may be substantial shifts within the category but overall levels of support have remained relatively constant.

Perhaps the category of expenditure that has been growing fastest proportionately is expenditure for general government and administration. This represents the general overhead expenditures for the maintenance and operation of government, and perhaps more importantly, the maintenance of the public bureaucracy. Although these expenditures represent a small portion of the total expenditures of government—the exact percentage depends upon the method of calculation used by the respective governments—these expenditures represent one of the fastest-growing categories of public expenditure. This would appear to indicate something about the growth of political strength in the bureaucracy. The bureaucracy is apparently capable of getting adequate and increasing expenditures for its own maintenance without direct relationship to specific programs.

In summary, the growth of government in terms of public expenditure cannot be neatly attributed to any one cause or any one policy area. Rather, expenditures for all areas examined have been increasing in absolute amounts. But if we look at the relative rates of increase, we see that defense—as perhaps indicative of the defining functions of government as well as defense per se—has shown relatively less increase than have resource mobilization and social expenditures. This may be regarded in part as a stage of policy development among political systems, and in part as an indication of political pressures in modern societies. Further, the relative strength of the bureaucracy in politics and policy choice is in part indicated by the relatively rapid growth of general government expenditures. Let us now explore that political power more closely.

THE GROWTH OF ADMINISTRATION

Our findings concerning the origins of governmental growth indicate that the bureaucracy is an increasingly influential political institution. As Krislov put it:

> Bureaucracies are the late bloomers of modern political structure. They grew silently, inexorably in the underbrush—seldom noticed, little analyzed. Convenience and necessity, not ideology and legitimacy, are their life-blood; they are not loved and respected, but rather tolerated and depended on.[18]

This is indicated by the size of public employment as well as by expenditures for general government. On a less-quantified level, the growth of bureaucratic power has been documented, discussed, and damned in a number of places. On one side, bureaucracy is seen as a Leviathan seeking aggrandizement of its powers and operating as an integrated, monolithic institution.[19] On the other hand, bureaucracy is pictured as the court jester: a fumbling, bumbling set of uncoordinated agencies who at best muddle through and at worst make absolute fools of themselves. The examples of court-jester behavior have been gathered in several places and include contradictory programs, meaningless memos, and assorted bumbling.[20] So, as one federal agency (OSHA) requires backup sirens on construction equipment, another (EPA) bans them as violating noise levels. In Britain, a nationalized industry goes into court to get approval for a program that had been blocked by a local government for environmental reasons. The examples proliferate, and the popular conception of bureaucracy persists. One school of analysts have in fact begun to argue that public policy formation can best be understood through the analysis of the conflict of bureaucratic agencies. To these scholars policy is more readily comprehensible—especially as a set of outputs and impacts on the population—by understanding bureaucracy than by understanding how a bill becomes a law in legislative institutions.[21] Likewise, the process of implementation is increasingly recognized as a fundamental political process that must be understood before public policy can be understood.[22] Thus, our understanding of both the quantitative and qualitative trends in policy formation lead us to a conclusion that we must understand bureaucracy in order to understand public policy, and further that the power of bureaucracy is increasing steadily. Our task here is to provide an explanation of these changes in the relative powers of institutions. To that end, we argue that the reasons for this change are primarily three: the quantitative growth of public problems and concerns, the qualitative growth of those concerns, and the failure of alternative institutions to cope with those changes.

The Quantitative Growth of Public Concerns

To say that the scope of government has increased because there are more things done in the public sector is tautological, but it is important to note the vast array of things now done by collective action that were either unheard of, or the subjects of private action, twenty years ago. The developmental scheme proposed by Rose is one indication of this as government added first resource-mobilization activities and finally social activities to its array of functions. One bit of his evidence, reproduced in table 2.5, shows how these functions have increased in several European nations. Thus, as well as increasing in the *level* of activity, e.g., the size of the budget, government is also extending the *scope* of its activities.

The increasing complexity of modern economic and social life is one obvious reason for the increase in the scope of governmental activity. This complexity is a function of the technological content of modern life, in which telecommunications, atomic energy, rapid commercial air service, space travel, and the mechanization of most production are but a few examples of dramatic increases in technology that impinge upon the citizen as consumer and voter. Further, increases in

TABLE 2.5

Growth of Government: Number of Agencies

Period	States	Defining (average number)	Functions Resource Mobilization	Social	Total
19th cent.	22	5.7	1.7	1.1	8.5
20th cent.	9	4.8	3.7	1.9	10.4
1913	25	5.9	4.0	1.6	11.5
1936	31	5.7	4.7	2.4	12.8
1972	32	5.6	9.1	4.4	19.2

SOURCE: Richard Rose, "On the Priorities of Government: A Developmental Analysis of Public Policies," *European Journal of Political Research* 4 (1976): 247–89, tables 1 and 2.

the rapidity of communication and transportation, and an increasing concentration of people in urbanized areas, have required collective decisions on matters that in simpler societies could be handled by individuals. Thus, in terms of economics, the externalities of individual behavior have tended to increase as the size and concentration of the population have increased.[23]

Not only have the externalities of individual behavior increased; so, too, have the perceptions of those externalities. Unfortunately, little research exists to document changes in perceptions of this sort, but by using somewhat softer evidence we can get some idea of the attitude changes. Such evidence is given by the increasing organization of individuals in a variety of national settings attempting to get regulation of things such as environmental pollution, deceptive and unsafe business practices, land use, and even economic foreign policy. Likewise, society is increasingly unwilling to allow individuals to live below certain minimum standards, so that the vast array of social functions represent, if not a perception of increased externalities, at least some concern for the ability of collective action to improve the lot of fellow citizens. Thus, modern society produces situations in which mechanisms of collective action are perceived as virtually necessary for a high quality of life. These necessities are apparently recognized by much of the population, although variably by both classes of individuals and by nations, and the bureaucracy has become the institutional manifestation of those necessities.

The Qualitative Growth of Public Concerns

As well as the increasing externalities of modern life and popular desire to have some regulation of economic and social problems, the technological content of life—already alluded to—has definite implications for bureaucratic dominance in decision making. Increasingly the things that government is called upon to regulate are matters having significant technological content. This is true not only of things involving the natural sciences and engineering, but also the developing "social technology," particularly in the economy. Experts in government tend to be concentrated in the bureaucracy, with very few if any legislative or executive structures having their own experts. As the concerns of government are increasingly influenced by the available technology, the public bureaucracy, as the possessor of the public's share of that technology, comes increasingly to the fore.

As well as influencing its relationship with other political institutions, the level of technological sophistication of the bureaucracy has also influenced relationships with the society. As programs such as atomic energy and space exploration have developed—requiring enormous capital investment, high levels of staffing, and some national-security concerns—few if any private institutions would be capable of engaging actively in the problem area even if they were legally able. This leaves government as the sole supplier of certain technological services. Private concerns that seek to engage in these technologically sophisticated activities—for example, a utility company building an atomic reactor—must seek the guidance, and more importantly, accept the regulation of the public bureaucracy. Further, research and development activities are diverted from what might be valued in the private marketplace into directions dictated more by political and bureaucratic demands. The "spinoffs" of these research efforts may have positive values for the citizens, but the interest here is in the change of location of the impetus and direction of that research from the private to the public sector.[24]

Institutional Change

The third major set of reasons for the increased power of bureaucracies in contemporary political systems is institutional, related to the characteristics of bureaucracy as a political institution, and the characteristics of other political institutions that are competitors for power. This competition is rarely overt, but it does have the effect of delineating the power relationships among institutions and the nature of the policies that are likely to be adopted.

The Legislature

The legislature has been the traditional locus of rule making for democratic political systems, and most nondemocratic systems use a legislative body to legitimate their actions to their own people and to the outside world. Given this traditional and normative role of legislatures, we must seek to understand why they are apparently losing, if not the formal powers of decision, at least the actual role-making powers within many political systems. The gainer in this decline of legislative powers is the bureaucracy.

Rather obviously, the quantitative and qualitative growth of governmental concerns has contributed to this decline in power. Legislatures, by placing their organizational effort into discussion, debate, and elaborate procedures for the open consideration of viewpoints, consequently limit their ability to consider more than a handful of issues in any one session. These may be the most important issues or may set very broad parameters of policy, but this still leaves a very large quantity of detail work to be filled in by administrators. Further, the qualities valued in legislative recruitment, popular elections, or advancement within the legislature are rarely those needed to handle technically complex materials in large quantity.[25] The non-legislative careers of most legislators are hardly those that would prepare them for such tasks except in terms of legalistic problems.

Going along with the questions of recruitment of legislators are questions concerning the structure of the institutions. Relative to the bureaucratic agencies whom they must confront, legislative bodies are understaffed and underspecialized. Even when well-developed systems of legislative committees exist, as in the United States and West Germany, the members of those committees have any number of other duties that prevent their specialization in narrow policy areas. Further, few legislative bodies are lucky enough to have specialization in committees to begin with, so that policy consideration in those bodies is often a haphazard thing. Finally, even when legislative committees exist as highly specialized bodies, rarely do they have independent sources of information to draw upon in considering policy; they must rely upon information gathered and processed by a bureaucratic agency, which presumably has some interest in a particular outcome.

Finally, the relative instability of legislative bodies as compared to the bureaucracy places the legislature at a disadvantage in any power competition.[26] Even in societies that have not had high levels of governmental instability or frequent elections, legislators and legislatures are certainly more transitory than bureaucracies. Thus a certain uncertainty surrounds the conduct of legislative business, and an opportunity arises for bureaucrats to engage in tutelage to new and inexperienced legislators. Further, the bureaucracy can always try to wait out the legislature, hoping that at the next election the people or parties in charge will change their minds, or not be there at all.

The Political Executive

Many of the problems of legislatures are also found in the political executive. This is especially true in parliamentary systems where executives suffer from the instability of regimes and must frequently rely on policy staffs of the legislature, such as they are. This has been described as the "problems of party government" and reflects the difficulty of any political executive imposing its will upon the ongoing administrative offices.[27] There are three particular problems that political executives have in seeking to impose their wills.

The first is a lack of skills relevant to understanding the policies that must be made, and a lack of time required to understand and manage those policies. Political executives must rely on their civil servants to shape policy and advise them about the operations of the ministry. Headey, for example, calculates that of the fifty-one appointments to departmental ministerial posts in the Wilson government of 1964–70, only five had any substantial prior knowledge of the policy area, with another five or six having some background in the area.[28] In the 1970 Heath government only four original appointees could claim specialist knowledge, with four more having some background.[29] Britain may be less well served than other countries in this regard, but recent hearings for cabinet posts in the United States, as well as cabinet reshuffles in any number of countries, would indicate that a knowledge of the policy area is by no means a prerequisite for a cabinet appointment.[30]

Lacking any specialized knowledge, it would be helpful if those in the political executive had sufficient time to spend in running their departments. In fact, most spend a "dog's life" in their ministerial posts.[31] Again, this may be especially evident in parliamentary systems, and even more particularly in Britain. Suleiman points out that revision of the French constitution preventing ministers from also being parliamentarians has greatly aided French ministers in running their ministries.[32] Likewise, the norms of other parliamentary systems concerning hours and the time spent in the legislatures may ease political burdens substantially.[33] Nevertheless, the minister remains at a disadvantage in attempting to understand and control the work of full-time and relatively specialized civil servants.

If the disadvantages of time and skill were not enough, the political executive also is seriously outnumbered in his attempts to impose external political goals upon a bureaucratic structure. Compared to the size of most administrative bodies, the number of political appointees who are imposed upon the top of the organization is quite small, but the appointees are expected to control all activities within the organization. This number is, of course, variable by political system; the United States, for example, has considerably more political appointees than the United Kingdom. But the numbers still pale in comparison to the size of the full-time bureaucracy. Disadvantages are minimized when a single political party provides direction for both bureaucratic and ostensibly political decision makers, but even here institutional loyalties may compete with party loyalties.

Finally, the need for civil servants to accept the will of their political masters and actually put into effect a partisan program is another obstacle to effective political control. Although few civil servants systematically sabotage or even obstruct the stated program of a minister, they still have their own departmental or ideological concerns, which may impede the smooth flow of work. From all that is known about human nature and behavior in organizations, it is unlikely that civil servants who disagree with, or are genuinely neutral toward, a policy will administer it with the same alacrity and vigor as they will toward a policy they like. Further, given the handicaps under which many ministers labor, civil servants are frequently able to control the agenda of the minister sufficiently so that few programs actually hostile to the interests of the civil service will be considered.[34] The tendency of administrators to drag their feet, or at least not administer vigorously, will be exacerbated in situations of high politicization both of particular policies and of the society in general.[35] For example, when a political system is divided communally and changes occur in the composition of the political leadership, frequently this may require the reshuffling of many senior civil servants so that the two may have the ability to cooperate somewhat effectively. Perhaps the most general point that can be made is that civil servants have little to gain by close cooperation with politicians. Their careers are largely untouched by politicians, and it may in fact be a detriment to be too closely identified with a particular political party or politician—especially if they lose office.

THE NATURE OF BUREAUCRATIC INSTITUTIONS

As well as being cognizant of the difficulties faced by competing institutions, we must also be aware of the behavior and motivations of bureaucratic agencies. Let us not adopt the totally cynical view that agencies are concerned only with the growth of the agency budget, but neither can we adopt the more naive view that agencies are concerned entirely with the performance of their constitutionally and legally designated tasks.[36] The truth probably lies somewhere in between. Further, attempts at bureaucratic "empire building" may be closely related to the desire of the agency not only to survive, but also to perform functions it considers essential to a high quality of life for the society. Thus, despite the obvious attempts of the Pentagon at times to increase the military budget to feed its own needs, it is only fair to say that officials in the Department of Defense sincerely believe that they are supplying an essential service to the society.

A second crucial component of the bureaucratic-aggrandizement model of policy making has been that agencies would compete over scarce resources—the budget—and for control of policy choices. This would seem to limit the extent to which any integrated bureaucratic government might emerge, given that the bureaucracy would tend to behave as a set of competitive entrepreneurs rather than as a unified political force.[37] However, more recent research has pointed out that bureaucracies are competitive primarily when core interests are threatened; they rarely engage in conflict at the edge of their "policy space." [38] Likewise, in the budgetary process, they can perhaps best be seen as satisficers rather than maximizers, again seeking to ensure survival of the agency rather than domination of the policy area.[39] Perhaps the best analogy is the balance of power in international affairs in which all actors involved seek to gain security through limited or tacit cooperation rather than overt competition.

Even if the bureaucracy as a whole does not constitute a unified political force, it may still constitute a formidable force within individual agencies. We have already noted the ability of the permanent staff essentially to determine the agenda for their presumed political masters. This becomes especially important in the presence of an agency ideology concerning proper agency goals and proper means of attaining those goals. Through the ability to control information, proposals for policy, and the knowledge concerning feasibility, the bureaucracy is certainly capable of influencing agency policy, if not determining it. It requires an unusual politician to be able to overcome this type of control within an agency.

Thus, we can view the bureaucracy as being in a powerful position in competition with its ostensible masters. Having control of information and of the instigation of policy alternatives, having an expert knowledge of the subject matter, and having a ministerial or departmental ideology concerning the manner in which the subject matter should be treated, the bureaucracy can control decisions actually adopted by the partisans at the top. Further, competition between agencies, which might serve to limit such powers, is usually confined to a small number of issues in which the basic interests of one or more agencies overlap. Within its purview, each agency remains supreme and can consequently dominate or control its own master.

COUNTERTRENDS IN GOVERNMENTAL GROWTH

Lest we think that all goes well for the statist position in modern society, we should briefly discuss several countertrends. The most general of these trends has been labeled a "new individualism." This trend is, as the name would imply, an attempt to reassert individualism and the rights and powers of the individual against the power of the state. This trend has had several political manifestations in the developed world. One has been the surge of voting strength for political parties expressing, at times in extremely strong terms, a rejection of governmental power.[40] Likewise, survey evidence from several political systems indicates an increasing unwillingness on the part of citizens to accept high taxation in spite of the positive benefits produced by government. For example, the data in table 2.6 from two of the more advanced Scandinavian welfare states indicates a decline in support for social programs, especially as they are perceived as imposing additional tax burdens on the population. There has also been some leveling off of popular support for programs such as nationalization in the United Kingdom. Although scattered, these data indicate some reversal of the trends toward greater popular support for social and economic programs in advanced industrial societies.

If the governmental role in society is to decrease, something must take its place, and it is here that the advocates of lessened governmental involvement come to grief. Most of the alternative institutions for public choice and social control—the family, the church, voluntary associations, economic organizations—have atrophied as the state has increased in power. Society would have to rejuvenate these institutions or develop alternative institutions if the role of government were reduced. As noted, the increasing interdependence of individuals in mass societies requires increased control—unless all people should suddenly become more saintly—and with this goes a need for institutions to provide that control. Unless alternatives can be found, government may just have to carry on.

Associated with the desire to limit the powers of government has been a special desire to curb the powers of the bureaucracy. The major intention has appeared to be a desire to break the bureaucratic monopoly over information, and to open bureaucracy to more public scrutiny. These efforts have encountered many of the difficulties

TABLE 2.6

Changes in Public Attitudes toward Various Public Policies

Sweden

Government should reduce social benefits. ("Social Reforms have gone so far in this country that in the future the State should *reduce* rather than increase social benefits and support for the citizen.")

	1968	1973
Agree	41%	60%
Ambiguous/DK	7	8
Disagree	52	32
	100%	100%

Denmark

Most Important Public Problem. ("Which problems do you think are the most important ones today which the politicians ought to take care of?")

	August 1971	October 1971	1973
Taxes	7%	9%	27%
Social problems	19	10	8
Housing	14	9	4

afflicting the political institutions previously, but increasing popular concern—and associated with it increased concern by political leaders —presents a definite challenge to the position and role of the bureaucracy.

There is also some interest in decentralizing government. The feeling is that government in the village would not be as remote, bureaucratic, or uninfluenceable as government in the national capitol.[41] Decentralization has been supported by both liberals and conservatives as a means of ameliorating some of the popular alienation from government. The results of attempts at decentralization are still too scattered for any real appraisal of costs and benefits in economic terms. Nevertheless, the symbolic values of local control may be more important than any real economic benefits that might be derived by keeping taxes closer to their source, and more efforts in this direction are underway.

Finally, one factor that must be taken into account in terms of a

TABLE 2.6 (*cont.*)

United Kingdom

Proportion of the Population Favoring Nationalization. ("Which of these statements comes closest to what you, yourself, feel about nationalization?")

(a) A lot more industries should be nationalized.
(b) Only a few more industries should be nationalized.
(c) No more industries should be nationalized but the industries that are nationalized should stay nationalized.
(d) Some of the industries that are nationalized should now be denationalized.
(e) Don't know.

	1966	June 1973	October 1973	May 1974	July 1975
A lot	8%	11%	10%	8%	5%
Some	17	10	11	11	8
Keep current	42	34	33	41	40
Denationalize	19	23	23	26	31
Don't Know	14	23	23	15	16
	100%	101% a	100%	101% a	100%

SOURCES: For Sweden, Bo Särlvik, "Recent Electoral Trends in Sweden" (Paper presented to Conference on Recent Political Trends in Scandinavia, American Enterprise Institute, Washington, D.C., February 1975), p. 24. For Denmark, Ole Borre, "Recent Trends in Danish Electoral Behavior" (Paper presented to above Conference), p. 15. For United Kingdom, *Gallup Political Index*, nos. 156, 159, 165, 180.

a Greater than 100% due to rounding.

lessening of support for the centralized state is the developing détente between East and West. Both sides retain massive military power, but there is apparently less acceptance of "the enemy" as a justification for both governmental power and massive military expenditures. Likewise, the withdrawal of virtually all former colonial powers from their former colonies and the associated lessening of those tensions will also serve to reduce some of the burdens on citizen from government. Certainly massive military forces and indirect involvement in former colonies still exist, but a lessening of tensions can help to control both expenditures and interference by government.

SUMMARY

This chapter can serve as a useful preface to what is to come. It has shown why it is necessary to understand public administration. Put simply, our daily lives are increasingly influenced by government, and what government does is increasingly determined by bureaucracy and bureaucrats. We have provided some introduction to the politics of bureaucracy and its structure that will be used throughout this book as a means of explaining the policy-making powers of bureaucracy. Our task then is to explicate these politics more completely, especially as they vary across nations, and to attempt to show what can be done to provide responsible and effective administration.

NOTES

1. See William Niskanen, *Bureaucracy and Representative Government* (Chicago: Aldine/Atherton, 1971); Anthony Downs, *Inside Bureaucracy* (Boston: Little, Brown, 1967); Randall Bartlett, *The Economic Foundations of Political Power* (New York: Macmillan, 1973).
2. A. Grosser, "The Evolution of European Parliaments," in *A New Europe?* ed. Stephen A. Graubard (Boston: Little, Brown, 1964); Gerhard Loewenberg, *Modern Parliaments: Change or Decline?* (Chicago: Aldine/Atherton, 1971).
3. For a review, see Daniel Tarschys, "The Growth of Public Expenditures: Nine Modes of Explanation," *Scandinavian Political Studies* 10 (1975): 9–31.
4. Ibid., pp. 19–21, 23, 25–26.
5. Ibid., pp. 21–23, 24–25.
6. See Niskanen, *Bureaucracy and Representative Government;* Downs, *Inside Bureaucracy.*
7. Richard Rose, "On the Priorities of Government: A Developmental Analysis of Public Policy" (Department of Politics, University of Strathclyde, 1975). Mimeographed.
8. See Harold L. Wilensky, *The "New Corporatism," Centralization and the Welfare State* (Beverly Hills: Sage, 1976).
9. See, for example, Anthony King, "Ideas, Institutions and the Policies of Government: A Comparative Analysis," *British Journal of Political Science* 3, nos. 3 and 4 (1973): 291–314, 409–24.
10. S. N. Eisenstadt, "Bureaucracy, Bureaucratization, Markets and Power Structures," in *Essays on Comparative Institutions,* ed. S. N. Eisenstadt (New York: John Wiley, 1965), pp. 172–215.
11. Gabriel A. Almond and G. Bingham Powell, *Comparative Politics: A Developmental Approach* (Boston: Little, Brown, 1966), pp. 195–96.

12. For example, in the United States employment in state and local government increased by 154% from 1950 to 1973, while employment at the national level increased by a modest 33%.

13. See, for example, Samuel P. Huntington, "Postindustrial Politics: How Benign Will It Be?" *Comparative Politics* 6, no. 1 (January 1974): 181–82.

14. The prestige factor is useful both internally and externally. Internally it helps to solidify the position of the ruling group or individual. Externally, it may serve not only as a deterrent to potential enemies but also establishes the nationhood of the new nation. It is, as Rose points out, a defining function of a nation to defend itself.

15. See Gavin Kennedy, *The Military in the Third World* (London: Duckworth, 1974), pp. 12–30.

16. In general, popular demand for social programs has been directed much more toward providing security than toward a redistribution of wealth or income. It would appear that many "welfare state" programs have had a negligible effect on the distribution of wealth. See J. C. Kincaid, *Poverty and Equality in Britain* (Hammondsworth, England: Penguin, 1973). Also, Harold Wilensky, *The Welfare State and Equality* (Berkeley: University of California Press, 1975).

17. Transportation expenditures were chosen as one resource mobilization measure that has had considerable importance for the time period reported. Obviously, if other indicators were selected, slightly different results would emerge.

18. Samuel Krislov, *Representative Bureaucracy* (Englewood Cliffs, N.J.: Prentice-Hall, 1974), pp. 40–41.

19. See B. Guy Peters, "The Problem of Bureaucratic Government" (Paper presented at annual meeting of Southern Political Science Association, Atlanta, Georgia, November 1976).

20. The most famous of these are the works of Parkinson, Peter, and Kharasch.

21. See Graham Allison, *The Essence of Decision* (Boston: Little, Brown, 1971); Morton H. Halperin, "Why Bureaucrats Play Games," *Foreign Policy* 5, no. 1 (1971): 70–90; "The Decision to Deploy ABM: Bureaucratic Politics in the Johnson Administration," *World Politics* 24, no. 1 (1972): 40–79.

22. Jeffrey Pressman and Aaron Wildavsky, *Implementation* (Berkeley: University of California Press, 1973).

23. Externalities are said to exist when "the production or consumption activities of one economic unit affect the productivity or well-being of another economic unit *and* no compensation is paid for the externally generated benefits or costs." David H. Hyman, *The Economics of Governmental Activity* (New York: Holt, Rinehart & Winston, 1973), p. 43.

24. Albert D. Biderman, "Social Indicators and Goals," in *Social Indicators,* ed. Raymond A. Bauer (Cambridge, Mass.: MIT Press, 1968), pp. 68–153.

25. See, for example, Richard Rose, "The Making of Cabinet Ministers," *British Journal of Political Science* 1, no. 4 (1971): 393–414.

26. Grosser, "Evolution of European Parliaments."

27. Richard Rose, *The Problem of Party Government* (London: Macmillan, 1974).

28. Bruce Headey, *British Cabinet Ministers* (London: George Allen & Unwin, 1974), pp. 83–109.

29. Ibid.

30. In her hearings for confirmation as secretary of housing and urban development, Carla Hills Anderson stated she knew little if anything about housing policy but expected to learn in office. *New York Times,* 25 February 1975.

31. E. Marples, "A Dog's Life at the Ministry," in *Policy-Making in Britain*, ed. Richard Rose (London: Macmillan, 1969), pp. 128–31.

32. Ezra N. Suleiman, *Politics, Power and Bureaucracy in France* (Princeton: Princeton University Press, 1974), pp. 164–70. Suleiman argues, however, that the nature of the party system is more important than the structural arrangement in determining relationships between ministers and civil servants in France.

33. For example, until recently the respective analogues of the Question Hour in France and West Germany have been easily disregarded by the government. In several parliamentary systems the Question Hour does not exist as a check on the executive.

34. Heady, for example, finds that the preferred minister among civil servants is a "policy selector" rather than a "policy initiator."

35. Dogan notes an apparent incompatability between high politicization and high independence of the public bureaucracy. Mattei Dogan, "The Political Power of Western Mandarins," in *The Mandarins of Western Europe*, ed. Mattei Dogan (New York: Halsted, 1975), pp. 12–16.

36. Robert D. Putnam describes these as the classical and the political bureaucrat. See his "Political Attitudes of Senior Civil Servants in Britain, Germany, and Italy," *American Political Science Review* 3, no. 2 (June 1973): 257–90.

37. Niskanen, *Bureaucracy and Representative Government*, pp. 155–68.

38. See, for example, Robert E. Goodin, "The Logic of Bureaucratic Back-Scratching," *Public Choice* 21 (1975): 53–68.

39. Richard M. Cyert and James G. March, *The Behavioral Theory of the Firm* (Englewood Cliffs, N.J.: Prentice-Hall, 1963). Goodin, "Logic of Bureaucratic Back-Scratching"; Downs, *Inside Bureaucracy*.

40. Most notable in this regard is Moegens Glistrup and his Progress party, who have advocated the virtual dismantling of the Danish government, and who received 15.9% of the votes in the 1973 Folketing election.

41. See, for example, W. A. Robson, "The Missing Dimension of Government," *Political Quarterly* 42, no. 3 (July–September 1971): 233–46. Timothy M. Hennessey and B. Guy Peters, "Postindustrialism and Public Policy" (Paper delivered at Annual Convention of the American Political Science Association, San Francisco, California, September 1975).

3 POLITICAL CULTURE AND PUBLIC ADMINISTRATION

Citizens do not interpret the behavior of their government in a vacuum. They are equipped by their society with an image of what constitutes good government and good administration. This "picture" of good government is actually comprised of a set of rather complex cognitive and evaluative structures that tend to be (relatively) common among all members of the society. We refer to these generally shared psychological orientations as *political culture*.[1] Although at times this common culture is directly imparted to children through civics courses and patriotic exercises, the acquisition of a political culture is usually part of the more general process of learning about the society. Thus, just as the child learns the prevailing norms concerning economic behavior, social interaction, and child rearing, he also learns how to understand and evaluate politics and government. Some evidence points out that this process begins early in life and is largely completed by early adolescence.[2] This process of learning political values and political culture is referred to as *political socialization*.

We have already seen that the social and economic systems of the society place boundaries on actions by government, and more specifically, on public administration. The political culture is equally important in setting boundaries of acceptable political action, although these limits are less tangible than are those of economic possibility. By defining those things that are valuable and for which the society should strive, the culture cannot only say what things are unacceptable, but it can also virtually require the performance of other actions. Despite the seemingly abstract and vague nature of these cultural boundaries, governments can violate the prevailing political norms only at risk. This is true no matter how antiquated and vestigial this element of the culture may be. This is not to say that a society's cultural values are immutable. Culture is subject to change, and there is a constant interaction of culture and politics that redefines the role of government. For example, the latitude of action allowed governments in developed countries at present would have been unthinkable before two world wars, one major economic depression, and a cold war fundamentally altered popular perceptions of the role of government.[3] Nevertheless, at the same time that the scope of government has been allowed to expand, some of the other values supporting a democratic political system, such as freedom and equality, have remained important, or have actually increased in importance to citizens.[4]

The remainder of this chapter examines the effects of political culture on the nature of the public administrative system. The comparisons made are of two varieties: (1) between political systems, commenting on the differences in administration in different countries, which may be a function of differences in their cultures; and (2) within systems across time.

ADMINISTRATIVE CULTURE

For our purposes, we can think of culture as existing at three distinct levels: societal, political, and administrative. The conceptual relationship between these three levels can be seen in figure 3.1.

FIGURE 3.1

The Culture of Public Administration

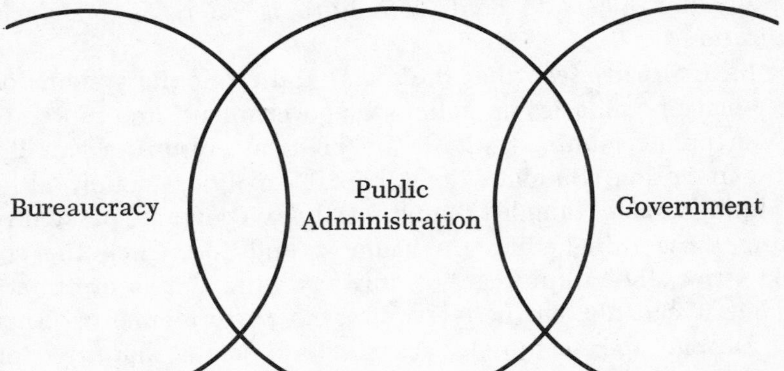

Bureaucracy   Public   Government
                   Administration

Notice in this diagram the relationship of administrative culture to the other two subsets of culture. We argue that the orientation of the society toward administration is a component not only of the general social culture, but also of the political culture; that is, some general social values either support or potentially undermine the effectiveness of administrative structures. This is true whether affairs are administered by government or by a private concern. However, we are particularly interested in those aspects of the political culture that affect the functioning of administration. Those aspects of political culture that either assist or impede the apparent transformation of politicized decision-making systems to administrative and technical decision-making systems are of crucial importance in understanding current trends in government.

General Societal Culture

Let us first look at several aspects of societal culture that affect the performance of administration. The first of these concerns the basic question of the acceptability of "bureaucracy" as a means of large-scale organization in the society. A culture will have a basic set of evaluations of bureaucratic structures not only in government but also in any large-scale organization. Likewise, those societies that tend to adopt bureaucratic forms of management for one type of enterprise will tend to adopt bureaucratic means for all types of enterprise. In discussing some aspects of these patterns, Bendix made the distinction between entrepreneurial and bureaucratic societies.[5] Great Britain is used as an example of an entrepreneurial society. The development and management of British enterprise has traditionally been an entrepreneurial action, despite the rather early acceptance of corporations and limited liability. The style of management tended to remain personal, the development of a rather extensive administrative apparatus notwithstanding. The administration of public policy in Great Britain would appear to follow many of the same entrepreneurial channels. Despite the development of the bureaucracy in Whitehall, the manner of functioning of public administration appears to be decision through personal bargaining and negotiation rather than through a bureaucratic imposition of authority. This process is evidently carried on in an informal, personalistic manner based on personal acquaintances and personal trust.[6]

The opposite of this entrepreneurial approach to administration is the institutionalized bureaucratic style of administration that has characterized Germany. This is, of course, a common stereotype of the culture of Germany (either East or West) but is also rather descriptive of styles of administration. Bureaucracy is the dominant form of social organization, just as the informality of the committee is the dominant form of organization in Great Britain.[7] This is true not only in government but also in economic, social, and cultural organizations. Likewise, authority and status relationships have been described as dominating the more general form of social relationships, including family relationships.[8] In such a society, bureaucracy and its emphasis on authority relationships is a natural and acceptable form of public organization. This is considerably less acceptable in a society more oriented toward personal and informal decision making as in the United Kingdom. This is especially interesting given that the two societies have approximately equal concern with the rule of law and the necessity of equal application of laws to individuals. The two societies simply choose different manners of ensuring this application of the rule of law. The effects of this difference may be important, however, as bureaucrats become increasingly involved in public decision making. This may be acceptable in Germany, but perhaps severely strain the authority of government in Britain.

Bendix was discussing primarily differences among Western industrialized nations, but there are perhaps even more significant differences between that set of nations and the non-Western and unindustrialized nations. In general, one finds that the non-Western world is less accepting of the use of bureaucratic methods than is the Western world. Attempts to import this Western concept into the non-Western world have often resulted in the adoption of formal aspects of bureaucracy but the circumventing of procedural norms. Riggs, in his discussion of the use of bureaucratic methods in underdeveloped countries, talks about the "sala" model of administration—having the form of a Western bureaucracy but actually filled with individuals operating according to more traditional norms of family and communal loyalty. Even in an economically developed albeit non-Western society such as Japan, the norms of personal loyalty tend to supplant any bureaucratic reliance on authority, achievement, and rules.[9]

Related to societal acceptance of bureaucracy as a means of organization is the acceptance of impersonality and universality of rules. Parsons has discussed this characteristic as one of his five pattern variables describing general patterns of cultural development.[10] Bureaucracies depend for their smooth functioning on the acceptance of impersonality and universality of rules. If rules must be renegotiated for each individual, bureaucracies become not only inefficient, they become superfluous as well. Bureaucracies have been developed to provide consistency and universality in the application of rules demanded by law as well as "modern" conceptions of fairness.

What sort of cultural systems tend to support this bureaucratic concept of universality and impersonality of rules? It can be associated with what we will call *rationalist,* or *deductive,* cultures.[11] These have become characteristic of most developed countries but are especially well developed in continental Europe. These cultures tend to emphasize the deduction of specific statements from general statements. It is only a short step from this type of argument in the general social culture to the bureaucratic style of decision making, in which decision about an individual case is made on the basis of deductive reasoning from a legal premise. In these cases, if the deduction of the specific is performed correctly, there is no basis for argument. Both client and administrator can accept the adequacy of the ruling. The client may not always like the ruling made by the administrator, but the correctness of the impersonal nature of the application is difficult to question within such a cultural context.

The rationalistic culture may be contrasted with the *pragmatic,* or *empirical,* culture that has been said to characterize the United Kingdom and much of Northern Europe.[12] In these cultures, generalities are derived from a series of individual decisions. This type of culture is perhaps best typified by English (and American) common law, built up from centuries of individual decisions. This culture is not so amenable to the development of bureaucracies or to impersonal decisions. Each case is, to some degree, a new case, and the particular individual circumstances may be sufficient to modify or overturn an apparent generality. Here, administrative and legal decisions are almost inherently personal and although precedent may rule, each case may be contested on its personal merits. This should not be taken to mean that the United Kingdom and the United States do not have bureaucratic organizations. By almost any definition of bureaucracy this would be a foolish statement. Rather, there will tend to be less rigidity and impersonality accepted in these more inductive cultures than would be true in the more deductive continental systems. The concept of individuality and individual rights, as one component of the more empirical culture, tends to make the job of the bureaucrat more difficult and forces more attention on specifics rather than on the generalities of the case.

Katz and Eisenstadt point to an interesting case in which the norms of impersonality developed by a bureaucratic system are undermined by an influx of clients unaccustomed to those norms.[13] Israel was settled initially by Jews of European origin accustomed to the norms of impersonal and universal rule applications. These same norms were not held, however, by later waves of immigrants from the Eastern branches of Judaism. Socialized into the largely personalistic and barter cultures of the underdeveloped nations, the new settlers were unwilling to accept even the most basic universal rules, e.g., that everyone who rides the bus should pay the same fare. Moreover, these immigrants were to constitute a major portion of the caseload for a number of social-service agencies in Israel. Interestingly, both the clients and the administrative structures found it necessary to modify their behavior in order to accommodate to the strains on their usual behavior patterns. The immigrants tended to adopt some of the basic ideas of impersonality, but the administrators also became more aware of personal differences among clients.

The above example brings to light two important aspects of the relationship of culture and administration. The first is the "barter" nature of the cultures of most of the underdeveloped world.[14] These nations present a variety and richness in cultural patterns, while impersonality and universality of rules remain largely attributes of developed and Western societies. In the non-Western world, all decisions are assumed to be subject to influence through personal bargaining and negotiation. Thus, any formal rules promulgated by the bureaucracy constitute merely a place to begin the bargaining. Likewise, Riggs has noted that societies in transition from traditional societies to modernity, which he terms "prismatic," adopt a style of decision making that he refers to as "double-talk." [15] He notes:

Even more typically prismatic is a law which provides for one policy although in practice a different policy prevails. A rule is formally announced, but is not effectively enforced. The formalistic appearance of the rule contrasts with its actual administration—officials are free to make choices, enforcing or disregarding the rule at will. We have already seen that over-conformity and non-enforcement of laws is typically prismatic. It makes possible prismatic codes which, while appearing to promulgate a rule, in fact permit a wide variety of personalized choices by enforcement officials. . . . Apparent rules mask without guiding actual choices.[16]

Thus, we can array cultures along a continuum from underdeveloped to rationalist on the basis of their willingness to accept impersonally made and applied rules. The Anglo-American pragmatic culture might be seen constituting something of a midpoint on this scale, although we would hypothesize it to be closer to the rationalist end of that scale. That is, compared to many non-Western political systems, the political culture of Great Britain would appear quite accepting of impersonal rules. When compared to other advanced and industrial countries of Europe, however, the culture of the United Kingdom is more personal and less bureaucratic than most other nations at similar levels of development.

The second point emphasized by the Katz and Eisenstadt research is interaction in the setting of the norms of administration. We have been stressing the importance of the lower echelons of administration and of contact with clients. Not only is this type of contact crucial for the client, it may also be crucial for the organization in the definition of its policies. Here we have the case of the organization modifying its basic orientation toward clients and toward administration on the basis of a problem in applying rules to specific clients. We can argue that at least formally the organizations could have continued to apply rules impersonally. In this case, however, the organization chose to innovate and innovated successfully to meet client needs. Organizations willing to make this type of innovation will be more successful in the long run than organizations that maintain rigid bureaucratic procedures even in the face of nonbureaucratic clients.[17] Evidence in this respect is limited, but it is important for the effectiveness of administration.

In summary, we have examined two aspects of the cultural values of society that are potentially important for understanding public administration. This is only a sample of these types of values, but any further enumeration runs the risk of being somewhat tedious. It would further distract attention from the more important relationships of the *political* culture of a society to the functioning of public administration. To the examination of these political aspects of the culture, and their relationships to public administration, we now turn our attention.

POLITICAL CULTURE AND PUBLIC ADMINISTRATION

In discussing political culture, we are concerned with the specific orientations of individuals toward politics as one type of social action and societal decision making. Public administration is a part of government and may therefore best be analyzed from this more politicized perspective.

Unfortunately for our purposes, the analysis and classification of political culture have been concentrated largely on the input side of the political system. Thus, attention has been given to attitudes and values concerning political participation, democratic procedures, political efficacy, and political involvement.[18] Much less attention has been given to classifying the orientations of citizens to the institutions of government, and to the outputs of the political system. In this respect, our knowledge of popular conceptions of administration is even weaker than our knowledge concerning people's feelings concerning legislatures, the political executive, and perhaps even the courts.[19] This field is not entirely vacant. In the American context, Jennings et al. have studied public conceptions of the civil service, especially the upper levels of the service.[20] They find an extremely high level of trust by citizens in these officials, as well as a recognition of their high levels of capability—perceived as being higher than that of congressmen. Levy, in another study, finds the general image of government and administration somewhat less positive.[21] Government is perceived as inefficient, filled with lazy officials; although individuals—especially top officials—may be respected as individuals, the composite image of the government and public administration is negative.

In a more strictly comparative sense, Almond and Verba have analyzed the perceptions of administrative competence of citizens in the United States, Great Britain, Italy, West Germany, and Mexico.[22] They sought to determine the degree to which these citizens feel capable of influencing administrative decisions. There was considerable variation among the countries, with over half the respondents in Germany and Great Britain feeling capable of exerting such an influence, while only 8 percent of Mexican respondents felt their protests would make any difference. Eldersveld, Jagannadham, and Barnabas, building on the work of Janowitz, Wright, and Delany, have been able to make some comparisons between citizens' attitudes toward administration in the United States and India.[23] Although the Indian sample was more willing to work in public jobs than private jobs, their general evaluation of public administration was much less positive than that of a sample in Detroit. The Indians felt that they were treated badly in their interactions with administrators and had a cynical view of corruption and favoritism in the public bureaucracy of India. This may be accounted for, in part, by the "prismatic" nature of India and of Indian administration, but it also points out that, despite Levy's findings, Americans are not entirely negative concerning their administrative structures, especially when compared to the attitudes of citizens of underdeveloped countries.

Leaving aside for the time being a lack of much direct evidence concerning popular orientations toward administration, we can undertake a more analytical discussion of the effects of political culture on administration. This should begin with some of the possible dimensions for analysis. As mentioned previously, the majority of analyses of political culture have dwelt almost exclusively with political participation. Thus, Almond and Verba speak of parochial, subject, and participant cultures on the basis of the willingness of the individual to participate on the input side of politics.[24] Almond and Powell use cultural secularization as one of their three variables to describe political development.[25] Although this is a broad concept, one of the primary components is an orientation toward politics involving manipulation and the attainment of individual goals through political action. We do not want to paint with too broad a brush, however. Some discussions of political culture have been concerned with problems of authority and of governmental institutions. Nettl has used "constitutional" and "elitist" as the two basic dimensions of his analysis of culture, with these two dimensions defined largely by the authority relationships within the society and polity.[26] This is therefore somewhat similar to Eckstein's discussion of authority as a crucial dimension of the analysis of political culture.[27] Likewise, Elazar's discussion of the dimensions of political culture in the United States rather explicitly involves a discussion of the cultural acceptability of certain types of public policies.[28]

Perhaps the most useful general categorization of the dimensions of political culture has been provided by Lucian Pye in the introductory essay to *Political Culture and Political Development*.[29] He develops four dimensions for the examination of political inputs, dimensions that are also useful for our analysis of the administrative and policy sides of government.

The first dimension is hierarchy and equality. Most administrative structures have a hierarchical structuring of personnel and authority in a formal organization, and cultural values concerning authority and impersonality of rules are important here. Several more basic political questions also come to mind when we think of hierarchy and equality in administration.

First, what are the means of recruitment into administrative positions? Parsons has used the terms "ascription" and "achievement" to describe how societies recruit people to positions.[30] In an achievement-oriented society, an individual's place in society is determined by ability. Advancement in society is determined by what the individual can do, not by who he is. Ascriptive societies recruit individuals to positions in society (and administration) on the basis of ascriptive criteria—class, status, race, language, caste—and the individual's position is determined by these largely immutable personal characteristics. As one would imagine, achievement criteria have generally been linked with "modern" society, while ascriptive criteria have been linked with "traditional" society. As discussed by Weber, as well as most other commentators on administration, bureaucracy and administration are inherently modern and achievement-oriented components of the political system.[31] Voters may choose a traditional elite to rule the country, but the bureaucracy would (in theory) still select the best people regardless of socioeconomic position or other ascriptive characteristics. This is true in theory, but the actual application of the principle varies markedly from society to society.

Equality in the recruitment of administrators is discussed at length in chapter 4, but some comment is necessary at this juncture. Equality of recruitment has been most thoroughly examined in the United Kingdom. Kingsley's seminal discussion of representative bureaucracy in Britain found that the middle classes are heavily overrepresented in the higher civil service.[32] The study was, however, ambivalent concerning the effects of that overrepresentation. It is probable that even bureaucracies recruited on the most achievement-oriented basis possible would still display this same dominance of the middle and upper classes because of the correlation between social class and the ability to take standardized tests, success in school, and so forth.[33] Nevertheless, the degree of equality or inequality in recruitment can be seen as a function of egalitarian norms in the society.

Equality is especially important given the composition of the clientele of most public bureaucracies. While a number of administrators are concerned with business and industry, agriculture, foreign policy, and defense, the majority of the clients of public agencies are from the relatively disadvantaged segments of the population. Thus we come to the common situation of middle-class administrators attempting to provide solutions for working-class problems. While there may be a common national culture, there may still be differences among social classes in their values.[34] This problem is especially important when class lines coincide with ethnic, linguistic, or other cleavages. On this basis, some have advocated the recruitment of administrators on a quota basis to ensure that administration accurately reflects the society it is attempting to govern. This solution, of course, can easily be interpreted as running counter to the concern for achievement-oriented recruitment.

Equality raises a second question for administration. As we have stated several times, bureaucratic organizations as they have been known in Western societies have involved the use of hierarchical authority. Superiors in the organizations have always attempted to exercise their authority to tell subordinates what to do. Various cultural groups have been more willing than others to accept this authority. Crozier points to distinct differences in the acceptance of authority among French, British, American, and Russian organizations.[35] He points out that French organizations are plagued by the inability of many of their members to accept authoritative commands from a superior, while patterns of deference in British culture make such an authoritative command quite acceptable. Likewise, several studies of administration in developing societies point out that orders from a superior may be obeyed as a function of the personal following of that individual, rather than from an acceptance of the authority of the position.[36] Despite these differences, acceptance of authority had declined in all developed nations. This may be seen as a part of the new individualism of the "postindustrial society."[37] Alternatives to the traditional hierarchical structuring of organizations have been proposed with such titles as "dialectical organizations" and "collaboration-consensus" organizations.[38] These, and myriad other proposed reforms, have had in common the replacement of authority with spontaneous forms of organization based on the equality of the members within the work group. The leaders and the led would be replaced by groups of collaborators.

Some of the most interesting efforts in the direction of equality in organizations have taken place in industrial management. Going under the label of "industrial democracy," these organizations have replaced the leadership of the foreman with the joint decision making of the work group.[39] For example, at the Gaines Meal plants in the United States, work groups are responsible for hiring and firing their own members. Workers at the Volvo and Saab plants in Sweden choose their own work leaders and their own working pace and times.[40]

These new forms of organizational management pose a unique

problem to the public organization: the position of the client in relationship to the organization. Public organizations tend to be "people-
processing" organizations in which the product has the same sort of
human needs as do the producers. As such, the position of the client
as either subordinate or participant must be defined by the organization. Few public organizations could afford the luxury of making the
client an equal partner in the decision-making process, no matter
how normatively desirable such a form of organization might be to
some observers (and clients). At the same time, the organization
does have the opportunity and ability to involve clients in some aspects of decision making concerning their cases and the general
functioning of the organization. The evidence coming from the first
decade of the postindustrial society indicates that clients are increasingly unwilling to accept a passive and subordinated position in the
organization. Just as do the employees, clients seek self-actualization
and some control over their lives. This plea for equality will probably
present public organizations with some of their most pressing problems in the next several years.

Liberty and Coercion

Closely allied with hierarchy and equality is the dimension of liberty and its opposite, coercion. As a gross generality, most of the
societies we have been discussing have been undergoing changes in
their value systems favoring decreased economic liberty and increased
liberty of expression and social action.[41] It is often the bureaucracy
that must decide the limits of both types of liberty. They must also
determine how much coercion is acceptable in enforcing their decisions. This is, of course, true for economic regulatory agencies, but
we often fail to remember that the police are themselves one of the
most ubiquitous forms of administration. We can make the argument
that the stability of a democratic society may depend upon the degree
of value consensus among the enforcers of those rules and the majority of the citizenry. As numerous student demonstrations during
the late 1960s demonstrated, there is apparently a great deal of
value dissensus, at least across generational lines, with respect to
the amount of liberty felt to be desirable and the amount of force
deemed necessary to enforce one side of that argument.

Despite the above-mentioned outbursts, the application of direct
physical coercion is becoming less frequent in modern societies. On
the other hand, the application of indirect coercion is becoming an

increasingly frequent and controversial technique of political control. Here we are not referring only to the potential use of psychological devices to exercise thought control, in the manner of an Orwell novel. Rather, we are speaking of the ability of administrative agencies to impose their wills on citizens without the opposition of that citizen. This is done in a variety of manners, the most common being the claim of efficiency and the appeal to technological criteria in decision making. It has become increasingly difficult for the average citizen, or even the exceptional citizen for that matter, to dispute the decisions made by a technologically competent and well-insulated bureaucracy. Government has therefore become an amalgamation of large organizations making decisions on their own terms and forcing them on individuals. Emmette Redford has said:

> The first characteristic of the great body of men subject to the administrative state is that they are dormant regarding most of the decisions made with respect to them. Their participation can not in any manner equal their subjection. Subjection comes from too many directions for man's span of attention, much less his active participation, to extend to all that affects him. Any effort of the subject to participate in all that affects him would engulf him in confusion, dissipate his activity and destroy the unity of his personality. Democracy, in the sense of man's participation in all that affects him is impossible in the administered society.[42]

We, and Professor Redford, may be guilty of overstating the case, but the possibility of administrative tyranny is apparent in even the best-administered modern societies. Here we comment on this only as a dimension of culture and leave the analysis of possible solutions to chapter 8.

Furthermore, while the possibilities for manipulation are certainly great in the administered or postindustrial state, we must not lose sight of the fact that the degree of control exercised over the individual through noncoercive means may be as great in traditional society. Thus the period of mass democracy and liberalism of the early and middle twentieth century may merely be a point of transition between two more "totalitarian" forms of government.[43] In the traditional society, this use of nonphysical coercion is justified on the basis of religious or ideological dogma. In the postindustrial society, it is justified through appeals to efficiency and technology, which constitute the dogma of the modern society striving for cumulative social and economic rationality.

Loyalty and Commitment

The third dimension mentioned by Pye is loyalty and commitment, meaning mainly the location of the terminal community to which the individual gives his ultimate loyalty.[44] For most traditional societies, and even for several developed societies, there is no identification with others outside the family.[45] Even where the commitment to the family is *not* paramount, loyalties to language, religion, caste, or ethnic group diminish individual commitment to the national political system and produce the potential for political unrest and instability.

The implications of a lower level of national commitment for administration are profound. This is especially true when those commitments are to subnational groupings outside the family. First, the existence of this type of social cleavage will tend to direct power upward toward the bureaucracy. Political decision making in situations of extreme cleavage is a difficult if not impossible process, although some countries of Europe have been developing structural and behavioral mechancisms to circumvent the problem.[46] In most cases, however, either immobilism or the necessity of imposed decisions will limit the effectiveness of legislative or executive decision making. In these cases, the public bureaucracy may be the only effective decision-making body in the nation. Moreover, if the bureaucratic ethos expressed by Weber and others that the bureaucracy is above politics is successfully inculcated into the population, the bureaucracy may be able to function effectively.[47] It can present the image of acting independently and rationally and at the same time make important policy decisions for the society when more conventional democratic institutions are inoperable. Certainly France in the Fourth Republic and modern Italy would fit this characterization, as would a number of underdeveloped countries.[48] As we have been seeing, however, the erosion of these conceptions of bureaucracy may limit the future effectiveness of the bureaucracy in immobilist or fragmented societies. The bureaucracy ceases to be an impartial arbiter of justice and becomes the object of manifest political appeals.

A second implication of the segmented nature of many political cultures for public administration concerns the relationship of administrator and client. As in discussing the relationship of social class to recruitment, so here we must give attention to differential hiring by ethnic groups. This is especially true if one subculture tends to dominate other subcultures. In such cases, typified by the domination of Protestants in Northern Ireland and the English-speaking community in Canada, the implications are not only for civil unrest but also for day-to-day tension.[49] One aspect of this tension between groups is the usual position of the dominant culture personnel in administrative agencies administering programs designed to aid people from the subject culture. As with social class, we find that the majority of administrators come from the dominant cultural groups in a society.[50] On the other hand, a disproportionate share of their clients tend to come from the subject cultures. This not only contributes to the underlying tension between the groups, but it may also place limits on the effectiveness of the administrative structures. Most public administration is people-processing. It involves the communication of desires and demands from client to administrator, the making of some decision on the part of that administrator, and the transmittal of that decision to the client. This is obviously a communication process, and as with all communication processes, it involves the use of common values, symbols, and cognitive structures.[51] This consensus does not necessarily exist between members of different subcultural groups. In these cases the probable result of interactions between administrators and clients is not the development of effective communication and empathy, but rather hostility, resentment, and the reinforcement of existing prejudices. This will be especially true when the program involved is a social program affecting the values of the client and administrator. The majority of direct evidence in this regard comes from the study of interactions of different social classes, but if we generalize, we can agree with Sjoberg, Bremer, and Faris concerning the "critical role of bureaucratic organizations in sustaining social stratification." [52]

Trust and Distrust: A Theory of Bureaucratic Power

The fourth and final aspect of political culture is the level of trust and distrust among the population. In our discussion of this dimension of culture, we attempt to develop a theoretical explanation for the differential development of the power of administration in different political systems.

We argue that differences in the rate of growth of administrative decision-making powers in modern countries are not due entirely to random or irrational forces, but instead are at least in part related to patterns of political cultures in these societies. The patterning of trust in the political cultures may play an important part in this explanation. To begin with, let us distinguish two separate components of social or political trust. The first of these components is a trust in individuals, as opposed to personal cynicism. This is conceptualized as the degree to which individuals in the society believe that others outside their immediate family can be trusted, as well as having a generally benign view of human nature. This trust of humanity is not at all evenly distributed across cultures. Almond and Verba offer some of the best direct evidence of this variation. In their survey they found that 55 percent of Americans, 49 percent of the British, but only 7 percent of the Italians in their sample indicated that they believed that "most people can be trusted." [53] Rather similar distributions of trust and distrust were found on several other items. Social distrust has been well described in the French context by Wylie, who notes that many of the French feel that

> . . . since all individuals are on the whole malicious and since society never tames the deeper self, every individual is actually motivated by hidden forces which are probably hostile.[54]

The importance of this attitudinal variable in the political culture for the growth of administrative power is that the lack of social trust removes the possibility, or at least the probability, of informal and self-regulative activities. In more trusting societies, these types of activities can be used to supplement the activities of government in regulating relationships within the society. In political systems such as the United States, the United Kingdom, or Scandinavia where social trust is high, nongovernmental alternatives to public administration emerge quite readily.[55] Individuals feel that they can safely form organizations and allow those organizations some control over the lives of the members. Some rather obvious examples of this are the use of bar and medical associations to regulate some important aspects of public policy. This can be further evidenced by the comparative powers of labor unions in these societies in the regulation of economic affairs. Thus, in cases where high levels of trust among individuals exist, we may expect a large number of otherwise public functions to be performed privately.

Using the willingness to form associations as one indicator of trust among individuals, we again find high levels of variation by countries. For example, Almond and Verba found that 40 percent of Amer-

TABLE 3.1

Proportion of Economically Active Population
Who Are Members of Trade Unions

Country	Percent
Australia	46
Austria	50
Belgium	46
Canada	26
Denmark	39
Finland	34
France	15
West Germany	31
Italy	18
Netherlands	27
Norway	41
Sweden	60
Switzerland	41
United Kingdom	41
United States	23

icans and 30 percent of the British preferred outgoing leisure-time activities, most of which involved some type of group membership.[56] In contrast, only 7 percent of the Italian sample and 11 percent of the Mexican sample preferred activities of this type. A survey of French respondents, reported earlier, displayed equally low interest in outgoing activities (11 percent preferring activities involving any sort of group membership.) [57]

Another indicator of the willingness to form groups may be taken to be the proportion of the work force that belongs to labor unions. Unions have emerged as probably the principal organizational groups in Western society, especially in terms of their influence on the political system. Thus if we look at the proportion of the economically active population involved in these organizations, we get some indication of the organizational skills and interest of the respective populations (see table 3.1). Here we see that the Scandinavian nations, the United Kingdom, and Australia display disproportionately larger percentages of memberships than the other nations. We have already mentioned the high levels of interpersonal trust in the United Kingdom, and the organizational propensities of the Scandinavian countries have been noted frequently.[58] The two most interesting aspects of this table are the low proportions reported for France and Italy and the low figure reported for the United States. As we have been seeing throughout this discussion of trust, Italy and France have low levels of social trust among their populations. This low trust is manifested here in low levels of organizational activities. Not only is this a quantitative indication of the lack of organizational propensity, but qualitative studies also indicate weakness within the organizations that do exist.

Given our findings concerning attitudes of social trust and the use of outgoing leisure-time activities, we might have expected somewhat higher levels of union membership among Americans. This is apparently an isolated manifestation of a lack of interest in joining a particular type of organization, rather than a more general indication of the propensity to join organizations.

A second aspect of trust is trust in government and political institutions. Here we are especially interested in the degree to which an individual believes that the "political" structures and politicians, as opposed to administrative structures, are worthy of trust.[59] Also involved in this conception of political trust, or its reverse of political cynicism, is the idea that politicians will take the citizen's viewpoint into account when making decisions. The implications of this type of trust for the development of administrative power are perhaps more obvious than the implications of generalized social trust. If the majority of the population, or even a significant minority, does not trust the government and politicians to be fair, honest, and impartial, then government will have at best a very difficult time in ruling the country. Decisions of a highly distrusted political system will be difficult for the population to accept as legitimate. The assumption would always be that some sort of corruption, deception, or favoritism was involved in the decision.

As with the social dimension of trust, we find considerable variation across cultures on the level of political trust. Almond and Verba present some directly comparable evidence as to the distribution of this trait. When respondents in the five countries involved in their survey were asked if they believed themselves capable of influencing local and national regulations, 75 percent of the American and 62 percent of the British respondents felt that they could influence national regulations, while only 28 percent of the Italian respondents felt that they could exert such an influence.[60] Also, in a study of political socialization in France, the Netherlands, and the United States, Abramson and Inglehart compared the trust expressed in a child's

FIGURE 3.2

Relationship of Dimensions of Social Trust to Administrative Power

Political Trust	Trust in Others	
	High	Low
High	Low Administrative Power	Moderate Administrative Power (positive affect)
Low	Moderate Administrative Power (negative affect)	High Administrative Power

father and in the head of state.[61] In the Netherlands and the United States, the children were very slightly more trusting of the political official; in France, the children were much more trusting of the father than the representative of the political system. Rather high levels of political trust have also been reported in the Scandinavian countries and in the Low Countries.[62]

Trust and Administration

We have now developed two different dimensions of trust—trust in individuals and trust in government. These two dimensions can be interrelated in a typological formation, as shown in figure 3.2. In this typology, we attempt to explain different levels of political power and of effect of the population toward administration from the positions on the two trust dimensions. In referring to political power of the administration, we mean the decision-making power of the public bureaucracy relative to other decision-making bodies (e.g., the legislature) in the political system, which over time has increased.

The second dependent variable in this typology is the affect felt by the population toward the administrative structures. It is basically difficult to love a bureaucrat, barring the outside chance that he is a

member of your immediate family. Yet there are instances in which
the general patterns of orientations toward the administrative structures are at least benign and actually somewhat positive. This may
be only a grudging respect for the administrative and technical abilities of the civil service, but it is still a positive view of administration.

As shown in figure 3.2, we do not include all possible combinations
of the two dependent characteristics of the typology in our predicted
outcomes. Instead we have chosen to hedge our bets and have labeled
two of the cells as having moderate administrative power. This is,
however, something more than a simple hedge and is related to some
characteristics of the political and social systems in question. We now
proceed with a discussion of each of the four cells of this typology,
with an attempt to explain and justify our predictions.

The first cell is comprised of societies that have high levels of interpersonal trust and high levels of trust in government. Here we shall
expect to find the weakest administrative structures. In these political
systems the normal "political" branches of the political system are
reasonably successful in ruling the country and tend to maintain a
strong hold on their decision-making prerogatives. They are able to
make and enforce rules without excessive assistance from their public bureaucracy. At the same time there are successful decision-making bodies outside government that are capable of performing a number of regulatory functions.

The most obvious example of a nation that would fit into this category of high interpersonal trust and high political trust is the United
Kingdom. Here, the Cabinet and to a lesser extent the Parliament com-
prise an effective political decision-making body.[63] As Nordlinger
points out, the level of political trust is sufficiently high in this system
to allow the political decision makers extreme latitude after an election.[64] The population thus expects to exert a direct political control
on their elected officials only at the time of election. Also, there has
been traditionally a good deal of regulation and self-regulation by
organizations within the society. Perhaps the best example of this is
the reliance on the affected groups to regulate most labor-manage-
ment difficulties until the passage of the Industrial Relations Act in
1971. In a nation with as large an organized labor movement and as
large an industrial sector, this type of self-regulation is rather amazing outside the cultural context.

This is not to say that the British bureaucracy is entirely dormant
and not involved in the making and implementation of policy. Recent
interpretations of the policy process in the United Kingdom have

placed a growing emphasis on the role of administrators in the formu-lation of policies.[65] However, unlike a number of other political sys-tems, the Cabinet and Parliament have not been relegated to the role of a virtual rubber stamp for the administrators, and the traditions of parliamentary control of ministers and their ministries have tended to prevent takeovers by bureaucratic authority experienced in other regimes, e.g., France. The United Kingdom therefore remains a po-litical system with a relatively low level of administrative power and control.

At the opposite extreme are several European countries and a number of societies in the Third World that have neither trust of the political system nor interpersonal trust. In Europe, this pattern can be attributed to France and Italy, and it fits probably a majority of the Third World, especially those nations with ethnic diversity that have been unable to build effective national institutions.[66] In these nations, there is little or no basis for the construction of effective extragovernmental organizations that could be useful in the regula-tion of some economic or social affairs. A number of authors have noted the relative weaknesses of these organizations in France and Italy.[67] These societies are certainly not devoid of interest groups, but the groups that exist tend to be fragmented and effective largely as defensive groups. They further lack the firm normative and po-litical commitment on the part of their members that is so char-acteristic of groups in other societies.

The political systems of these countries are also relatively weak. This weakness certainly diminished in France under the Gaullists, but it is still potentially a crippling factor in the French government.[68] Politics in these countries are characterized by fragmentation, ideo-logical argument, and immobilism. This is due in part to the weak-nesses of the political institutions, but it is also due to the cultural traits of individualism and "amoral familialism." [69] Thus the popu-lation is unwilling to accord legitimacy to the actions of government, preferring the family, or the local *patron,* as the source of authority. Parliaments and Cabinets in these situations tend to be so afflicted with division and conflict that the effective making of policy becomes a secondary concern to the preservation of ideological purity. In these cases, the bureaucracy may be required to step in to fill a power vacuum in the political system. The country must be run somehow, and the logical heirs to powers ordinarily held by Parliament or the Executive is the bureaucracy. Unfortunately, perhaps, this pattern tends to be self-reinforcing. As more power and decision making pass to the bureaucracy, the popular image of government as authoritarian and impersonal is reinforced. This further reduces the legitimacy of the political system in the eyes of the population and further prevents the legislative and executive bodies from becoming effective rule-making bodies. Thus a cycle of bureaucratic domination tends to perpetuate itself, being broken mainly by "charismatic personalities" who are capable of producing effective political action either through or around normal political channels.

The similarity between the situations of France and Italy and some of the countries of the Third World is rather striking. The new nations tend to lack interpersonal trust among the population.[70] This is often traceable to the predominance of ethnic cleavages in the society and the use of protective as opposed to promotional groups. Each segment of the society tends to protect its interests against all others, rather than offering an alternative means of social decision making. Likewise, the long history of colonial rule and the lack of a social and economic infrastructure usually associated with democratic government have made the bureaucracy and the army the two logical contenders for power in these societies.[71] As well as being the choices by default, the bureaucracy and the army also have some of the characteristics of modernity that would qualify them for the management of developing economies and societies.[72] Both institutions tend to have had relatively extensive contacts with more modern nations and to have values and attitudes that conform more closely to those of the modern state than do those of other political elites. Thus, just as with the "developed" countries of France and Italy, the bureaucracy in the underdeveloped world fills a power vacuum when it exists. One question that remains is whether this will be a continuing phenomenon or whether the underdeveloped countries will be able to develop the political and interpersonal trust that a large proportion of the developed world has been able to generate.

We move now to the two cases with mixed degrees of trust. These have been characterized as having moderate levels of administrative power, but they differ in the affect felt by the population toward the administrative system. The first is the case of low interpersonal trust and high trust for government. This would appear to be typical of the "consociational democracies" of the Low Countries, Austria, Switzerland, and (once) Lebanon.[73] In these societies, strong cleavage between religious and linguistic groups in turn produces relatively few feelings of interpersonal trust. Lorwin notes that in Belgium:

Flemings know little of Walloons thinking: Walloons know little of Flemish thinking. People of each side therefore tend to see and resent the others as a solid bloc arrayed against them.[74]

Likewise, much of Dutch sociology tends to emphasize the "pillarization" of their society, with the three major groups (Catholic, Protestant, and nonreligious) vertically integrated but having little contact with members of the other communities, or "families." [75] This arrangement tends to reinforce feelings of separation and distrust among the population.

These societies obviously have the ability to develop the immobilism and the conflict that has been characteristic of French and Italian governments. Fortunately, however, there is a well developed sense of mutual trust among the elites of each of the "families," as well as a general feeling of political trust for the government.[76] Thus, although vertically integrated, compromise and interaction at the elite level enable the political system to function effectively. It is also able to function with only a moderate level of administrative power. The legislative bodies are fragmented politically but at the same time have formed lasting coalition governments with the continuing support of the population. This feeling of trust and respect for the government is carried over into the generally positive feelings of the population toward the administrative structures.

The final set of nations are those with relatively low trust in the political system but high levels of interpersonal trust. This pattern would appear to be displayed in the United States. The political culture of the United States has traditionally been one preferring individual and group action to governmental action.[77] A number of functions that might be performed by government, or at least with extensive governmental intervention, are still performed privately in the United States. The most notable example of this is health care, although a number of other professions and businesses have retained the right to administer their own affairs and make decisions that in other societies would be considered a matter of public concern.[78] Despite this, survey evidence has shown that Americans at least expect fair treatment from the political system, although this expectation is not so high as in the United Kingdom.[79] Moreover, when compared to levels of interpersonal trust, the government comes out a rather poor second. Thus, if we use the level of interpersonal trust as an "expected" level of trust, the level of trust found for government is low.

Whether or not the United States can be said to be indicative of this pattern, what are the consequences for administrative power? In the first place, we may expect a moderate level of administrative power. The use of nongovernmental organizations for a variety of regulatory tasks lessens the workload of the administration; at the same time, the relatively bad image of the political arms of government forces a number of questions to be decided administratively rather than politically. The "political" branches of governments tend to be so weighted down with checks and balances that the bureaucracy must again be called on to fill something of a decision-making vacuum. This is apparent in the increasing usage of administrative regulation and can also be evidenced by the apparent weakness of Congress in dealing with the Presidency and with the administrative bureaus. But, even given this growth of power, the general viewpoint of the American system vis-à-vis the public bureaucracy is rather negative. Americans may have some respect for individual administrators, but the dominant theme of the culture is perhaps all too well indicated by George Wallace's desire to throw the "bureaucrats and their briefcases" into the Potomac River.

In summary, we have seen that a relatively simple typology of variations in the levels of trust among the population toward two different social objects—individuals and the government—can be useful in explaining differences in the degree of administrative power in modern governments. This typology and its conclusions are rather obviously an oversimplification of a complex reality. A number of other cultural and political factors must be taken into account in the final explanation or prediction of administrative power. However, the relatively high correspondence between the predictions of the typology and this descriptive analysis of representative political systems offers some credence to the relationships hypothesized.

CULTURE AND THE INTERNAL MANAGEMENT OF ORGANIZATIONS

To this point we have been looking largely at the relationship of the political culture of the society and the performance of the administrative system. That is to say, we have been looking more at what the bureaucracy does for the political system rather than the manner in which it chooses to perform those tasks. We now turn our attention to the effects of culture on the internal management of complex administrative organizations. This is a complex topic worthy of several volumes in itself. Here we limit the scope of this discussion by dealing with only two topics. The first of these is the relationship between superiors and subordinates in an organization, related to general patterns of authority in the society. The second topic is the cultural basis of motivation for workers. As with most other aspects of this book, we are especially interested in the effects of these internal management practices on the policy outputs of the organization.

Culture and Authority

The definition and acceptance of the authority of one individual by another is a function of culture and society. As with virtually all cultural norms, there are individual interpretations of the norm, and hence individual variation, but certain modal patterns emerge. The use of impersonal and "rational-legal" authority as a means of controlling individuals, as suggested in formal models of bureaucratic management, is a culturally determined concept. First, it is intimately connected to the social cultural patterns of the West, and even then to a rather small segment of Western thought. This managerial strategy, to be successful, would require the support of a generally hierarchical and bureaucratic society. A culture that stressed the ideas of individualism and personal equality would find it difficult to support such a system of management.

Weber has presented the classical discussion of the sources of authority in society.[80] Much the same can be said of patterns of authority in organizations. Weber argued that authority had three sources: tradition, charismatic personality, and rationality. The first was taken to characterize most traditional societies. The authority exercised by an individual in government or in an organization (such few as might exist) would be a function of the individual's position in the traditional hierarchy in the society. This hierarchy is ordained by some alleged divine connection, or it may be a function of property, but the source of authority is not subject to any rational challenge. The charismatic authority is a transitional variety of authority. The source of authority is the force of personality of the individual. Weber spoke of this largely in terms of social leadership, but the same category could apply to organizational leaders who were capable of commanding respect and obedience through the force of their individual personality.[81] Weber notes that over time charisma tends to be institutionalized and to be converted into rational-legal authority. In this third class of authority the individual willingly accepts the authority of his superior simply because of the hierarchy of the organization or society. Thus, if the superior is in a superior position within the organization, that is sufficient to provide the individual with authority. In Simon's terms, the subordinate willingly suspends judgment and accepts the direction of the superior.[82]

Much management and management thinking is still bound to this Weberian conception of rational-legal authority, and of the right of the superior to command the subordinate. This, in fact, would appear to be one of the major causes for discontent in most large organizations in the Western world today. The cultural values of these societies have changed decidedly in favor of the right of people to decide their own futures. Workers, especially younger workers, are seeking involvement in decision making. This has largely been phrased in terms of the management of industrial enterprises, but much the same can be said of public organizations. The lower echelons of these organizations are also seeking new forms of management that will allow participation by those affected by decisions. This is often taken to include clients as well as the lower levels of administration.

Another challenge to hierarchical authority is expertise. The appeal of technology and expertise in modern society is almost ·hypnotic in its effects. Expertise has become a new basis of charisma for leaders of an organization. The problem is that this source of authority often (usually?) conflicts with the rational-legal basis of authority. Victor Thompson has argued that this divergence between expertise and formal authority is the fundamental problem of modern organizations.[83] Authority is concentrated at the top of the organizational pyramid while expertise is concentrated at the bottom. The conflicts intrinsic in such a situation are obvious. In public organizations expertise is often not only technical, but is also direct knowledge of the clientele and their problems, which is considered unimportant by those in the upper levels of the organization. The conflict, over both knowledge and values, in such a situation is virtually unavoidable.

The problems of authority and management in underdeveloped nations are rather different. The acceptance of hierarchy and rational-legal authority in these cases is formalistic at best. This pattern of authority conflicts with the traditional basis of authority in most other relationships. Even under colonial rule, the traditional authority structure was often borrowed by the colonial power for its own uses,[84] and attempts to modernize places new strains on traditional power structures. In many cases, the ideology of modernization would require the destruction or bypassing of older systems of authority. The destruction of this authority has created a vacuum that the rational-legal basis of authority has found it difficult to fill. Riggs notes the formalism of administrative structures in these societies, with apparent rationality in the pattern of organization, but a general reliance on traditional criteria of decision making.[85] Pye notes the same formalism in the bureaucratic system of Burma.[86] Thus modern institutions may often serve as a thin disguise for traditional practice.

Culture and Motivation

How do you activate workers to join an organization and to produce once they are members? To some degree, this is a part of the prior question of authority, in that Weber tended to assume that authority was itself a sufficient motivation for performance.[87] Beyond this seemingly naive expectation, how can the manager of a public organization activate his subordinates to do their jobs effectively? Answers range from the use of physical coercion, either real or threatened, to involvement in decision making. In each case, the choice of motivational strategy will be to some degree a function of the culture of the society. In general, we can think of four basic motivational techniques that are available to managers. The first technique, if it may be given such a euphemistic title, is coercion. Fortunately, the modern world has largely left behind the period in which direct coercion might be used as a means of gaining organizational compliance. The use of indirect or implied coercion is still an actively used technique, however. The coercion is rarely physical but involves other types of deprivations to the employee. In particular, this involves the loss of prestige, status, and acceptance through either loss of office or demotion. Newspapers carry stories of the deportation of disfavored administrators to the country's functional equivalent of Siberia (e.g., Cut Bank, Montana, in the United States). While this is certainly better than a public flogging in most people's minds, it can still be a severe deprivation in both physical and psychological terms.

A somewhat more subtle form of coercion is the use of ideological or religious doctrines as a motivating force. Perhaps the two most famous examples of this are the Protestant ethic and the thoughts of Chairman Mao. The former religious and ideological doctrine has been cited as one of the principle reasons for the development of Western industrial society.[88] By equating success in business or profession with Salvation, the Protestant ethic constituted an important motivating force for the growth of Western business and commerce. Even now, when direct belief in the correlation of success and divine election has waned, the culture of the West has been sufficiently influenced by this doctrine that success is valued as a good in itself.

The thoughts of Chairman Mao, although less widespread, constitute perhaps the best example of the use of a secular ideology as a motivating device. Exhortations to progress, development, and efficient production through this ideology have been an important if not crucial factor in China's economic development. This has been true despite a number of economic inefficiencies dictated by the doctrine. On a more personal basis, the desire to fulfill the thoughts of Mao and to please him and the people of China have served as important means of motivating the individual. As with the Protestant ethic, the threat of coercion has been internalized by the individual. The deprivations for the individual are more often than not internal, so that personal pressures of compliance constitute the major motivation for the individual.

It should be noted here that the use of ideology and religion can be at once a very expensive and a very inexpensive means of motivation. On the one hand, once the ideology is accepted by the population, it requires largely symbol manipulation in order to be effective. This is certainly less expensive than having to pay people money to motivate them or to involve them in decision making. Thus, as with any cultural device, the ideology of a society (or organization) provides a set of symbols that can be manipulated by those in power. The ideology also provides a set of psychological deprivations for the individual for failure to comply with the ideology. At least psychologically, the manipulation of symbols can constitute something approaching coercion. Ideology used as a means of motivation becomes expensive when it restricts forms of action available to the organization.[89] One of the defining characteristics of an ideology is that it prescribes and proscribes actions for individuals and groups that in turn limit the flexibility of action for the organization and society. Political leaders have been quite adept at justifying virtually any policy in terms of the dominant ideology, but this is costly both in the time required and in the probable weakening of commitment by some individuals. The same types of problems are encountered when attempting to change an ideology to meet changing social conditions. Thus an ideology can be an exceedingly inexpensive motivational method in the short run, but it may impose a number of long-range costs. The rational assessment of the net benefits of this motivational strategy will therefore depend upon the discount attached to long-range costs as well as the level of short-range demands.

The third motivational technique available to managers is monetary reward. Probably the prevailing concept of management in Western societies has been that monetary rewards are a sufficient inducement to gain the compliance of workers with the demands of the organization. The importance of money as a means of management and motivation is that in many ways it is the cheapest means of motivation, particularly in administrative organizations. Here, the main "product" is not goods or services, but rather it is decisions. If the majority of the work force can be motivated through their paychecks, then the need to allow their participation in decision making is eliminated. This will allow greater latitude of action for decision makers than can be found in ideological or involvement systems of management. This type of motivation was, in fact, a major assumption of Weber's ideal-type of the bureaucracy.[90] It makes bureaucracy virtually a neutral instrument that can be used for almost any purpose by its managers. While this assumption is rather obviously overstated, the latitude granted to managers through monetary motivation is an important consideration for any manager. The choice, however, is probably not individual but cultural.

The question of the latitude of decision making brings us to the fourth source of motivation. This is the involvement of the workers in decision making in the organization. The use of this method of management has varied across time more than across cultures and is generally considered to be a product of the "postindustrial" or "postwelfare" society.[91] In general, this method of management employs the ability of the worker to perceive that he has greater control over his life and work as a means of motivation. Studies of motivation have shown that the major source of motivation for professional and white-collar employees is the individuals' ability to perceive that they are doing something significant and the ability to feel that they could control what happened to them in their jobs.[92] Given the level of education and training required for most administrative jobs, the same type of motivational structure can be expected among administrators. Moreover, the ideology of participation is apparently increasing in importance as an increasing number of workers at all levels of administration demand an influence in the decisions made which affect them. This development is rather obviously in contradiction to the ideal-type bureaucratic model and to a significant body of literature in public management stressing the importance of executive control and the duty of leadership at the top.[93]

One interesting aspect of this increasing demand for involvement is that it has spread not only among administrators, but also among the clients of administration. Thus a new force has to be taken into account by management, and managers must think of motivating the clients of the organization to gain their compliance in much the same way that managers must think about motivating workers. The inducements are not only of the monetary (services) variety, but now also include involvement in decision making.

With both workers and clients, involvement is an especially costly means of gaining organizational compliance. It reduces the latitude allowed for action on the part of the managers and provides them little in return. Unlike an ideology that can be readily used in "normal" times to satisfy employees, involvement requires a constant redefinition of goals and priorities. And, as with ideological change, these types of changes are generally quite costly to the organization in terms of both time lost and personal costs to the losers in the struggle. In public organizations, this also involves a redefinition of some aspects of public policy that may require negotiations of other political institutions. Thus the losses in continuity of programs, in the reanalysis of priorities, and in the personal reshaping of work priorities make the granting of involvement an exceedingly expensive means of motivation. Nevertheless, in some cases it may be the only means of motivation that will be successful. Increasingly, labor has sought less in terms of increases in wages and hours benefits and more in the way of determination of job and work priorities. Teachers and others in professional positions have also struck for considerations of this type. We can only expect that much future labor negotiation will be directed at this problem rather than at the more traditional pecuniary concerns.

We should not be totally negative concerning the use of involvement as a motivational device. In terms of human values it is probably the best means of management devised. Furthermore, it may be one means of solving Thompson's dilemma concerning the comparative misplacement of expertise and authority in organizations. In the short run, this means of management has been successful, although its long-range effects have yet to be gauged. Involvement with little real consequent change for the individual may actually be an alienating experience. Given the demands of the present culture, however, the demands for involvement can no longer be readily denied.

We have, to this point, avoided the traditional notion of the motivation of the public servant being solely the public interest. This was not done to denigrate the long service of a number of committed individuals in organizations.[94] Thus we view the majority of individuals in public organizations to be little different in their motivational structure (but perhaps in their value structures) from individuals in any other organization. The idea of the public service would, therefore, be classified analytically as just another of the many ideological convictions that have motivated individuals in organizations.

CONCLUSION

This chapter has attempted to show the influence of patterns of political culture and general cultural values on the operation of the administrative system. We have examined this influence as it affects not only the outputs of the administrative system, but also the internal management of the organizations. In both cases, we find that culture has a significant impact on the behavior of public administration. Unfortunately, the assessment of this impact had to remain in a somewhat impressionistic level because of the lack of much hard evidence on these relationships. One of the main problems with the concept of culture, and especially of political culture, is that it generally tends to be a vague and amorphous concept that can be twisted to include virtually anything a researcher wishes. We hope we have avoided this pitfall as much as possible and have presented the evidence in as unbiased a manner as possible. But we are the products of our own culture and see the world from our own perspective. It is difficult if not impossible to escape the imperatives of a culture taught to us from birth. Any significant progress in the field of relating cultural values and their effects on administration (or other aspects of politics) must come from a more complete empirical delimitation of culture and an examination of its dimensions. We hope this discussion has been a step in the direction of analyzing the potential and probable effects of culture so that more informed empirical analysis can test for these effects.

NOTES

1. Lucian W. Pye and Sidney Verba, *Political Culture and Political Development* (Princeton: Princeton University Press, 1965).

2. For a recent review, see David O. Sears, "Political Socialization," in Fred I. Greenstein and Nelson W. Polsby, *The Handbook of Political Science*, vol. 2 (Reading, Mass.: Addison-Wesley, 1975).

3. Just as with expenditure levels, major public events may have a "displacement effect" on the more general sphere of government activity. See Alan T. Peacock and Jack Wiseman, *The Growth of Public Expenditure in the United Kingdom* (2nd ed.; London: George Allen & Unwin, 1967), pp. 27–28.

4. Ronald Inglehart, "The Silent Revolution in Europe: Intergenerational Change in Post-Industrial Society," *American Political Science Review* 65 (December 1971): 991–1017; Alan Marsh, "The 'Silent Revolution,' Value Priorities, and the Quality of Life in Britain," *American Political Science Review* 69 (March 1975): 21–30.

5. Reinhard Bendix, *Work and Authority in Industry* (New York: John Wiley, 1956).

6. Hugh Heclo and Aaron Wildavsky, *The Private Government of Public Money* (Berkeley: University of California Press, 1974).

7. See Sidney Verba, "Germany: The Remaking of Political Culture," in Pye and Verba, *Political Culture*, pp. 151–54.

8. Ibid. Verba does point to significant long-term changes in the family structure. See also Kendall L. Baker, "Political Participation, Political Efficacy and Socialization in Germany," *Comparative Politics* 6, no. 1 (October 1973): 73–98.

9. Robert E. Ward, "Japan: The Continuity of Modernization," in Pye and Verba, *Political Culture*, pp. 27–82.

10. Talcott Parsons and Edward A. Shils, *Toward A General Theory of Action* (Cambridge, Mass.: Harvard University Press, 1951), p. 77.

11. Giovanni Sartori, "Politics, Ideology and Belief Systems," *American Political Science Review* 63 (June 1969): 398–411.

12. Ibid.

13. Elihu Katz and S. N. Eisenstadt, "Some Sociological Observations on the Response of Israeli Organizations to New Immigrants," *Administrative Science Quarterly* 5, no. 1 (June 1960): 113–33.

14. Riggs refers to this as the "bazaar" nature of these cultures. Fred W. Riggs, *Administration in Developing Countries: The Theory of Prismatic Society* (Boston: Houghton Mifflin, 1964).

15. Ibid., pp. 200–202.

16. Ibid., p. 201.

17. See S. N. Eisenstadt, "Bureaucracy, Bureaucratization and Debureaucratization," *Administrative Science Quarterly* 4 (December 1959): 302–20.

18. This has been true not just of studies of political culture, but of most contemporary comparative politics. See Roy C. Macridis, "Comparative Politics and the Study of Government: The Search for Focus," *Comparative Politics* 1 (October 1968): 79–90.

19. For example, there are regular polls on presidential popularity, on the job that Congress is doing, and even on the role of the Supreme Court, but few queries about the bureaucracy.

20. M. K. Jennings, F. P. Kilpatrick, and M. C. Cummings, "Trusted Leaders: Perceptions of Appointed Federal Officials," *Public Opinion Quarterly* 30 (Fall 1966): 368–84.

21. S. J. Levy, "The Public Image of Government Agencies," *Public Administration Review* 23 (March 1963): 25–29.

22. Gabriel A. Almond and Sidney Verba, *The Civic Culture* (Princeton: Princeton University Press, 1963), pp. 70–73.

23. Samuel J. Eldersveld, V. Jagannadham, and A. P. Barnabas, *The Citizen and the Administrator in a Developing Democracy* (Glenview, Ill.: Scott, Foresman, 1968).
24. Almond and Verba, *Civic Culture*, chap. 1.
25. Gabriel A. Almond and G. Bingham Powell, *Comparative Politics: A Developmental Approach* (Boston: Little, Brown, 1966), pp. 57–63.
26. Peter Nettl, *Political Mobilization* (New York: Basic Books, 1967).
27. Harry Eckstein, *Division and Cohesion in Democracy* (Princeton: Princeton University Press, 1966).
28. Daniel J. Elazar, "The States and the Political Setting," in his *American Federalism: A View from the States* (New York: Crowell, 1966), pp. 85–104.
29. Lucian W. Pye, "Introduction: Political Culture and Political Development," in Pye and Verba, *Political Culture*, pp. 3–26.
30. Parsons and Shils, *General Theory of Action*.
31. H. H. Gerth and C. Wright Mills, *From Max Weber: Essays in Sociology* (New York: Oxford University Press, 1946), pp. 198–200.
32. J. Donald Kingsley, *Representative Bureaucracy* (Yellow Springs, Ohio: Antioch Press, 1944).
33. See, for example, OECD, *Social Objectives in Educational Planning* (Paris: OECD, 1967).
34. One view of the difficulties created thereby is given by Edward Banfield, *The Unheavenly City* (Boston: Little, Brown, 1970). A very different view is given by Gideon Sjoberg, Richard A. Bremer, and Buford Faris, "Bureaucracy and the Lower Class," *Sociology and Social Research* 51 (1966): 325–37.
35. Michel Crozier, *The Bureaucratic Phenomenon* (Chicago: University of Chicago Press, 1964), pp. 213–36.
36. Lucian W. Pye, *Politics, Personality and Nation Building* (New Haven: Yale University Press, 1962); Edgar L. Shor, "The Thai Bureaucracy," *Administrative Science Quarterly* 5, no. 1 (June 1960): pp. 66–86. Though clearly not underdeveloped, Japanese administration has the same tendency toward personal followings and cliques.
37. Inglehart, "Silent Revolution."
38. See Orion F. White, "The Dialectical Organization—An Alternative to Bureaucracy," *Public Administration Review* 39 (January–February 1969): 32–42.
39. See Paul Blumberg, *Industrial Democracy: The Sociology of Participation* (London: Constable, 1968). Business International S.A., *Industrial Democracy in Europe* (Geneva: Business International, 1974).
40. See Charles H. Gibson, "Volvo Increases Production Through Job Enrichment," *California Management Review* 15 (Summer 1973): 64–66. Nils Elvander, "Democracy in Large Organizations," in M. Donald Hancock and Gideon Sjoberg, *Politics in The Post-Welfare Society* (New York: Columbia University Press, 1969), pp. 302–24.
41. Inglehart, "Silent Revolution."
42. Emmette S. Redford, *Democracy in the Administrative State* (New York: Oxford University Press, 1969), p. 66.
43. This is certainly the feeling one gets from the recent spate of "crisis" literature. See Michel Crozier, Samuel P. Huntington, and Joji Watanuki, *The Crisis of Democracy* (New York: New York University Press, 1975).
44. This usage is quite similar to that of Deutsch and Haas in discussing political integration. See Karl Deutsch, et al., *Political Community in the North Atlantic Area* (Princeton: Princeton University Press, 1957); Ernst B. Haas, *The Uniting of Europe* (Stanford: Stanford University Press, 1958).

45. See, for example, the argument of Edward Banfield, *The Moral Basis of Backward Society* (New York: Free Press, 1958); Daniel Lerner, *The Passing of Traditional Society* (New York: Free Press, 1958).

46. Arend Lijphart, *The Politics of Accommodation* (2nd ed.; Berkeley: University of California Press, 1975). Martin O. Heisler with Robert B. Kvavik, "Patterns of European Politics: The 'European Polity' Model," in *Politics in Europe: Structures and Processes in Some Postindustrial Societies,* ed. Martin Heisler (New York: David McKay, 1974), pp. 27–89.

47. Gerth and Mills, *From Max Weber.*

48. Diamant argues, however, that only routine decisions get made and that few significant innovations are made. Alfred Diamant, "Tradition and Innovation in French Administration," *Comparative Political Studies* 1 (July 1963): 251–74.

49. See, for example, Richard Rose, *Governing Without Consensus: An Irish Perspective* (London: Faber, 1971).

50. See chapter 4.

51. See, for example, John T. Dorsey, "A Communication Model for Administration," *Administrative Science Quarterly* 2, no. 3 (December 1957): 307–24.

52. Sjoberg, Bremer and Faris, "Politics in Post-Welfare Society," p. 325.

53. Almond and Verba, *Civic Culture,* p. 213.

54. Laurence Wylie, "Social Change at the Grassroots," in Stanley Hoffmann et al., *In Search of France* (New York: Harper & Row, 1963), p. 203.

55. See chapter 6.

56. Almond and Verba, *Civic Culture,* p. 270.

57. SOFRES, *Sondages* 25, no. 2 (1963).

58. Nils Elvander, *Intresseorganisationera i dagens Sverige* (Lund: CWK Gleerups, 1966); Lars Madsen, *Interressorganisationerne og det offentlige* (Copenhagen: Handelshøjskolen, 1969).

59. Again, relatively fewer studies have focused upon trust in administration than upon trust in more political institutions.

60. Almond and Verba, *Civic Culture,* p. 142.

61. Paul R. Abramson and Ronald Inglehart, "The Development of Systemic Support in Four Western Democracies," *Comparative Political Studies* 2, no. 4 (January 1970): 419–42.

62. Arend Lijphart, *Politics of Accommodation;* Dankwart A. Rustow, *The Politics of Compromise* (Princeton: Princeton University Press, 1955); Eckstein, *Division and Cohesion.*

63. For some contrary evidence, see Richard Rose, *The Problem of Party Government* (London: Macmillan, 1974).

64. Eric Nordlinger, *The Working Class Tories* (Berkeley: University of California Press, 1967).

65. Rose, *Party Government;* James B. Christoph, "High Civil Servants and the Politics of Consensualism in Great Britain," in M. Dogan, *The Mandarins of Western Europe* (New York: Halsted, 1975), pp. 25–62.

66. Effective "democratic" political institutions might be a more appropriate term. See Cynthia Enloe, *Ethnic Conflict and Political Development* (Boston: Little, Brown, 1973).

67. A good review is provided in Henry W. Ehrmann, *Politics in France* (3rd ed.; Boston: Little, Brown, 1976), pp. 181–214. Joseph LaPalombara, *Interest Groups in Italian Politics* (Princeton: Princeton University Press, 1965).

68. Philip M. Williams and Martin Harrison, *Politics and Society in DeGaulle's Republic* (Garden City, N.Y.: Doubleday, 1973), pp. 169–74.

69. Banfield, *Moral Basis of Backward Society.*

70. See, for example, Victor Olorunsola, *The Politics of Cultural Sub-Nationalism in Africa* (Garden City, N.Y.: Doubleday, 1972).
71. This role has generally been exercised by the army rather than the bureaucracy. An interesting case study is Robert M. Price, "Military Officers and Political Leadership," *Comparative Politics* 3, no. 3 (April 1971): 361–80.
72. Lucian W. Pye, "Armies in the Process of Political Modernization," in *The Role of the Military in Underdeveloped Countries*, ed. J. J. Johnson (Princeton: Princeton University Press, 1962), pp. 77–80.
73. Arend Lijphart, "Consociational Democracy," *World Politics* 21 (January 1969): 207–25.
74. Val R. Lorwin, "Belgium," in Robert Dahl, *Political Oppositions in Western Democracies* (New Haven: Yale University Press, 1966), p. 174.
75. Val R. Lorwin, "Segmental Pluralism: Ideological Cleavages and Political Cohesion in the Smaller European Democracies," *Comparative Politics* 3 (January 1971): 141–75; Hans Daalder, "The Netherlands," in Dahl, *Political Opposition*, chap. 6.
76. Arend Lijphart, *Politics of Accommodation*.
77. The impact of these views is well illustrated in Anthony King, "Ideas, Institutions and Policies of Government: A Comparative Analysis," *British Journal of Political Science* 3, nos. 3 and 4 (July and October 1973): 291–314, 409–24.
78. See chapter 6.
79. Almond and Verba, *Civic Culture*, pp. 70–75.
80. Gerth and Mills, *From Max Weber*, pp. 295 ff.
81. Ibid.
82. Herbert A. Simon, *Administrative Behavior* (New York: Free Press, 1957), pp. 124–28.
83. Victor Thompson, *Modern Organizations* (New York: Knopf, 1961).
84. This was especially true of the British rule in Africa. See L. Rubin and B. Weinstein, *Introduction to African Politics* (New York: Praeger, 1974), pp. 34–41.
85. Riggs, *Administration in Developing Countries*, pp. 182–84.
86. Lucian W. Pye, *Politics, Personality and Nation Building: Burma's Search for Identity* (New Haven: Yale University Press, 1962).
87. Gerth and Mills, *From Max Weber*, pp. 199–202.
88. Richard H. Tawney, *Religion and the Rise of Capitalism* (New York: Harcourt, Brace & World, 1926); Max Weber, *The Protestant Ethic and the Spirit of Capitalism* (London: George Allen & Unwin, 1930).
89. Harold Wilensky, *Organizational Intelligence* (New York: Basic Books, 1967), chap. 2.
90. Gerth and Mills, *From Max Weber*.
91. See, for example, the articles by White and Sjoberg, Capps, Hancock, and Elvander in Hancock and Sjoberg, *Politics in Post-Welfare Society*.
92. Perhaps the most thorough study of this type is G. Gurin, J. Veroff, and S. Feld, *Americans View Their Mental Health* (New York: Basic Books, 1960).
93. Two rather classic works in this regard are Chester Barnard, *The Functions of the Executive* (Cambridge, Mass.: Harvard University Press, 1938); Ordway Tead, *The Art of Administration* (New York: McGraw-Hill, 1951).
94. See a more thorough discussion of reported motivations in chapter 4.

4

THE RECRUITMENT OF PUBLIC ADMINISTRATORS

Before anyone can make much progress toward administering a public program, the political system must enlist and train a group of public administrators. This is common sense, but it is used simply to point to the importance of recruitment in a study of public administration. In order to be able to say what a public agency will do, we must first have some idea of who will do it and for what purposes—public or personal. Unlike earlier assumptions concerning organizational management, such as Weber's ideal conceptualization of the bureaucrat or the Taylors' scientific-management school, the individuals who occupy organizational positions are not interchangable parts.[1] This is widely understood when discussing more strictly political leaders—Presidents, prime ministers, and judges—but is often not understood for administrative personnel, even for those clearly in policy-making positions of bureaucratic structures. Bureaucrats bring with them to their jobs a host of values, predispositions, and operating routines that will greatly affect the quality of their performance in a bureaucratic setting.[2] Again we must emphasize that public administrators, even those at relatively low levels in the organizational hierarchy, are indeed decision makers. The proverbial story of the judge having burned toast for breakfast and then sentencing the defendant to death may be as true, albeit in less extreme situations, of thousands of administrators passing on thousands of requests or demands for services from government. In this particular chapter we are interested in the manner in which governments go about selecting administrators, and thereby the ways in which they narrow the range of possible outcomes of the policy-making process.

MERIT VERSUS PATRONAGE

Several somewhat conflicting themes have dominated the discussion of administrative recruitment. The first of these has been the search for efficiency through merit recruitment. One of the defining characteristics of Weber's model of bureaucracy was that the bureaucrats should be selected on the basis of merit rather than the ascriptive criteria of caste, race, or class, or on what Kaufman termed "neutral competence." [3] The underlying assumption was that the bureaucracy had to be able to recruit the best personnel possible, and merit recruitment was the logical means of filling the available positions with the most qualified personnel.

In developmental terms, a second impetus for the adoption of merit recruitment was the desire to remove the appointment of administrative positions from political patronage and to require merit qualifications.[4] Thus, in addition to removing the inequalities and possible inefficiencies of ascriptive recruitment, the merit reforms of civil service were intended to remove the inefficiencies and favoritism of political appointment.

As desirable as the idea of employing the best person possible for each job in the public service may be from the point of view of enforcing the achievement norms of a modern society, and perhaps of achieving new goals of social equality in a developing society, some important inefficiencies may result from merit recruitment. These may be especially noticeable when contrasted to the alternative political appointment. Merit recruitment appears to imply the more mechanistic conception of the administrator or bureaucrat as the value-free administrator of programs who will administer public policies regardless of their intentions or impacts on society. It is assumed that sufficient technical criteria will guide their choices and that commitment to a program or rejection of it will have little influence on behavior. This conception of the administrator simply does not conform to the realities. Individuals were at least more disposed toward the programs of the political party in power than the supposedly neutral appointees of a merit system who may, in fact, be hostile to that program.[5] This requires that political appointees be selected for some combination of political disposition and administrative talent, however, and not for political predisposition alone.

This discussion of political versus merit appointment is, of course, one of degree. Virtually all political systems have some level at which appointments are quite clearly political—frequently referred to as "policy-making" positions—and they also have jobs for which appointment is made on a relatively routine basis on some sort of merit system. The question, then, is how far up the ladder of the administrative hierarchy merit, or at least not overtly political appointment, is intended to go, and conversely, what are the limits of political appointment? Let us take two countries as examples: the United States and the United Kingdom.[6] The United States chooses to provide some rather wide discretion to the President to appoint political officials in the federal government.[7] Approximately 1,200 posts currently exist in the federal government, and frequently four or five echelons of political appointees are in command of the career civil servants in the executive departments. The United Kingdom chooses to place virtually no political officials between the ministers in political command and having political responsibility for the department and the upper echelon of the career civil service—the permanent secretaries.[8] What accounts for these differences? One argument is that bureaucratic structures have simply evolved in the course of history, and no one has seen any real reason to alter them. A more rationalist hypothesis might be that the more fragmented the decisional structure of a political system, the more likely it is to provide its ministers (or secretaries) with a number of political appointees to attempt to provide some degree of integration of political motive and actual administration. The relative integration of the political elite and policy system in the United Kingdom, contrasted with that of the United States or the continental European systems that also tend to have large numbers of political appointees, would appear to argue that the United Kingdom does not need to attempt to enforce conformity with policy or discussion of policy as far down the administrative hierarchy as is true in those other systems.[9]

REPRESENTATIVE BUREAUCRACY

A second dominant theme in a discussion of recruitment into public administrative positions is the question of equality of opportunity and representativeness of the public bureaucracy.[10] Since Kingsley coined the term "representative bureaucracy" there has been concern over the extent to which the bureaucracy does, or should, represent the characteristics of the population in whose name it administers policy. Thus, just as some scholars have emphasized the necessity of merit in the recruitment of public administrators, others have stressed the importance of producing a set of administrators whose social and economic characteristics are similar to the people with whom they will be working. The arguments are twofold. The first is that narrow recruitment from any social stratum will tend to bias programs and policies. This is especially important in social programs because there is a higher probability that these personnel will be working with members of minority communities and may tend to impose dominant group values. Studies of teachers, social workers, the police, and other types of public employees indicate a tendency to reward those clients who correspond to accepted dominant values and punish those who do not.[11] This difference in value structures may not only impair the personal interaction of client and administrator, but will also tend to prevent a number of qualified individuals from receiving services.[12]

The second argument on behalf of greater representativeness is that the ability of the public bureaucracy to hire personnel should be used as a positive weapon to alter the social and economic structure of the society. Thus, hiring minority community members can serve not only to break any bonds of prejudice within the society, but also to provide a means of economic advancement for members of the minority community.[13] In ethnically plural societies in which the differences between the communities are not necessarily those of dominance or submission, or in which the ethnic cleavage is rather intensely politicized, this argument is generally altered to say that representative recruitment can be used to *preserve* the social structure and the rights of each of the ethnic communities in administering policy.[14] In both versions of this argument, however, is the underlying premise that bureaucracies should be representative not simply because it is democratic for them to be so, but because the pattern of recruitment will have a fundamental effect on the shape of the social structure and social stratification across time.

Before one goes too far with the idea of representative bureaucracy, however, several important caveats must be advanced. The first is that research on representative bureaucracy has consistently found an overrepresentation of middle-class (broadly interpreted) backgrounds among civil servants. This is to be expected. The civil service is in itself a middle-class occupation, and the sons and daughters of the middle class tend to have a much higher probability of attaining middle-class occupations than do the sons and daughters of the working class. This is in part due to the nature of educational recruitment which, even in modern "welfare states," tends substantially to overrepresent the middle class, and in part due to the nature of the motivations and incentives inculcated in middle-class households.[15] In either case, the number of middle-class offspring in the civil service is not a particularly damning finding for the nature of the bureaucracy but is rather reflective of more general patterns of social stratification and mobility in the society. Interestingly, this pattern persists in societies that have sought to eliminate class barriers in public life, e.g., the Soviet Union. Such evidence as we have would indicate that those occupying positions in the upper echelons of the Soviet civil service tend to come from families of fathers who also held "middle-class" occupations.

A second caveat is that concern for representative recruitment—other than in its purely democratic form—assumes that the social class of parents will tend to determine behavior. This is the underlying assumption in a large amount of elite research, but such research as attempts to link background with behavior provides quite disappointing results.[16] In the first place, administrators have acquired or retained middle-class standing and, therefore, their behavior may be more directly determined by the standards and norms of that class rather than any class from which they have been mobile.[17] And although members of minority groups may not be able to change their status quite so rapidly, one could argue with some support that they would tend to adopt the values of the dominant community at a higher rate than would other members of their minority. This puts us in a somewhat paradoxical situation. Regardless of the degree of ostensible representativeness of the bureaucratic structures, there may still be a high level of homogeneity of attitudes among bureaucrats, especially if the same personnel remain in the same structures across time.

Finally, we must realize that there may not of necessity be as broad a gap between merit recruitment and programs of "affirmative action" as there might appear to be at first glance. To some degree, the possession of certain ascriptive criteria may be an important qualification for the efficient administration of public programs, especially at the client-contact level of the bureaucracy. Language, race, or class differences may prevent the adequate administration of public programs; to prevent those differences from becoming too significant in administration, some attention to ethnic balancing of personnel must be given. Thus, to some degree, defining the person best able to carry out a job can depend upon ethnic characteristics just as it can depend upon formal education and the possession of certain skills.

PUBLIC AND PRIVATE EMPLOYMENT

A final question that often arises with respect to recruitment and retention of civil servants is the relationship between the advantages of governmental and private employers in providing salaries, benefits, and working conditions that will attract good personnel. There is, however, some question as to whether government should directly compete with the private economy. This argument rather naturally arises most often in free-market economies. The argument made is that through taxation, employers are actually coerced into supporting their competition in the labor market; further, the public sector lacks any effective means of pricing most of its products.[18] Therefore, governments can, to a point, drive up the price of labor to an unreasonable level from the viewpoint of actual productivity of personnel if employed in the market economy. This diseconomy may be especially evident when public personnel are allowed to unionize.[18] Thus we come down to a rather simple question of the relative demand for public and private goods and the consequent willingness to pay for each type of goods. The evidence would appear to argue that there is considerably less demand for publicly produced goods—especially as they take on the characteristics of public goods—compared to the demand for private goods.[19] This may accentuate the diseconomies of public hiring. There may be no ready solution for this problem, but it is one that must be considered when discussing the extent and type of recruitment into the public bureaucracy.

METHODS OF RECRUITMENT

As well as the rather broad questions concerning recruitment outlined above, several questions deal with the more specific methods of recruitment and the judging of qualifications for positions. These questions are, of course, greatly simplified if political patronage or other sorts of nonachievement criteria are used, for then only simple appointment by the appropriate political official is required.

Education and Training

The first question is the type of training required for a position, and associated with it, the type of testing employed. Here we are interested primarily in the recruitment of the upper echelons of the bureaucracy rather than the clerical positions for which relatively uniform skill requirements can be established. In general, recruitment to policy-making positions requires some sort of postsecondary education, with the major question being the degree of specialization of that education. This brings us to the rather classic argument between

TABLE 4.1

University Majors of Direct Entrants to
Administrative Class of the Civil
Service in the United Kingdom, 1961 and After
(in percentage) [a]

Arts and Humanities	Social Sciences	Natural Sciences and Applied Science	Other
69	27	12	4

SOURCE: A. H. Halsey and I. M. Crewe, "Social Survey of the Civil Service,"
The Civil Service (The Fulton Report) (London: HMSO, 1969), vol. 3,
pt. 1, p. 93.

[a] Greater than 100% due to dual concentrations.

the advocates of generalists and specialists in bureaucratic hiring.[20]
The generalist school, as perhaps best typified by practice in the
United Kingdom, selects individuals for these bureaucratic roles
largely on the basis of general abilities and success in any program of
formal postsecondary education. The famous Northcote-Trevelyan
Report of 1854 not only called for the establishment of a merit-based
civil service in Britain, but also noted that training in the classical
disciplines was perhaps the best preparation for any aspiring administrator.[21] This tradition of the talented amateur has persisted
even in the face of the increasing technological content of public
programs.[22] The assumption remains that general intelligence is
all that is required to sift the technical information supplied to the
ministries from their technical staff and a few outside experts and
that the role of administration is the application of intelligence to the
sifting of that information. This tendency to seek talent, whether
trained in technical specialities or not, is well reflected in the academic backgrounds of senior civil servants, as compared to the top
executives in the American civil service, and to executives in British private industry (see table 4.1). An overwhelming proportion of
the British civil service have arts and humanities degrees, with almost no degrees in applied sciencies or other technical fields. This is
in marked contrast to the American pattern, although somewhat less
so to the pattern of recruitment of managerial talent in British industry. The British civil service, despite vast increases in the technological content of its programs, persists in assuming that the

talented amateur can muddle through. The need for increased technological sophistication on the part of the administrative class of the
civil service was one of the principle findings of the Fulton Commission, but it will require years to implement this. Until then, British
government must continue to rely on talented amateurs.[23]

American public administration has opted for more specialized recruitment into the public bureaucracy. The American system, however, performs this recruitment after the education of the applicant in
his academic speciality. France, the German Länder, and several other
continental European administrative systems take this practice somewhat further by educating administrators in specialized schools either
completely or partially managed by the state. In France, the École
Nationale d'Administration (ENA) is the principal means of entry
into the upper levels of the administrative corps.[24] The general legal
and administrative training provided at the ENA is supplemented by
more technical training provided at several other Grandes Écoles. In
this system, the state can decide exactly what type of training it wants
its future administrators to receive. After all, it is footing the bill. This
system of training is capable of providing a corps of highly specialized
administrators with the technical knowledge of the law, financial administration, or applied science that may be required by the modern
state.

The British and French cases, as is so often true, are the extreme
poles of the training question. The majority of administrative systems
operate somewhere in the middle in terms of degree of specialization.
The United States, the Scandinavian countries, Switzerland, and
Austria tend to recruit personnel who already possess some form of
required training and then train them in service for some of the more
particular functions of public administrators. In all of the above except the United States, the role of administrator is quite similar to that
of jurist, so the most common requirement is a legal degree. Thus, to
some extent these officials are also generalists; they have no specific
training other than law but are required to administer programs that
may have a scientific or technical complexion.

The underdeveloped countries of the world are in a more difficult
position when it comes to a choice between specialist and generalist.
In the first place, they are frequently left with a civil service trained
by the former colonial power and thereby trained according to the
traditions of that European country.[25] Further, underdeveloped countries generally lack technical talent and must opt for a more generalist stance in recruitment into new positions. Some countries have

attempted to replace an indigenous technical force with one drawn from Western countries—usually the former colonial power—but the demands of national pride and the need for jobs for their own people frequently require that jobs be given to less technically quali- fied individuals from the new nation.[26] At the same time that the ad- ministrative system may be somewhat deficient in specialized talent from an absolute point of view, they may have a relative monopoly on such talent within the country. A principal characteristic of many developing countries is that the political system is forced into the posi- tion of becoming the major directive force in social and economic reform. As one commentator put it:

> While there is no uniform pattern, the experience of many newly independent countries shows a growing emphasis on cen- tralized planning, direction, and implementation of development programs. Thus, the government relies more on the bureaucracy than the private sector to carry out the task of nation and state building, economic growth, and social reforms—activities which are preeminent in the consciousness of the rulers and the ruled.[27]

The Western model of development—speaking broadly, as the Western economic and social systems evolved by several significantly different paths—assumed a long time span and the absence of de- velopmental pressures from mass publics and organized segments of the society.[28] The developing countries today are faced with pro- ducing change within the context of widely disseminated informa- tion on the glories of development and consumerism. Their leaders face demands for increased production of consumer goods at the same time that they know the need for investment in capital projects, which will bear greater productive benefits in the long run but which require a short-term retreat from a consumer-oriented economy toward a more state-directed economy. Given these problems, it is rather apparent that these societies have a pressing need for spe- cialized administrators capable of proposing some solutions to these problems and a large number of skilled personnel actually to manage economic enterprises that may be run directly by the state.

The above description of administration and administrative func- tions, if in the undeveloped countries taken to its logical extreme, might be a relatively accurate description of administrative functions in the Soviet Union and, to a lesser extent, other communist coun- tries.[29] As the state becomes not only an economic planner, regulator, and adviser, but also the chief entrepreneur, the need for specialized talent tends to increase. Thus the average Soviet administrator, even if not administering a highly technical project, tends to have scientific or social science training. Interestingly, the more generalist talents of ideological argument and broad knowledge of the intended purpose of the Soviet state appear to be devalued by this set of upper-level administrators, who may differ little in this respect from administrators in other societies.[30] They have the same—if not greater—demands for production and efficiency that face other managers, and are often faced with highly technical problems that only someone with a technical background may fully understand.

Job Placement

Related to the question of the type of training that a prospective civil servant is expected to have is the question of the means through which the position and the applicant are expected to find each other. Again, we find two principal answers: a centralized personnel organization and recruitment by each individual agency that seeks employees. The first model is practiced by the United States, the United Kingdom, France, Belgium, Italy, and the majority of the underdeveloped countries. The last set of countries are engaged in this means of recruitment in large part as a function of their inherited systems of administration coming from former colonial rulers. In the centralized pattern of recruitment there is a central civil service organization of some sort that is responsible for advertising new positions, testing applicants, and selecting some smaller set of applicants for final selection by the agency seeking the employee. The usual procedure is that the agency notifies the personnel organization of the position, a competitive examination is held, and then the agency seeking the person is sent a list of three or more names from which they select their new employee. The latter selection may be made on the basis of personal interviews or simply by taking the individual with the highest score on the examination or by any other rational or irrational criteria. This means of recruitment obviously fills the requirements of merit recruitment. Competitive tests are used to fill the position, these tests are centrally administered to prevent bias, and the hiring organization accepts only those deemed qualified on the basis of the examination. In practice, there may be ways around the merit system, especially for those who have professional qualifications, e.g., physicians, lawyers, librarians, and the like. They may be qualified simply on the basis of their degrees and certificates and require no further examination.

The second means of hiring and recruitment is used primarily by the Northern European countries, Spain, and many of Latin American countries. In these systems there is no central personnel organization; rather, each agency is responsible for hiring its own personnel. The most common procedure is for the agency to publish notice of a vacancy and accept applications from prospective employees. These applications are generally judged on the basis of their containing the appropriate minimum qualifications for the job—especially legal training in the Scandinavian countries (Sweden, Denmark, Norway), West Germany, and Austria. After the individual is deemed minimally qualified, selection may be made on the basis of less achievement-based criteria. This system of decentralized recruitment obviously allows considerable latitude for the use of partisan and ascriptive criteria in hiring public officials, who can become tenured in office and virtually impossible for subsequent regimes to remove. Charges of partisanship are indeed made in these systems, even in Sweden and Denmark with their long histories of civil service independence and prestige.[31] Very frequently, the charges have more than a little truth in them. It is a simple matter to hire partisans when there are no formal restrictions to prevent it, and the parties in power would be extremely foolish if they did not try to provide employment for their own supporters and employ administrators likely to be favorably disposed toward the programs they will be administering. As with many administrative practices, this is not a simple case of recruitment by merit or by patronage, but rather something of an intermediate means of recruitment that combines some features of both ideal-type methods. There is the potential for substantial patronage, but these opportunities are restrained in practice by the norms, procedures, and pride of the administrators. In each country in Europe in which the recruitment of administrators by agency is practiced—with the possible exception of Spain—the civil service is a sufficiently respected profession that few practitioners would seek to demean it by an excessive or blatant use of the power they find themselves possessing.

The nature of recruitment by agency is made more complex when federalism is introduced as another variable. In Germany and Switzerland recruitment to public administrative positions is done not only by the individual agencies, but also by separate and in some cases highly independent subnational political units, who are in turn responsible for the administration of national programs.[32] This is further complicated by Swiss bureaucracy's need to preserve some balance among regional, linguistic, and religious subpopulations among civil servants. In general, the use of subnational bodies to perform the recruitment function may provide even greater possibilities for the use of nonmerit criteria in recruitment. Nevertheless, in Germany and Switzerland we find again that the norms of the bureaucratic system are sufficiently ingrained so that merit criteria are strenuously enforced. Those who are hired will have the necessary qualifications for the position—legal training and prior legal experience—and they will be made to undergo some sort of postentry training in the work of administration before they are granted permanent positions as administrators.[33] There is an attempt, and actually a rather thorough attempt, to employ people who are formally qualified according to the requirements of the law. Thus, in this case as in others, although the rigidity of bureaucracies is often an impediment to innovation, it can also serve as an important protective device for the society in preventing illegal or immoral actions on the part of government.

Career Distinctiveness

A third question concerning recruitment is the degree to which the public service is a distinct career, one for which the individual must train specifically and that is viewed as a separate career hierarchy from the rest of the economic structure of the society. It is interesting to note that movement back and forth between public and private employment—especially in policy-making positions—has been used as an indicator of two rather different relationships between society and the political systems. On the one hand, such movement is frequently taken to indicate a healthy congruence between the value structures of polity and society, a means of ensuring the representativeness of the bureaucratic structures, and even a means through which "typical" citizens can exert some influence on public policy. On the other hand, such movement can also be taken to indicate the colonization of the society by bureaucrats, or conversely, the colonization of the public service by representatives of certain vested interests in the society. The former of these negative perceptions is best illustrated by the concern of the French over the *pantouflage*, or "parachuting," of upper-echelon civil servants into important and lucrative positions in the private economy.[34] This is taken as an

indication of the attempt on the part of *fonctionnaires* and technocrats
to manage the whole of society and not just the governmental apparatus. It also means that a great deal of executive talent developed
at public expense is exported to the private sector free of charge.
The second negative conception of lateral movement between public
and private management is more representative of thought in the
United States where, at times, the feeling is voiced that too much of
the government is being run by administrators currently on leave
from major corporations, major unions, and other significant interests
in the society.[35] Consequently, there is a belief that much of government is run for the benefit of those interests rather than for the
benefit of the public at large.

The degree of concern over, or distrust of, lateral movements between public and private sectors would appear to be a function of
several normative concerns of the society, especially as they relate to
the administrative roles of government. One concern is the perception of the values, job, and norms of the public bureaucracy as distinct
from those of the private sector. In the French case, the *fonctionnaires* are perceived as a special set of the population. This perception
contains some positive and some negative elements, but the most
common is that *pantouflage* is a means through which they may seek
to impose their conception of society onto the society. In other societies that seek as much as possible to distinguish bureaucratic
careers from private careers, it is rather clear that employment as a
public administrator is *supposed* to carry with it a rather distinct set
of values and decisional premises. For example, in Germany and
Sweden the public administrator has been traditionally conceived of
in a modified legal role. It is assumed that he will act much as would
a judge in impartially administering programs *pro bono publico* and
in accordance with the letter of the law. This may be too much to
expect from a mere human, but this separation and idealization of
administrator and career patterns has been useful in justifying decisions made by administrators in societies that rely heavily on administration in the conduct of public business.

A second and related normative concern is the extent to which
the society fears bureaucracy and therefore seeks to prevent the development of a large and inflexible bureaucratic structure atop society. There are a number of means of controlling the development
of such a bureaucracy, and lateral entry at the upper echelons is
certainly one of them.[36] This is perhaps the logical extension of
the idea of the amateur in administration, but it is one way in which

general social values can be injected into the conduct of government and administration, recognizing all the while that this will likely reduce the efficiency of organizations already attacked as being inefficient.

Incentives and Motivation

We have already mentioned the question of incentives when discussing one of the more general aspects of recruitment in public bureaucracies. We now discuss more of the methods available to public administration to recruit and maintain their personnel. In a general overview of organizations and membership in organizations, Clark and Wilson developed a classification of the types of incentives that an organization can offer members; the three types mentioned were material, purposive, and solidary.[37] Material incentives are pay, benefits, and direct financial rewards. Purposive incentives are related to the ability of the individual within the organization to have some influence over the shape of public policy adopted and implemented by government, or simply to get something done on the job. Finally, solidary incentives derive from the social aspects of employment and group membership, which in the case of public employment may at times involve belonging to one of the more prestigious organizations in society.

Any organization will potentially provide some of each of these incentives to employees. We are interested here in some cross-national differences in the extent to which each of the three is perceived as an effective means of motivation by current and potential administrators. Some evidence of this type can be gained by survey data, although such data are available for only a limited number of systems, largely from Western nations. As shown in table 4.2, there are some differences in response patterns even in this relatively homogeneous set of countries. In the first place, it is interesting to note that purposive incentives, which might have been thought to be the most significant means of influencing people to join the bureaucracy, are not. In the cases for which we have data, one of the other incentives, most usually solidary, is mentioned by a larger percentage of the respondents. The relative undervaluing of purposive incentives may, however, be in part a function of the subgroup within the public service about whom we have information. These were largely administrators near the top of the bureaucratic hierarchy; they had been in office for some time and may, therefore, be expected to have

TABLE 4.2

Incentives in Recruitment and Retention of Administrators
(in percent)

Incentives	United Kingdom (1967) [a]	France (1969) [b]	New Zealand (1966) [c]	Spain (1967) [d]	Italy (1965) [e]	Turkey (1965) [f]
Material	20	24	36	21	61.1	25.3
Purposive	19	32	27	39	4.7	12.1
Solidary	56	34	21	30	27.0	56.7
Other	6	10	16	10	7.2	5.9
	101 *	100	100	100	100	100

* due to rounding.

SOURCES:

[a] Brian Chapman, "Profile of a Profession: The Administrative Class of the Civil Service," in The Civil Service (Fulton Report) (London: HMSO, 1968), vol. 3, pt. 2, p. 12.

[b] Ezra N. Suleiman, Politics, Power and Bureaucracy in France (Princeton: Princeton University Press, 1974), p. 120.

[c] R. L. Green, M. R. Palmer, and T. J. Sanger, "Why They Leave," New Zealand Journal of Public Administration 30, no. 1 (Summer 1967): 27.

[d] Manuel Gomez-Reino and Francisco Andres Orizo, "Burocracias Publica y Privida," in Anales de Moral Social y Economica, Sociologica de la Administración Publica Española (Madrid: Raycar, 1968), p. 267.

[e] Frederica Garzoni Dell'Orto, "I funzionari e la cavriera," in Ammassari et al., Il Burocrate Di Fronte Alla Burocrazia (Milan: Giuffre, 1969), p. 68.

[f] Leslie L. Roos and Noralou P. Roos, Managers of Modernization: Organizations and Elites in Turkey (Cambridge, Mass.: Harvard University Press, 1971), p. 123.

developed a greater identification with the organization than with the *cause* of the organization. Thus we might need to know the reasons given by those just entering the public service in order to have a better idea of the extent to which the ability to influence policy may have an impact on recruitment. This may be especially true in the last decade when many younger people have apparently sought careers in public service for purposive reasons.

The differences between the several sets of administrators for which we have data are not particularly striking, but we can note three rather interesting things. The first is the extremely high percentage of administrators in the United Kingdom who gave answers in terms of solidary incentives when questioned about their jobs. This would appear to conform nicely with the stereotype of British administration as a set of "old boys" who conduct administration in a collegial, gentlemanly fashion and whose role as amateurs may prevent any effective policy initiative from arising from the bureaucracy. Of course, numerous recent studies of the administrative apparatus of the United Kingdom indicate that although they may not be experts in any particular technical specialty, many administrators discharge quite significant roles in the formation of policy—in fact, that has been known by the practitioners themselves for quite a long time.[38] Still, it is interesting to note the extent to which the practitioners give more social reasons for either joining or staying in their positions. Of the countries on which we have data, the French upper-echelon administrators reported the highest levels of purposive incentives. This too conforms to the prevailing conception of the French bureaucracy as the *groupe diregante* of the society.[39] Traditionally, the way of getting things done in French government has been through administration, and we may expect that administrators would perceive a relatively great ability to accomplish things through their jobs. Finally, the Italian administrators gave a very high proportion of material answers, indicating the often cited tendency to use the bureaucracy as a means of personal advancement rather than as a force for policy change.

If the evidence on incentive structures for Western administrative systems is rather spotty, then the information on non-Western administrative systems appears virtually nonexistent. The data for a sample of Turkish administrators, however, show a close similarity to Western nations. Further, from a number of more descriptive studies, we can rather quickly develop the hypothesis that the major incentives for joining bureaucratic systems in non-Western societies are solidary and material rather than purposive. In the first place, given the colonial backgrounds of most of these societies, the pattern of goal achievement through administration was not well ingrained into these systems at the time of independence. Moreover, in the Latin American systems, which have been independent longer, the administrators are not protected by merit systems and tenure so that any attempt to use administration to alter the existing social and economic arrangements often meets with a prompt dismissal from office.[40]

There are also more positive aspects to the attraction of the bureaucracy for many prospective employees. The public bureaucracy is a stable and relatively remunerative institution of the society, and compared with opportunities that may exist in the private economy, the opportunity to work in the public bureaucracy is frequently an extremely attractive economic option.[41] The operation of the solidary incentives are perhaps less obvious. One of the social and cultural bases of many underdeveloped countries has been an emphasis on status and rank in defining social behavior. Also, in most of these societies the public bureaucracy has been able to establish itself as a high-status occupation. This may be in part related to the relatively brief separation in time from the period in which recruitment to these governmental positions—the authorities—was determined almost entirely by ascriptive criteria, and in fact the best families frequently chose to send their sons into the public service. As Kearney and Harris said when speaking of Ceylon:

> The great prestige enjoyed by the public servant has, however, probably contributed at least as much as material advantage or employment security to the attractiveness of a bureaucratic career. The social prestige of the modern bureaucrat is in large measure a heritage of Ceylon's feudal and colonial past.[42]

These authors go on to point out that the "social exclusiveness and supreme confidence" of colonial administrators tended to reinforce the impression that administrative positions were to be equated with superior social position.[43] Further, in societies that value social position above the more achievement-based criteria usually associated with Western societies, one may expect a high level of solidary incentives among those joining the bureaucracy.

The above discussion of the incentives of administrators joining the bureaucracy in the underdeveloped world is obviously different from the types of incentives that we would expect to characterize bureaucrats charged with bringing about important social and economic changes. We have already noted the load being placed upon administration in these transformations, and we find here a great disparity between the requirements of social change and the motivation of the people being recruited.[44] This cannot, of course, provide an optimistic outlook for the future of administered change.

To conclude this discussion of incentives, we may also make some highly conjectural statements about the nature of the bureaucracy in the Soviet Union and other communist countries. On the basis of descriptive accounts and descriptions of prior administrative systems, we can hypothesize that the incentive structures of these bureaucrats will be rather similar to those found for administrators in Western societies, i.e., a balance of material, purposive, and solidary. The purposive incentives are rather obvious, given that the Soviet Union, like most Western societies, has become a heavily administration-oriented political system. It might be expected that people would feel the ability to accomplish certain goals through working in the administrative structures. The material incentives may appear rather odd in a supposedly classless society, but we know well that there are, if not classes, at least groups for whom there are differential economic rewards.[45] The public bureaucracy is one such group; being a member of the "apparatus" of the state will generally pay off not only directly, but also indirectly through access to scarce consumer goods. Finally, one traditional description of Russian administration was as a set of small and closely knit primary groups operating within the context of a larger administrative structure.[46] We may hypothesize that this same sort of small group is still operating in the Soviet bureaucracy so that there will be a high level of solidary motivation for the worker within such a group. Of course, these are only conjectures about the motivations of these administrators, but we have some idea that each of the incentives is likely to be effective. What we do not know is the relative strength of these motivations and incentives.

PATTERNS OF RECRUITMENT

We have been discussing the methods by which administrators are chosen and some of the issues involved in the choice of methods. This section looks at the effects of these choices by examining the actual patterns of recruitment of administrators. Again, we are somewhat constrained by the lack of availability of data for administrative systems, especially those of the less-developed countries. Despite these constraints, we are able to find substantial recruitment information on the administrative systems of twenty-one countries on several dimensions of social background, preparation, and representativeness that can give important information about how administrators are chosen. We must, however, offer some important caveats to the reader. This information was gathered by different individuals, at different times, and on somewhat different segments of the bureaucratic population. The majority concentrates on upper-echelon administrators, but in some cases definitions are broader. Therefore, care must be exercised in the interpretation of differences among

TABLE 4.3

Social-class Background of Senior Civil Service Personnel (in percent)

Social-class Origin	United Kingdom (1968)[a]	United States (1959)[b]	France (1953–68)[c]
Upper	21	19	19
Middle	56	44	61
Working	19	21	17
Other	5	16	3
Total	100	100	100

* 9.7% did not answer.

	Switzerland (1969)[g]	Italy (1965)[h]	Canada (1957)[i]
Upper	—	17.4	18.1
Middle	85	65.4	68.7
Working	15	4.7	13.2
Other	—	12.5	—
Total	100	100	100

	Spain (1967)[m]	Pakistan (nd)[n]	Zambia (1969)[o]
Upper	—	22.4	5
Middle	96	76.1	43
Working	4	1.5	23
Other	—	—	27
Total	100	100	100

SOURCES:

[a] A. H. Halsey and I. M. Crewe, Social Survey of the Civil Service, vol. 3, pt. 1 of The Civil Service (The Fulton Report) (London: HMSO, 1969), p. 19.
[b] W. L. Warner, et al., The American Federal Executive (New Haven: Yale University Press, 1963), p. 29.
[c] Ezra N. Suleiman, Politics, Power, and Bureaucracy in France (Princeton: Princeton University Press, 1974), pp. 87–88.
[d] Wolfgang Zapf, Wandlungen der Deutschen Elite (Munich: Piper, 1966), p. 180.
[e] Henry Stjernguist, "Centraladministrationens Embedsmaend 1948–1946," in Centraladministrationen 1848–1946 (Copenhagen: Ministerialforenigen, 1948), p. 282.
[f] Sten-Stuve Landstrom, Svenska Ambetsmans Sociala Ursprung (Uppsale: Almqvist och Wiksell, 1954), p. 42.
[g] Ulrich Kloti, "Die chefbeamten der Schweizerischen Bundesverwaltung: Ein Forschungsbericht," in Annuairre Suisse de Science Politique (1971) 2:57.
[h] Paolo Ammassari, "L'Estrazione Sociale dei funzionari dello Stato e degli enti locali," in Ammassari et al., Il Burocrate di Fronto Alle Burocrazia (Milan: Giuffre, 1969), p. 21.
[i] John Porter, The Vertical Mosaic (Toronto: University of Toronto Press, 1965), pp. 445–46.

TABLE 4.3 (continued)

Social-class Background of Senior Civil Service Personnel (in percent)

Social-class Origin	West Germany (1955)[d]	Denmark (1945)[e]	Sweden (1947)[f]
Upper	13	38.3	9.1
Middle	68	48.9	81.9
Working	0	4.3	3.0
Other	0	8.5	6.0
Total	81 *	100	100

* 19% did not answer.

	India (1947–63)[j]	Turkey (1962)[k]	Republic of Korea (1962)[l]
Upper	29.2	29.0	13.2
Middle	67.1	61.5	70.3
Working	—	1.0	6.8
Other	4.7	8.5	—
Total	100	100	90.3 *

	Netherlands (1973)[p]
Upper	59
Middle	26
Working	15
Other	—
Total	100

SOURCES (cont.):

[j] V. Subramanian, Social Background of India's Administrators (New Delhi: Ministry of Information, 1971), p. 145.

[k] C. H. Dodd, "The Social and Educational Backgrounds of Turkish Officials," Middle Eastern Studies 1 (1964): 271.

[l] Dong Suh Bark, "Korean Higher Civil Servants: Their Social Background and Morale" in Byung Chul Koh, Aspects of Administrative Development in South Korea (Kalamazoo, Mich.: Korea Research Publication, 1967), p. 27.

[m] Juan J. Linz and Amando de Miguel, "La Elite Funcionarial Espanola Ante La Reforma Administrativa," in Anales de Moral Social y Economica, Sociologica de la Administracion Publica Espanola (Madrid: Raycar, 1968), pp. 208–9.

[n] Ralph Braibanti, "The Higher Bureaucracy of Pakistan," in Asian Bureaucratic Systems Emergent From the British Imperial Tradition, ed. R. Braibanti (Durham, N.C.: Duke University Press, 1966), p. 271.

[o] Dennis L. Dresang, "Ethnic Politics, Representative Bureaucracy and Development Administration: The Zambian Case," American Political Science Review 68, no. 4 (December 1974): 1609.

[p] Samuel Eldersveld, Sonja Hubée-Boonzaaijer and Jan Kooiman, "Elite Perceptions of the Political Process in the Netherlands Looked at in Comparative Perspective," in The Mandarins of Western Europe, ed. M. Dogan (New York: Halsted, 1975), p. 136.

these countries, but the data serve an important function of illustrating the general directions of recruitment in each country. In each case, we take care to note the source, year, and definition of the administrative population (if different from "top" administrators).

The first dimension upon which we have data is the socioeconomic background of the administrators. Given that the administration is essentially a middle-class occupation, the major variance here is in the occupation of the fathers—or the class of origin—of these administrators. We see from table 4.3 that not only is administration a middle-class occupation, but the origins of the administrators are also primarily middle class. The definition of class origin here is somewhat fuzzy, especially the difference between upper class and middle class, but the largest single class of origin in each case is middle class. This is even more striking when the categories are collapsed into working class and bourgeois (by adding together middle and upper classes). In each case, few if any children of workers ever make it into the ranks of upper administration, with the most open system apparently being that of the United States where almost one-quarter of the federal executives came from working-class backgrounds. Despite the elitist image, the French civil service also had a relatively large percentage of inductees from the working class.[47] West Germany would appear to be the most unrepresentative of the civil services, for in the sample taken by Zapf of upper administrators, none came from working-class backgrounds.[48] Lest we become too critical of the bureaucratic systems, we should note that this pattern of elitist recruitment is far from entirely the fault of these institutions. The bureaucracies are at the mercy of the educational system, and despite attempts to make postsecondary education more available, it still remains a sanctuary of the upper and middle classes. Given the job requirements for the vast majority of higher administrative positions, be they for specialists or generalists, a postsecondary education is a virtual necessity, and in most countries few working-class children are provided that opportunity. This educational nexus is, in fact, the probable reason for the rather positive showing of the United States. Postsecondary education is more available in the United States than elsewhere, so the pool of potential applicants is that much larger.

We should not, on the other hand, be too quick to absolve the bureaucracies of all guilt when it comes to their rather unrepresentative nature. Like all organizations, they tend to replicate themselves, and there is a strong tendency to recruit people who are like those already in the positions. This type of organizational bias is per-

haps especially strong during the personal interviews generally required for appointment to upper-echelon positions.[49] Further, the
formalistic requirements of a legal degree or even a college degree
for some administrative positions are somewhat superfluous. Likewise,
the rather stringent restrictions on movement between different
classes in administrative hierarchies (the old administrative and
executive classes in Britain, for example) tend to prevent good
working-class talent from working its way up through the ranks.[50]
These are all important, but they probably could not overcome by
themselves the fundamental problem of educational inequality.

Education

We now have some inkling that education may be an important
characteristic in describing public administrators, and again especially those at the upper levels of the hierarchy. We again have problems with less than comprehensive data, but we can get the same
sort of impression about the educational levels that differ across cultures and educational systems. As much as possible, we have attempted to group the data into categories that would be meaningful
to American readers. This may lose something in precision, but it
should be compensated by an increased comparability of the data.

The previous discussion of the relationship of education and class
in the selection of administrative personnel should have led us to
expect a well-educated group of people serving as upper-echelon
administrators. This expectation is well justified by the data. Almost
universally, administrative personnel tend to have some form of postsecondary education, with the majority having completed the equivalent of a bachelor's degree. In some cases, this education may be
within the confines of a specialized administrative college, but there is
nonetheless a definite postsecondary phase of education for most
administrators. This is to be expected in many cases simply because
such education is a requirement for appointment. Interesting here is
that the United States and Canada, which are frequently cited as having more "democratic" political cultures, tend to have larger percentages of their upper civil services without any postsecondary education.[51] Israel has by far the most open administrative structures,
in part because of the newness of the country and in part because of
the relatively poor pay levels.

As well as having completed college or its equivalent, these administrators have frequently attended the more prestigious colleges

TABLE 4.4

Educational Levels of Senior Civil Servants (in percent)

	United Kingdom (1967)[a]	United States (1959)[b]	France [c]	West Germany (1955)[d]	Sweden (1947)[e]
High School	2	5	0	0	23
Some College	27	14	7	23	
College Grad	52	57	93	77	77
College +	19	24	0	0	
Total	100	100	100	100	100

	Switzerland (1969)[f]	Canada (1957)[g]	USSR (1950–66)[h]	Japan (1949–59)[i]	Republic of Korea (1962)[j]
High School	7	17	10	1.2	10.1
Some College		4	50	98.8	8.6
College Grad	82	79	40		54.3
College +					26.9
Total	89 *	100	100	100	100

* 11% did not answer.

	Turkey (1962)[k]	Pakistan (1948–64)[l]	Burma (1962)[m]	Israel (1969)[n]	Netherlands (1973)[o]
High School or Less	1.5	0			15
Some College		35.2	23.8	49.4	
College Grad	98.5	64.8	76.2	28.2	85
College +				22.4	
Total	100	100	100	100	100

SOURCES:

ᵃ A. H. Halsey and I. M. Crewe, *Social Survey of the Civil Service*, vol. 3, pt. 1 of *The Civil Service* (The Fulton Report) (London: HMSO, 1969), p. 64.

ᵇ W. L. Warner et al., *The American Federal Executive* (New Haven: Yale University Press, 1963).

ᶜ Ezra N. Suleiman, *Politics, Power and Bureaucracy in France* (Princeton: Princeton University Press, 1974), p. 67.

ᵈ Wolfgang Zapf, *Wandlungen der Deutschen Elite* (Munich: Piper, 1966), p. 178.

ᵉ Sten-Stuve Landstrom, *Svenska Ämbetsmans Sociala Ursprung* (Uppsala: Almqvist och Wiksell, 1954), p. 129.

ᶠ Ulrich Kloti, "Die Chefbeamten der Schweizerischen, Bundesverwaltung: Ein Forschungsbericht," in *Annuairre Suisse de Science Politique* (1971) 2:59.

ᵍ John Porter, *The Vertical Mosaic* (Toronto: University of Toronto Press, 1965), pp. 433–34.

ʰ Philip D. Stewart, *Political Power in the Soviet Union* (Indianapolis: Bobbs-Merrill, 1968), p. 142. This is a sample of Obkom First Secretaries who hold politico-administrative posts.

ⁱ Akira Kubota, *Higher Civil Servants in Postwar Japan* (Princeton: Princeton University Press, 1969), p. 69.

ʲ Dong Suh Bark, "Korean Higher Civil Servants: Their Social Backgrounds and Morale," in Byung Chul Koh, *Aspects of Administrative Development in South Korea* (Kalamazoo, Mich: Korean Research Publication, 1967), p. 29.

ᵏ C. H. Dodd, "The Social and Educational Background of Turkish Officials," *Middle Eastern Studies* 1, no. 2 (1964): 273.

ˡ Ralph Braibanti, "The Higher Bureaucracy of Pakistan," in *Asian Bureaucratics Systems Emergent From the British Imperial Tradition*, ed. Ralph Braibanti (Durham, N.C.: Duke University Press, 1966), pp. 279–81.

ᵐ James F. Guyot, "Bureaucratic Transformation in Burma," in ibid., p. 425.

ⁿ Nimrod Raphaeli, "The Senior Civil Service in Israel: Notes on Some Characteristics," *Public Administration* (London) 48, no. 2 (Summer 1970): 174.

ᵒ Samuel Eldersveld, Sonja Hubée-Boonzaaijer and Jan Kooiman, "Elite Perceptions of the Political Process in the Netherlands Looked at in Comparative Perspective," in *The Mandarins of Western Europe*, ed. M. Dogan (New York: Halsted, 1975), p. 136.

TABLE 4.5

College Majors of Senior Civil Servants
(percent with college backgrounds)

Major	United Kingdom (1967) [a]	United States (1959) [b]	West Germany (1955) [c]	Japan (1949–59) [d]
Natural Science	13	42.9		14.3
Social Science	28	16.9		
Humanities	71	10.7	31	0.8
Economics and Business	—	7.8		5.5
Law	—	13.6	69	69.3
Other	2	8.1		10.1
Total	114 *	100	100	100

* Greater than 100% because of dual majors.

	Republic of Korea (1962) [e]	Turkey (1963) [f]	India (1947–63) [g]	Sweden (1947) [h]
Natural Science	29.9	34.2	32.5	19.2
Social Science	11.7	6.2	9.4	1.2
Humanities	—	13.1	20.9	17.7
Economics and Business	12.0	15.8	36.4	9.7
Law	25.3	17.5	—	52.3
Other	21.1	13.2	0.8	—
Total	100	100	100	100.1

	Netherlands (1973) [i]
Natural Science	25
Social Science	28
Humanities	—
Law	45
Other	2
Total	100

SOURCES:
[a] A. H. Halsey and I. M. Crewe, *Social Survey of the Civil Service*, vol. 3, pt. 1, *The Civil Service* (The Fulton Report) (London: HMSO, 1969), p. 91.

SOURCES (*cont.*):

b W. L. Warner et al., *The American Federal Executive* (New Haven: Yale University Press, 1963), p. 363.

c Wolfgang Zapf, *Wandlungen der Deutschen Elite* (Munich: Piper, 1966), p. 178.

d Akira Kubota, *Higher Civil Servants in Postwar Japan* (Princeton: Princeton University Press, 1969), p. 79.

e Dong Suh Bark, "Korean Higher Civil Servants: Their Social Backgrounds and Morale," in Byung Chul Koh, *Aspects of Administrative Development in South Korea* (Kalamazoo, Mich.: Korean Research Publication, 1967), p. 11.

f Republic of Turkey, Office of the Prime Minister, State Institute of Statistics, *The Government Personnel Census* (Ankara: State Institute of Statistics, 1965), 1:32–39.

g V. Subramanian, *Social Background of India's Administrators* (New Delhi: Ministry of Information, 1971), p. 155.

h Sten-Stuve Landstrom, *Svenska Ämbetsmans Sociala Ursprung* (Uppsala: Almqvist och Wiksell, 1954), p. 130.

i Samuel Eldersveld, Sonja Hubée-Boonzaaijer and Jan Kooiman, "Elite Perceptions of the Political Process in the Netherlands Looked at in Comparative Perspective," in *The Mandarins of Western Europe*, ed. M. Dogan (New York: Halsted, 1975), p. 136.

and universities in their country. As shown in table 4.4, for example, almost two-thirds of the British administrative class had attended Oxford or Cambridge. In his study of the backgrounds of Indian administrators, Subramanian reported that "the majority of recruits come from the six older and better known [universities]. . . . The significance of education in the right college is unmistakable." [52] Suleiman also reports that the majority—and in fact over three-fourths—of the entrants to the ENA had had their university education in Paris.[53] Forty-two percent of these entrants have had their entire education in Paris. Thus, in these cases, the importance of not only attending college but also the right college is indeed unmistakable. Here again, the American experience is somewhat different from the other systems reported. The analysis by Warner et al. of the college attendance of American career executives shows a rather strong influence of large state-supported universities in the education of administrators.[54] If foreign-service executives are excluded, none of the Ivy League schools is among the top ten in terms of number of degrees held, and only three are in the top thirty. Among foreign-service executives, however, three of the Ivy League are in the top ten, and all eight schools are in the top thirty. This evidence would appear to offer some support for the conception of American society and its administrative system as being somewhat more open than most. It further supports the contention that the public service in the United States has become an important means of social mobility.

The last question we want to ask concerning the educational backgrounds of these administrators is the type of degree obtained. Here we are interested in the degree of technical or functional expertise that the administrators are likely to be carrying into their work as a function of their college education. We have already reported some data of this type for the United Kingdom, and they are reproduced in table 4.5 along with data for such other countries as were available. We find considerably more variance in the *types* of education received than we did in the *level* of education. There are apparently three rather distinct groups of educational degree types in this non-random sampling of administrative systems. The first is represented by the United Kingdom, with a great emphasis on general education, the arts and humanities, and consequently less emphasis on technical ability. As noted, this is indicative of the generalist conception of administration in the United Kingdom. A second type is typified by West Germany and Sweden. These systems place heavy emphasis on legal training, and consequently about two-thirds of their administrators have legal backgrounds. Many of the remainder also possess some form of professional qualification, such as engineering, medicine, or educational degrees. France is somewhat similar but goes a step further by providing most of the upper-echelon legal and financial training through ENA. The final pattern of educational backgrounds is typified by the United States and several underdeveloped countries. The major characteristic here is the high percentage of natural science (including engineering) students in the administrative hierarchy. For the United States, as an economically developed country, this is the result of a tendency to staff programs rather than identifying personnel who have great promise and then providing them a career in the public service. Thus, the United States tends to hire more specialized talent, and since many of the programs of the government involve some level of technical training, a relatively large percentage of natural scientists are in the public service. The findings for the underdeveloped countries are similar, but this would tend to be for the developmental reasons outlined earlier. There is a need for these societies to concentrate the available technical talent in the country and attempt to make the greatest use of this scarce resource.

One way of doing this is to hire as much talent as possible in government and then use the government as a means of allocating resources. Moreover, given the relatively underdeveloped state of the economies of many of these countries, there may in fact be little option for the trained person but to work for government. Many political considerations may prevent the public bureaucracy in underdeveloped countries from fulfilling their potential for administering programs of social and economic change, but it would appear from these data that many of the countries have the raw material, in terms of personnel within bureaucracies, that might make those reforms successful.

Ethnic Representativeness

The final question to be looked at in the presentation of background data on civil services is that of the ethnic representativeness of the bureaucracies. Just as there is some cause for concern over the representativeness of public bureaucracies according to social class, so is there concern over their equality in recruitment of various minorities within the society. We may expect the same sort of pattern as was found with respect to class, with the dominant community having a disproportionate share of the members of the civil service, especially in elite positions. As the data in table 4.6 show, these suspicions are confirmed. In most cases, there is a distinct overrepresentation of the dominant racial, language, or religious group. As with class, this may not be the result of overt discrimination but the result of the application of the usual educational criteria, which may more subtly discriminate.

Two special points should be made with respect to ethnic representation. The first is that these data are for upper-echelon personnel; as we go farther down the bureaucracy, the importance of the representativeness of the organization should increase rather than decrease. We have noted the importance of the client-contact personnel of agencies for the success of the agency and for the success and positive image of the clients. Such limited information as does exist on lower echelons of public agencies does indicate that they are more representative than are upper-management positions.[55] They may therefore be expected to be more successful in dealing with their clientele than would top management. Also, they may not be perceived as being as unrepresentative as they are, simply because the clients may deal only with the relatively more representative lower echelons.

TABLE 4.6

Ethnic Representativeness of Public Bureaucracies (in percent)

Ethnic Groups	United States [a]	Canada (1972)[b]	Israel (1967)[c]	Malaysia (1960)[d]	India[e]
Dominant	79	81.8	70.6	67	87.7
Minority	21	18.2	6.6	33	12.3
Total	100	100.0	77.2 *	100	100

* 22.8 listed "other."

	Lebanon (1955)[f]		Switzerland (1969)[g]			
		Language		Religion	aa	bb
Maronite	40.0	French	27.0	Catholic	12	42
Sunni	27.0	German	69.6	Protestant	88	58
Shi'ite	3.6	Italian	3.4		100	100
Greek Orthodox	11.7	Romansch	—			
Greek Catholic	9.0		100			
Druze	7.2					
	98.5					

SOURCES:

[a] Milton C. Cummings, Jr., M. Kent Jennings, and Franklin P. Kilpatrick, "Federal and Non-Federal Employees: A Comparative Social-Occupational Analysis," *Public Administration Review* 27 (December 1967): 399.

[b] P. K. Kuruvilla, "Administrative Culture in Canada: Some Perspectives," *Canadian Journal of Public Administration* 16, no. 2 (Summer 1973): 295. Minority—Francophone.

[c] Nimrod Raphaeli, "The Absorption of Orientals into Israeli Bureaucracy," *Mid East Studies* 8, no. 1 (January 1972): 55–91. Dominant, European; minority, Oriental.

[d] Robert O. Tilman, "Public Service Commissions in the Federation of Malaya," *Journal of Asian Studies* 20 (February 1961): 194. Minority—non-Malay Asians and British.

[e] V. Subramanian, *Social Backgrounds of India's Administrators* (New Delhi: Ministry of Information, 1971), p. 146. Minority—Non-Hindus.

[f] Ralph E. Crow, "Confessionalism, Public Administration and Efficiency in Lebanon," in *Politics in Lebanon,* ed. Leonard Binder (New York: John Wiley, 1966), p. 172.

[g] Ulrich Kloti, "Die Chefbeamten Der Schweizerischen Bundesverwaltung: Ein Forschungsbericht," *Annuairre Suisse de Science Politique* (1971) 2:58. The religious representation varies by ministry. Ministry (aa)—Volkswirtschaft—is heavily Protestant, while ministry (bb)—PTT—approaches proportionality.

The second point about ethnicity and representativeness is that this is frequently a point of bargaining in societies attempting to manage severe internal ethnic divisions. In some societies, most noticeably Belgium, this has gone to the extent of dividing several ministries by ethnicity (in this case, language) and actually providing two ethnically homogeneous units instead of one integrated unit that might tend to advantage one group or another.[56] Another variant of the same pattern is the Austrian method of carefully dividing the posts in each ministry according to ethnicity, or more exactly in this case, religious or nonreligious preferences.[57] Similarly, the division of posts in the Lebanese administrative system between the numerous religious groups in that society was an important part of the bargain holding that otherwise tenuous union together.[58] Thus there is no necessity for having unrepresentative bureaucracies in ethnically plural societies, but the equalization of the service often requires explicit bargaining and a recognition of the role of the bureaucracy in institutionalizing ethnic cleavage.

SUMMARY AND CONCLUSIONS

We end with several more general points about the composition and the representativeness of public bureaucracies. The first is that although these may be highly unrepresentative institutions, they are generally less unrepresentative than other public elites in the same countries. Parris notes, for example, that in Britain the membership of the House of Commons is at least as unrepresentative, if not more so, than the administrative class of the civil service.

If there are an excessive proportion of Oxbridge graduates in the Administrative Class, so is there in the House of Commons. The electorate ought to be blamed for making the wrong choice just as much as the Civil Service Commissioners. If too few civil servants have scientific and technological backgrounds, the same criticism can be made of industrial managers.[59]

The simple point is that elites are unrepresentative by the very function of their being elites. Success in society is related to social background, educational opportunities, and interests, and the elite that a society may choose to govern will differ only at the margins in most cases from an elite appointed to govern—at least in terms of social and educational backgrounds. The dangers of elitism and unrepresentativeness in public life are therefore general and confined simply to the public bureaucracy. They are only more apparent in the bureaucracy where the emphasis on merit criteria and open recruitment makes it a more ostensibly democratic institution in its selection. But, as Weber pointed out:

> Democracy takes an ambivalent attitude toward the system of examinations for expertise. On the one hand the system of examination means, or at least appears to mean, selection of the qualified from all social strata in place of rule by the notables. But on the other, democracy fears that examinations and patents of education will create a privilege "caste" and for that reason opposes such a system.[60]

These words should not be taken as an exoneration of bureaucracies for their often elitist practices, but rather as a means of placing the problem of representative and unrepresentative bureaucracy in more perspective.

The second point is that all the furor over social class and ethnic background of administrators, especially top administrators, may be a somewhat misplaced attack on the institutions. Much analysis has shown that social background tends to have a rather slight effect on behavior in public office. This is true of legislators, judges, and administrators. A more important determinant of behavior would appear to be the nature of the organization and the goal of the agency. Again, this may be especially true at upper echelons; there may need to be greater representativeness at lower levels simply to be able to cope adequately with the clientele that an agency may serve. This is not to say that this need be simply a cosmetic gesture on the part of the agency; rather, it is a real need to be effective in interacting with and serving the clientele. But the more general point remains that in order to change the policy outcomes from the public bureaucracy, one may have to do more than simply gradually replace administrators drawn from one social class with administrators recruited more broadly from society. The operating routines of agencies, the tendency toward conservatism in organizations in general, and the process of organizational socialization all tend to reduce the variability of individuals in the organization regardless of their social background. Thus, changing policy may be a considerably more complex topic, and it is one that we shall spend a good deal of time on during the remainder of this volume.

Policy does involve a human element. We began this chapter by discussing the failure of traditional models of bureaucracy to take into account human differences and variability. The differences, however, may be more in values, motives, and goals than in social background. We have touched on this briefly when discussing the incentive structures of public bureaucracies, and also when discussing the administrative cultures of society. Thus, studies of recruitment need to delve somewhat into the nature of the personnel recruited to administrative careers, to determine not only where they came from, but more importantly where they think they (and the society) are going.

NOTES

1. Max Weber, "Bureaucracy," in H. H. Gerth and C. Wright Mills, *From Max Weber: Essays in Sociology* (New York: Oxford University Press, 1946), pp. 196–244; Frederick W. Taylor, *Principles and Methods of Scientific Management* (New York: Harper, 1911).
2. Some direct cross-cultural evidence of this is given in Robert Putnam, "The Political Attitudes of Senior Civil Servants in Western Europe," *British Journal of Political Science* 3, no. 3 (July 1973): 257–90.
3. Weber, "Bureaucracy," pp. 198–203.
4. Ari Hoogenboom, *Outlawing the Spoils* (Urbana: University of Illinois Press, 1968).
5. Two clear examples of this possibility are first the concern of some Britons that the civil service, generally recruited from the middle and upper classes and possessing generally conservative political views, might balk at administering the program of the Labour party after that party gained office in 1945. These fears proved to be groundless. A second example is the concern of many people in the developing areas that the public bureaucracies, many of whom were recruited during colonialism, are not committed to the ideas of reform and may actually be slowing down the process of social changes. See K. Mathur, "A Committed Bureaucracy for India: Notes Toward A Theory," *Political Science Review* 10, no. 2 (July 1971): 113–23.
6. Richard Neustadt, "White House and Whitehall," *The Public Interest* 2 (1966): 55–69.
7. The President currently has appointment powers over about 1,200 administrative positions.
8. See J. S. Harris and T. V. Garcia, "The Permanent Secretaries: Britain's Top Administrators," *Public Administration Review* 26 (1966): 31–44.
9. See Hugh Heclo and Aaron Wildavsky, *The Private Government of Public Money* (Berkeley: University of California Press, 1974).
10. J. Donald Kingsley, *Representative Bureaucracy* (Yellow Springs, Ohio: Antioch Press, 1944); V. Subramanian, "Representative Bureaucracy: A Reassessment," *American Political Science Review* 61, no. 4 (December

1967): 1010–19; Samuel Krislov, *Representative Bureaucracy* (Englewood Cliffs, N.J.: Prentice-Hall, 1974).

11. See Peter Rose, Stanley Rothman, and William J. Wilson, *Through Different Eyes* (New York: Oxford University Press, 1972).

12. Conflict between clients and administrator, despite its recent vogue, has been a subject of research for some time. See Gabriel Almond and Harold Lasswell, "Aggressive Behavior by Clients toward Public Relief Administrators," *American Political Science Review* 28, no. 4 (August 1934): 643–54; Peter M. Blau, "Orientation Toward Clients in a Public Welfare Agency," *Administrative Science Quarterly* 5 (1960).

13. See Samuel Krislov, *The Negro in Federal Employment* (Minneapolis: University of Minnesota Press, 1967), pp. 86–106.

14. See Martin O. Heisler, "Patterns of European Politics: The European Polity Model," in *Politics in Europe*, ed. Martin Heisler (New York: David McKay, 1974), pp. 27–89. Recruitment of administrative personnel in supranational bodies is another obvious example of this type of representativeness.

15. OECD, *Social Objectives in Educational Planning* (Paris: OECD, 1967); Richard F. Tomasson, "From Elitism to Egalitarianism in Swedish Education," *Sociology of Education* 38, no. 3 (Spring 1965): 203–23.

16. See Lewis J. Edinger and Donald D. Searing, "Social Background in Elite Analysis," *American Political Science Review* 61, no. 2 (June 1967): 428–45.

17. This problem of "administrative pricing" is felt to contribute to many of the problems of public bureaucracy and the alleged inefficiencies of public bureaucracies. See William Niskanen, *Bureaucracy and Representative Government* (Chicago: Aldine, 1971).

18. See Samuel P. Huntington, "Postindustrial Politics: How Benign Will It Be?" *Comparative Politics* 6, no. 2 (January 1974): 179–82.

19. Albert Breton, "A Theory of the Demand for Public Goods," *Canadian Journal of Economics and Political Science* 32 (November 1966): 455–67; Anthony Downs, "Why the Government Budget Is Too Small in a Democracy," *World Politics* 12 (July 1960): 541–63.

20. See F. F. Ridley, *Specialists and Generalists: A Comparative Study of the Professional Civil Service at Home and Abroad* (London: Routledge & Kegan Paul, 1968).

21. E. N. Gladden, *The Civil Services of the United Kingdom 1855–1970* (London: Frank Cass, 1967), pp. 18–21.

22. Brian Chapman, one of the leading commentators and critics of British administration, once referred to the "luxuriant amateurism and voluntary exclusion of talent" in British administration. The Fulton report on reform suggested that specialized training be given more weight in recruitment but that recommendation was ignored. See Brian Chapman, *British Government Observed* (London: Allen & Unwin, 1963).

23. John Garrett, *The Management of Government* (Harmondsworth: Penguin, 1972), pp. 259–68.

24. There are a number of studies of the ENA and its effects on public administration and administrators. See Jacques Mandrin, *L'Enarchie ou les mandarins de la societe bourgeoise* (Paris: La Table Ronde de Combat, 1967); also the discussion in Suleiman, *Politics, Power*, pp. 42–71.

25. See, for example, Ralph Braibanti, ed., *Asian Bureaucratic Systems Emergent from the British Imperial Tradition* (Durham, N.C.: Duke University Press, 1967).

26. See, for example, L. G. C. Wallis, "Nigerianization of the Public Services in Western Nigeria," *Journal of African Administration* 12, no. 3 (July 1960):

144–46; Krislov, *Representative Bureaucracy*, pp. 88–92; J. Donald Kingsley, "Bureaucracy and Political Development, with Special Reference to Nigeria," in *Bureaucracy and Political Development*, ed. Joseph LaPalombara (Princeton: Princeton University Press, 1963), pp. 301–17.

27. Fred A. Clemente, "Philippine Bureaucratic Behavior," *Philippine Journal of Public Administration* 15, no. 2 (April 1971): 119–47.

28. For a discussion of these several paths and the relationship of administration to development in Europe, see John A. Armstrong, *The European Administrative Elite* (Princeton: Princeton University Press, 1974); Fritz Morstein Marx, "The Higher Civil Service as an Action Group in Western Political Development," in LaPalombara, *Bureaucracy*, pp. 62–95.

29. Merle Fainsod, "Bureaucracy and Modernization: The Russian and Soviet Case," in LaPalombara, *Bureaucracy*, pp. 233–67; Armstrong, *European Administrative Elite*.

30. Jerry F. Hough, *The Soviet Prefects* (Cambridge, Mass.: Harvard University Press), pp. 292–305.

31. The recruitment by agencies is, in fact, governed by statutes requiring certain qualifications, etc. See Poul Meyer, "The Administrative Aspects of the Constitutions of the Northern Countries," *Nordisk Administrativ Tidskrift* (1960), pp. 254–65.

32. Brian Chapman, *The Profession of Government* (London: Allen & Unwin, 1959), pp. 82–85.

33. See Herbert Jacob, *German Administration Since Bismarck* (New Haven: Yale University Press, 1963), pp. 212–15.

34. See Jean Meynaud, *Nouvelles etudes sur les groupes de pression en France* (Paris: Armand Colin, 1962), pp. 187, 230.

35. Felix A. Nigro, *Modern Public Administration* (New York: Harper & Row, 1970), pp. 272–75.

36. See Peter E. Sheriff, "Outsiders in a Closed Career: The Example of the British Civil Service," *Public Administration* (London) 50, no. 4 (Winter 1972): 397–418.

37. Peter B. Clark and James Q. Wilson, "Incentive Systems: A Theory of Organizations," *Administrative Science Quarterly* 6, no. 2 (September 1961): 129–66.

38. Most notably, Heclo and Wildavsky, *The Private Government;* Michael R. Gordon, "Civil Servants, Politicians and Parties: Shortcomings in the British Policy Process," *Comparative Politics* 4, no. 1 (October 1971): 29–58.

39. B. Gournay, "Une groupe dirigente de la societe francaise: les grandes fonctionnaires," *Revue francaise de science politique* 31, no. 2 (April 1964): 215–42.

40. J. L. Weaver, "Expectativas de los functionarios latinoamericanes en relacion con la administracion publica," *Aportes* 25 (July 1972): 119–45.

41. See, for example, James F. Guyot, "Bureaucratic Transformation in Burma," in Braibanti, *Asian Bureaucratic Systems*, pp. 382–84.

42. Robert N. Kearney and Richard L. Harris, "Bureaucracy and Environment in Ceylon," *Journal of Commonwealth Political Studies* 2, no. 3 (November 1964): 254–55.

43. Ibid., p. 255.

44. See J. R. Nellis, "Is the Bureaucracy Developmental: Political Considerations in Development Administration," *African Studies Review* 11, no. 3 (December 1971): 389–401.

45. Frank Parkin, *Class Inequality and Political Order* (New York: Praeger, 1971), pp. 137–59. Djilas, however, points out that recruitment into the

"new class" tends to be rather broad based. See M. Djilas, *The New Class* (New York: Praeger, 1957), p. 61.

46. Michel Crozier, *The Bureaucratic Phenomenon* (Chicago: University of Chicago Press, 1964), pp. 228–29.

47. The development of the second "concours" as a means of entry into the ENA was intended as a means of widening the social basis of recruitment. As noted by Suleiman, this effort has been far from entirely successful. See Suleiman, *Politics, Power,* p. 59.

48. Wolfgang Zapf, *Wandlungen der Deutschen Elite* (Munich: Piper, 1966), pp. 180–82.

49. R. K. Kelsall, *Higher Civil Servants in Britain* (London: Routledge & Kegan Paul, 1955), pp. 70–71, provides a good description of the effects of interviews on recruitment in Britain.

50. Another of the recommendations of the Fulton Commission was that this sort of advancement through the ranks should be made less difficult.

51. Seymour Martin Lipset, *The First New Nation* (New York: Basic Books, 1963), pp. 226–31; John Porter, *The Vertical Mosaic* (Toronto: University of Toronto Press, 1965), presents a different picture of Canadian society. Presthus shows that the Canadian bureaucracy has higher rates of social mobility than other institutions in the society. See Robert V. Presthus, *Elite Accommodation in Canadian Politics* (Cambridge, England: Cambridge University Press, 1973), p. 277.

52. V. Subramanian, *The Social Backgrounds of India's Administrators* (New Delhi: Ministry of Information and Broadcasting, 1971), p. 39.

53. Ezra Suleiman, *Politics, Power,* p. 67.

54. W. Lloyd Warner, *The American Federal Executive* (New Haven: Yale University Press, 1963), p. 372.

55. Pierre Escoube, "Les Hommes dans l'Administration," in Ecole Practique des Hautes Etudes, *Traite de Science Administrative* (Paris: Mouton, 1966), pp. 359–72; Krislov, *Representative Bureaucracy,* pp. 112–14; Republic of Turkey, Office of the Prime Minister, *The Government Personnel Census,* vol. 1 (Ankara: N.P., 1965).

56. Martin O. Heisler, "Institutionalizing Societal Cleavages in a Cooptive Polity: The Growing Importance of the Output Side in Belgium," in Heisler, *Politics in Europe,* pp. 212–15.

57. See Kurt Steiner, *Politics in Austria* (Boston: Little, Brown, 1972), pp. 390–97.

58. Ralph E. Crow, "Confessionalism, Public Administration and Efficiency in Lebanon," in *Politics in Lebanon,* ed. Leonard Binder (New York: John Wiley, 1966), pp. 71 ff.

59. Henry Parris, *Constitutional Bureaucracy* (London: Allen & Unwin, 1969), p. 315.

60. Gerth and Mills, *From Max Weber,* p. 240.

PROBLEMS OF ADMINISTRATIVE STRUCTURE

Concern over the structure and design of organizations has traditionally dominated the study of public administration. This may have resulted from the lack of any readily quantifiable measures of organization—such as profit—in public organizations, so that greater attention was placed on theoretical questions. Moreover, the responsibility of public organizations to external political forces and the general opprobrium associated with the word "bureaucracy" also placed pressure on public administrators to design the perfect organization. For whatever reason, public administration has been almost obsessed with constructing the best organizational structures for implementing public programs.[1] This tendency reached its height with the theories of administration, dismissed by Simon as the "proverbs of administration," based on such concepts as unity of command, span of control, and POSDCORB management.[2]

This chapter cannot hope to provide a comprehensive review of theories of organizations in the public sector, nor of the empirical variations in public administrative establishments. Rather, it is an introduction to the problems associated with the structure of government and public administration as well as some description of major structural variations across political systems. Finally, an attempt is made to assess the relationship of organizational structure to organizational performance.

THE STRUCTURE OF ADMINISTRATION

One of the most general questions of administrative structure concerns the basis of organization for the administrative apparatus as a whole. How will the entire public service be structured to achieve its tasks? Rather early in the formal study of public administration, Luther Gulick proposed that the organization of public administration could be founded on four alternative principles: purpose served, processes employed, types of persons or things dealt with, or geographical area covered.[3] Examples of these forms of organization are readily apparent. The purposes served are clearly the most frequent basis of organization, as departments or ministries of defense, education, and health would indicate.[4] Organization by process is more commonly found at subministerial levels, with divisions or bureaus of accounting, legal services, engineering, and the like. Types of persons or things dealt with would include organizations such as the Veterans Administration in the United States, similar organizations in other countries, the Bureau of Indian Affairs, and various boards and commissions for (or against) foreign workers in European countries. Finally, the area served is frequently used as an organizational principle at the subdepartmental level, as in the use of regional offices, but may also be institutionalized at the departmental level, as in the Scottish and Welsh Offices in the United Kingdom.

Each of these modes of organizations has some assets and some liabilities, which have been rather thoroughly discussed by Gulick and others working on the problem. We need not engage in an extensive discussion of that literature here. Rather, let us begin to examine how these four categories of organization can be used to analyze differences in administrative systems cross-nationally, and what the implications of these differences are for administration. The bulk of our analysis is on modes of organization other than by purpose, since that mode is the most common and the one with the least comparative differences.

Organization by Area Served

Area provides the most interesting comparative differences across cultures. These differences in administration are largely related to broader organizational questions for the entire political system, especially the degree of centralization to be imposed upon the country by the central government. In fact, the two most important variants of areal administration emanate from quite different solutions to this problem. One solution is for the central government to attempt to control and supervise closely the execution of its policies throughout the nation. One of the most powerful means to ensure such uniformity is the use of prefectoral officers in localities. In a general sense, prefects are officers of the central government responsible for the execution of national programs at the subnational level. Each ministry may have its own field service, but these are coordinated and to some degree supervised by the prefect. In France, the prefect has also been responsible traditionally for the conduct of local government and has had veto power over most local programs and finances.[5] There are differences in the precise ways in which prefectoral systems operate, but the common thread running through such systems—as in France, Italy, and Japan—is that one officer will coordinate and be responsible for public policies in one subnational area.[6]

Prefectoral systems often operate quite differently from the formal model of central control. As well as serving as a representative of the national government to the locality, prefects also represent their locality—and themselves—to the center. That is, prefects may frequently be coopted by their localities and will support claims for local variances in national programs. Worms notes four points of convergence between the interests of the prefect and interests of local politicians.[7] The prefect, in practice, is often the man in the middle, linking the demands of the local constituency for special treatment and rapid action to the demands of the central government for uniformity. He also must think of his own career, so that it may benefit him to cooperate with the locality in order to obtain smooth and successful execution of the tasks of the local authorities.[8]

At the other end of the spectrum are several schemes for administrative devolution and administrative federalism. These either transfer control of administration downward to a subnational unit or provide deconcentrated control of the administration. Probably the most extreme version of this form of organization is found in West Germany, where the functions of the national bureaucracy are confined primarily to program development in the ministries in Bonn and the running of the state railroad, post office, and several nationalized industries. The majority of the work of administering public policies is done at the level of the states, or Länder.[9] Although the federal ministers must assure that the programs of their ministry are administered properly and uniformly throughout the country, in practice they have few means of enforcing such uniformity. The system allows for considerable autonomy in the Länder with respect not only to the organization of their own civil service systems, but also to the manner of executing public policies. The logic behind such a system —from the administrative rather than political point of view—is that different local conditions and problems may require marginally different solutions.[10] Further, different local historical factors and differences in the religious composition of the Länder may require variations in the internal procedures of administration. Such a system raises a number of important problems concerning public accountability for policy, and associated with that, public control of policy and administration. The centralized system may be inflexible and possibly autocratic, but at least responsibility for policy is clear. Thus, as with the internal management of organizations, the conflict between centralization and its associated responsibility for decision, and decentralization and its associated flexibility, rages at the broader level of the organization as a whole.

A less extreme version of administrative federalism is currently evolving, or devolving, in Great Britain, particularly with respect to Scotland. Although formally the powers of decision in Scottish affairs still reside largely in London, increasing political control and substantial amounts of administrative control are being passed on to Edinburgh.[11] This system is far from federal in that the administrators in Edinburgh are still members of the same civil service apparatus and still essentially responsible to the same political authorities as those in London. But the system offers some opportunity for regional variation as well as removing some of the isolation of government. Pressure for administrative and political reforms of this type are now common in most European countries, with some based on ethnic considerations and others simply on desires to make government closer to the people and to improve the efficiency of service delivery.[12] Whether regionalization or devolution will be successful in attaining those two ends is an empirical question.

Finally, in the United States and virtually all other political systems there is deconcentration of administration, if not real decentralization. That is, an attempt is made to move some decision making out of Washington into regional offices—most notably the ten "regional capitols"—so that some attention to local conditions can be given and perhaps some variations made. This is intended to produce greater feelings of administrative efficacy among the population, perhaps speed up response to demands, but interestingly may also be used as a means of providing greater control and supervision of programs.

In addition to the question of centralization of administration, another areal question that arises with respect to the organization of the political system and public administration is the size of administrative units, and indeed the size of governments themselves.[13] There has been a consistent tendency for governments in recent years to reorganize administration and local governments (these two are often synonymous) to make larger and larger units. Sweden, for example, has reorganized over 2,700 local governments and administrative units into just over 270, with similar changes occurring in other Scandinavian countries, Great Britain, and Germany.[14] These reforms have generally been justified by economies of scale in the production of public goods and services, and in terms of the ability of larger units to support a broader array of public services. However, some evidence points to a certain inefficiency within larger units. First, as the size of governmental units increases, there is a tendency for overhead expenditures to increase as a proportion of total expenditures; after some point, any gains from the economies of scale are absorbed by increases in overhead costs.[15] As the size of the governmental unit increases, there is a need for intermediary levels of administration between decision makers and field services, which adds to the overhead without actually adding to the productive output of the agency. Further, as some point is passed for each service, increases in size may actually decrease efficiency in service provision, as costs per unit of service may increase.[16]

Leaving aside economics, as the size of the unit increases, there may also be a drop in satisfaction with the services.[17] This is perhaps a function of the relationship of the costs of government to the services actually provided. On the other hand, as Fesler noted, and as advocates of regionalization reiterate, as the size of government increases so does its remoteness; consequently, so does the alienation of the population.[18] In either case, arguments can be made for the retention of small and "inefficient" local governments and administrative divisions, even in the face of demands for increased service and increased efficiency.

Organization by Process

Government can be organized by process, or by the communality of the processes employed by the members of the organization and the communality of their professional skills, rather than by purpose of the organization. Taken to an extreme this principle might mean, for example, that all accounting or purchasing activities for government would be concentrated in single agencies, or that all engineers or lawyers would be concentrated in bureaus of engineering or law, and their services provided to other agencies as required.[19]

The above examples might appear inefficient—and they probably are—but the point is that such an option does exist for the organization of government. Ostensibly it can be justified as a means of acquiring concentrations of skilled individuals, a means of imposing relatively uniform professional practices, and a means of stream-lining the operations of other agencies. The most common distinction of the process type made in public administration has been between "line" and "staff" agencies. Initially, the concept of staff was reserved primarily for personal advisers to an executive, to an Ehrlichman, Haldeman, and Haig in the Nixon White House. As the tasks of the executive broadened, so did the definitions of staff. Executives soon found their own staffs expanded to a point where they could no longer be adequately supervised personally, so that differentiated organizations performing staff functions developed. For example, currently the Executive Office of the President of the United States employs over 1,500 people. This is perhaps the largest existing staff agency in the world.

We have been employing the term "staff functions" rather glibly. Just what are the functions that a staff person or agency is expected to undertake? Personnel from line or operating agencies might be tempted to say that their principal function is to prevent those actually providing a public service from having access to the executive. This is hardly their real function, but it points to a potential conflict between staff and line agencies. The ostensible purpose of staff agencies is to do those things that line agencies have neither the time, the power, or the competence to do. Perhaps the most important of these tasks is coordinating the programs of line agencies. Obviously line agencies, having a limited scope of operations and consequently narrow perspectives on the tasks of government, are not really in a position to attempt to coordinate their own programs. In fact, their incentives—if we assume that agency growth is a prime bureaucratic goal—are to attempt to spread their services into policy areas already occupied by other agencies and thereby to provide, if not duplicate services, at least competing services.[20] Thus the executive and his staff (here interpreted broadly as either personal staff or staff agencies) must intervene in order to prevent unnecessary duplication.[21]

One of the principal means used by staff to control duplication is the use of budgeting and accounting agencies with extensive discretion over programmatic concerns.[22] Associated with coordination and budgetary tasks is the task of planning for future public programs. Line agencies tend to be so heavily involved in their ongoing work that they frequently lack the time for nonessential things such as planning what to do in the future, and any sort of comprehensive planning may involve a wider viewpoint than that of a single agency.

Planning agencies tend to be directly attached to the executive and to provide a broader overview of the future.

A number of differences appear in the use of staff agencies. Self provides an interesting discussion of staff functions in the United States and Great Britain. He notes that staff functions have not been institutionalized in Britain as they have in the United States, in part as a function of the differences in the forms of government. Specifically, in British Cabinet government, problems of coordination are in the main horizontal rather than vertical, with a number of (allegedly) equal departments competing for funds and programs.[23] As the heads of these departments are all members of the Cabinet, the problem of coordination becomes one of imposing collective decision, rather than analysis and coordination by executive decree. Further, rather than being done by some isolated executive agency such as OMB, most coordination is done by one of several departments —the Treasury—whose leader is one among many ministers in the Cabinet.[24] As Self and others note, however, such a system would not be practical with an administrative system less homogeneous and less well integrated than that of Britain.[25] Self further notes that, with the exception of Treasury control, there is virtually no formal means of coordination within government, and other devices have to be adopted to bring about the desired level of coordination. The most common response to this problem has been the creation of very large departments; any potentially duplicating or competitive services can be included within the confines of a single department and be subject to hierarchical coordination by a single minister.[26] Likewise, there have been attempts to impose "overlords," or superministries, on the existing Cabinet structure to ensure effective policy control. In practice, it would appear that as the size of the ministries is increased, the old administrative "proverb" of span of control would be increasingly violated, so that in practice one might actually get less coordination, or at least the need for more extensive staff work within the department.[27]

We have at several points intimated conflict between line and staff agencies. Conflicts are almost inherent in this system of organization. The line agencies tend to regard the other side as ivory-tower planners far removed from the day-to-day problems of program administration but still able to sell themselves as experts and have more access to decision making than the operating agencies. The staff agencies are also seen as formidable obstacles to bureaucratic growth.[28] On the other side of the conflict, staff agencies often become highly suspicious of the motives of line agencies in resisting attempts to coordinate and "rationalize" public services and may resent the ability of the line agencies to mobilize political support for their programs outside the bureaucracy. Staff may come to regard the line agencies as spendthrifts, raiders on the public purse. Thus, one of the inherent limitations that organization by process, especially in terms of line and staff, may have is the tendency for intra-organizational conflict and resistance to coordination and streamlining of services.

The problem of line and staff occurs not only at the level of the whole government, but also at the level of each individual department. Just as national executives require staff services to do things that their operating agencies cannot do, executives of operating agencies have the same need. At the departmental level, these staff services are also concerned with coordination of programs and activities. One of the more notable examples of staff services within a department is the ministerial *cabinet* in France and Belgium. Each minister in the French government has the opportunity to appoint a *cabinet* consisting of up to ten members to provide a variety of staff services such as policy advice, press relations, control of potentially recalcitrant civil servants, communications, and planning.[29] Although appointments to these *cabinets* are ostensibly at the will of the minister, in practice they involve extensive political considerations in addition to concerns over the quality and political reliability of the staff work produced.[30] Especially important in terms of the actual direction of policy is the job of the *conseilleur technique*, who serves as a political appointee linking the formal organization of the ministry to the politically appointed *cabinet*.

The use of ministerial *cabinets* is even more extensive in Belgium, to the point that they have been termed "counter administrations." [31] The divisions of Belgian society along several dimensions make it necessary to employ *cabinets* staffed by people known to be reliable, as opposed to civil servants who are highly politicized and consequently may not be politically loyal to the minister.[32] Again, some contrast with British and American practice may be in order. One might argue the need for the ministerial *cabinets* in large part because of the relative inability or unwillingness of French and Belgian ministers to rely on their civil servants. This in turn necessitates the use of political appointees to drive the control of the minister farther down into the organization than would otherwise be possible, and provides more of a check on the execution of ministerial directives within the organization. In the United States, the existence of several layers of political appointees between the cabinet officer and the upper echelons of the civil service is an indication of the use of "staff," although the appointees may actually hold positions in "line" agencies, to ensure political control over presumably independent civil servants. Britain is somewhat unique in terms of the apparent willingness of political ministers to accept the advice of career civil servants readily and be willing to allow those civil servants to control many operations of the agencies.[33]

One interesting variant of organization by staff and line, or more generally organization by process, occurs in Sweden. Here the two usual functions of the public bureaucracy—the development and the execution of public policy—are organizationally divided into two separate organizations. First, the staffs of the ministries are charged with the development of public policy. The ministries are small, and their work is confined to staff-type work—planning, coordination, and program development.[34] The actual execution of public programs is left to a set of administrative boards, or *styrelsen*. The boards are independent of the ministries—although linked through the budgetary process and a number of other not particularly subtle ways—and perform "line" functions of actually implementing programs. This method of organization points to the extent to which organization by line and staff corresponds to the old adage about the separation of politics and administration.[35] Staff functions can be equated with the political functions of advocating programs and formulating policy, and assuring that the independent civil servants do what their political masters intended. Line functions are more normally associated with the execution of policy in a rather routine fashion. As we have pointed out—and will deal with more extensively later—the dichotomy between politics and administration is largely a false one, but it is important to note the extent to which it has been incorporated into public administration.

A final possibility for organization by process is organization by corps, or by some other internally homogeneous administrative bodies. The corps system is best developed in France but has been copied by a number of other countries, especially those derivative from a French or Napoleonic administrative tradition. The concept of the corps is a body of administrators with similar educational backgrounds and similar professional skills. In France, there are three *grands corps*—the Cour des Comptes, the Conseil d'État, and the Inspectorate des Finances—plus three technical *grands corps*—Ponts et

Chausses, Travaux Publiques, and Mines. These six corps constitute the cream of the domestic French administration. The top graduates of the ENA—the National School of Administration—generally take posts in the *grands corps*, while the technical corps have their own specialized and publicly supported training grounds.[36] Each of the *grands corps* is, in theory, specialized by function; in practice they have a pervasive influence on French administration and have adopted somewhat broader roles. Suleiman notes that it is virtually obligatory to have a member of the Inspectorate of Finances as a member of a ministerial *cabinet* or for *directeur*, if for no other reason than to have a ready avenue for appeal or consultation on the budget.[37] Members of the other corps are also included in a number of *cabinets*. These corps are specialized by function but together provide a high level of leadership within the public service, which might be lacking without the corps structure and the *esprit de corps* that such a system engenders. Moreover, the isolation of the *grands corps* from a number of the usual administrative pressures, their prestige, and their individual abilities allow them to enforce standards of uniformity throughout the administration, so that this form of organization by function contributes to the maintenance of centralized government in France.[38]

Outside France, several functions are amenable to organization by corps or process. Engineering has been one, and any number of countries have specialized engineering corps within their national civil services or militaries, e.g., the Army Corps of Engineers in the United States.[39] If we look at administration broadly, the military officer corps and the diplomatic services could be considered as specialized corps, and as rather obvious cases of organization by function or process. Also, as with the Inspectorate of Finance in France, financial inspectors are frequently organized as a separate branch of administration, to ensure their impartiality in auditing public accounts. This goes so far, in the United States, as to isolate them almost entirely from the rest of the public service (in the General Accounting Office). Thus we can say that those functions that tend to be organized by process tend to be those that require: (1) technical training or highly professional skills, or (2) a high degree of internal commitment and *esprit de corps*, or (3) impartiality and isolation from other portions of the bureaucracy and from political pressures.

In summary, organization by process can make some useful distinctions between the tasks of various civil servants and agencies, but as a general organizing principle it appears to be unwieldy. Even in its limited form, it tends to engender political conflicts between those who (at least from their own perspective) do the work of the civil service, and those who merely (?) plan, coordinate, and control. Likewise, organization by corps as a special example of organization by process can engender similar political conflicts and rivalries directed against an elite group with broadly defined competencies who appear all too ubiquitous in the exercise of their tasks and all too close to those who are responsible for decision. Thus, as will be said again, the organization of the public service, as well as being a problem for the administrative scientist, is a problem for the politician as well. Both must attempt to provide smooth and efficient government, and both must try to protect their own interests through organizational devices.

Organization by Clientele

The third possible basis for organization is the clientele to be served by the agency. Clientele groups who are presumed to have special needs or whose life styles, situations, or other characteristics are considered sufficiently distinctive may justify an organization for them and their interests. There have been two apparent reasons for developing clientele-based organizations: (1) to be able to provide better services for a special set of clients (especially those with political clout), e.g., veterans, urban dwellers, farmers; or (2) conversely, to at once assist and *control* segments of the population lacking such clout, e.g., Indians, foreign workers, aliens. The important fact about both these justifications is that they result in an organization that is an obvious avenue for influence by the clientele on government. That is, organization by clientele, even when undertaken for the purpose of regulation, generally results in more direct group influence on administration than might be found in other forms of organization. The reasons for this are perhaps obvious; they will be developed more fully when we discuss the politics of administration.[40] But we should point out here that in client-based organizations, a process of exchange and mutuality almost inherently results. The clientele group needs the access to government decision making provided by the public organization, and the agency in turn requires popular support from its clientele in political conflicts. Further, those public organizations may owe their existence to the activities of particular clientele groups and must therefore cater to the demands of those groups more than might be thought by others to be in the "public interest."

Perhaps the most important manifestation of this tendency toward cooptation and symbiosis between clientele and administration occurs in so-called independent regulatory boards. The underlying conception of these boards, as they are constituted in the United States and elsewhere, is that they should serve as administrative *qua* judicial bodies controlling the activities of some portion of the economy or society. The boards are made independent to prevent excessive partisan influence from being exerted over their decisions. They are intended to regulate in the public interest and without regard for political considerations.

No matter how commendable these ideas may be in theory, they are almost certainly doomed to failure in practice. Many of the activities that these boards were intended to regulate are among the most sensitive and societally important, including transportation, energy, and communication.[41] But, by being isolated from political demands in their tasks of regulating these industries, the boards are isolated from political supports as well. They essentially lack any strong and direct connection with the executive and cannot therefore easily appeal for assistance in financing, staffing, and general support for their regulatory functions. Any such executive interference might be regarded as antithetical to the depoliticized and nonpartisan conception of these boards. Thus the independent regulatory boards must seek other sources of political support, with the most likely source being the very interests they were designed to regulate. The point of this argument, then, is that organization *by* clientele may rapidly change into organization *for* clientele.

Organization by client may also be made at the subdepartmental level, and may have many of the same consequences although they may be manifested primarily through intraorganizational conflict rather than through isolation and subversion of the public purpose.[42] As a department or agency develops bureaus devoted to assisting or even regulating a particular client group, those bureaus frequently become captives of that group and become a spokesman for them in policy-related matters. As with the organization of departments by client, the subdepartmental agencies may also need political support for political conflicts. Their clientele can provide such support, but the price of that support is favorable treatment or regulation.

Two interesting and countervailing examples of the way in which organization by clientele can influence an agency are those of forest rangers and the engineering corps. In these examples, local communities, or more specifically local business interests, operate as client groups.[43] The Forest Service is an attempt on the part of the organization to counteract possible local influences on regulation. One task of a forest ranger is to regulate the use of national forests for commercial purposes such as lumbering and grazing. The Forest Service uses as a general guideline that no ranger should remain in the same community for more than two years. This is to prevent him from becoming too closely integrated into the local community and therefore too sympathetic to pleas from local businessmen for excessive use of the forests.[44] Civil engineering corps in both France and the United States—and probably elsewhere—get a significant portion of their political support by integrating themselves into local communities and at times providing special treatment for the localities. This provides a huge reservoir of political support should the executive or legislature seek to curtail the autonomy of the corps.[45] The first of these examples shows an attempt to prevent clientele organization from subverting the formal goals of the organization; the second shows a use of client organization to enable the agency to succeed in its political conflicts.

Organization by clientele is at times difficult to avoid. There are powerful political pressures to organize to benefit certain groups, and there is a certain logic to such organization when the needs of a clientele are distinctive. On the other hand, this form of organization has a number of possible dangers. It is difficult for the public agency to remain at all detached from its clientele and to be able to administer programs objectively and in the "public interest."

Organization by Purpose

The final possibility for organizing administration is the principal purpose, or goal, of the organization. This mode of organization is not always clearly distinguishable from the others already discussed. For example, is a Department of Agriculture organized on the basis of its major purpose—the promotion of agriculture—or is it organized around a ready-made clientele group—farmers? Organization by purpose, perhaps more than the others mentioned, points up the lack of exclusiveness of this set of categories.

There are, however, more important topics to be discussed with respect to organization by purpose. The first is, where do organizational goals and purposes come from? Presumably, the legislation establishing an organization will specify the tasks to be performed by that organization. In most cases, however, these tasks are put forth in only the barest outline, allowing substantial latitude for future elaboration and interpretation. In theory at least, the elaboration of these organizational goals will be largely a political process involving the imposition of externally developed goals upon the organization by its political masters.[46] A number of scholars have undertaken to look at this process somewhat more realistically; they find that because of the weakness of those alleged to impose the goals and the resistance of the administrative organizations, there is relatively less impact of political masters on public organizations than was thought to be true.[47]

If the purposes of the organization do not come from the outside, as previously thought, where do they come from? The most obvious answer then is that they are generated internally. If that is true, we come to one of the most commonly noted pathologies of formal organizations: the displacement of goals.[48] There is a tendency in organizations gradually and almost imperceptibly to shift from what might be called public goals to what may be termed private goals. Even though the organization was established to fulfill some need in society, over time organizational survival and possibly organizational development may supersede that societal goal. Downs discusses this in terms of the tendencies of individuals within organizations to shift from zealot to conserver roles.[49] When young, they seek to achieve societal goals through their actions in the public service, but over time, because of a natural aging process, the growth of personal responsibilities, and perhaps cynicism about the possibility of social change, they become less interested in producing change but more interested in personal gain and security. Their major goals in office become: (1) to continue the existence of the agency, (2) possibly to expand its role and budget, and (3) finally to do something for the society.

Even if we do not accept the cynical view that after some (unspecified) point in time agencies become self-serving, we must understand that over time the goals pursued by an agency generally come to mean what the incumbents of the roles want them to mean. In other words, departments develop ideologies concerning the tasks that lay before them and the means of completing those tasks. Further, by controlling selection, socialization, and to some degree retention of members, they tend to preserve this ideology even when confronted with new members.[50] The organizational conception of goals and the means of achieving those goals are often functions of the period of political and organizational socialization of the incumbents to the leadership positions within the organization.

For example, most social-service agencies in the United States were developed or expanded dramatically during the New Deal era. The basic philosophy of social improvement was to throw money at the problem, and to some extent the imposition of middle-class values on clients of the agency.[51] These organizations were not particularly receptive to innovative or client-centered approaches to social problems, and so new organizations had to be created outside the existing framework to take new initiatives in social policy. In the same way, the foreign offices of many Western nations are still heavily influenced by a "Munich mentality," which dictates that any attempt at compromise with an enemy is a sign of weakness and a prelude to further threats and demands. As a final example, one might cite the essentially conservative and elitist civil services inherited by many Third World countries from their former colonial masters. These civil services were not organized or staffed to undertake the massive programs of economic and social development that they faced, and some were opposed to them ideologically. Thus there have been frequent expressions of hostility from the political leaders of these countries toward these seemingly recalcitrant civil servants who were impeding programs of rapid social change.[52] The major point to be made in this discussion of goal setting is that the purpose of a public agency is not necessarily the one outlined in the enabling legislation or in official policy statements. Setting goals is a political process, and very often it is an intraorganizational political process hidden from public scrutiny and public control.

Following the question of origin of goals is the question of what the agency does when it runs out of things to do. There are a number of rather amusing examples of agencies that have long outlived their stated purposes and have become essentially sinecures for the remaining employees. The few remaining widows and orphans of Garibaldi's campaign still rate an agency in Italy. Our concern is not with blatant inefficiency and redundancy, but rather with the problem of the succession of goals in an organization. That is, how can an agency shift its principal concerns and orientations from one objective to another? Given the discussion above, we must first assume that this would be a difficult task, but we do know that organizations undergo such shifts in order to survive. There are a number of examples of this type of goal succession in private organizations; two com-

monly cited examples are the March of Dimes and the YMCA.[53] The
examples from public organizations are perhaps less clear, but they
exist. One of the most common in European nations of late has been
the transformation of agencies formerly concerned with the management of colonial territories into offices of overseas development
and aid to underdeveloped countries. While still dealing with essentially the same clienteles geographically, the goals, operations, and
politics of these agencies have been greatly changed. Similarly, the
restructuring of American aid programs has necessitated a rather
massive shakeup within the Agency for International Development,
necessitating retraining of almost all the field staff. We can see that
agencies can and do shift goals, but it requires some strong impetus
to do so, with the loss or decline of agency support—both from the
budgetary process and the public—being the most important impetus
in public organizations.

Summary

We have now discussed four broad methods of going about the
business of organizing government and public administration. As
noted, the lines between each of these categories are not always
clear. What is clear is that none of these forms offers the perfect
solution to the problem of organizing the public service. Each has
advantages and disadvantages as a means of organization, and each
may conform better with the cultural values and social and economic
requirements of a particular nation. Thus the rather obvious but often
forgotten point that the structure of government must conform not
only to the wishes of the organizational theorists, but also to the political realities of the nation. There are certainly a number of organizational options, but these must be carefully weighed before being accepted and implemented, particularly as the costs of reorganization in
both personal and organizational terms are high.

INTERNAL ORGANIZATION

To this point we have been largely examining the problems of
organizing the public service at the national level with some attention
to problems within agencies that are analogous to those at macroscopic levels. We turn now to a brief discussion of internal organization and management. More particularly, we will be looking at problems of hierarchical control and communication within agencies.

These problems appear universally, and we therefore deal with them first as a general phenomenon. Toward the end of the discussion we try to bring out the comparative dimension both in terms of the differences between nations and the differences between types of policies and agencies.

Hierarchical control, or the chain of command, and the communication of information and decision form a central part of the study of organizations.[54] The drawers of organization charts assume that those at the top of the hierarchy are responsible for making decisions, that their decisions are binding for all members of the organization, and that it is the task of subordinates to communicate all relevant information upward so that decisions can be reached by those at the top. Unfortunately, these neat organization charts have to be staffed with real people, and this neat hierarchy is rarely seen in practice. In practice, a number of impediments disrupt the smooth flow of authority and information within the organization; they must be either accepted, overcome, or corrected by management. These problems may be especially acute in public organizations. In the first place, public organizations lack any ready mechanism by which to judge their effectiveness and consequently have nothing that can trigger "search activity" to find a better organizational framework.[55] Private organizations, especially businesses, can look at the balance sheet and use the level of profit, but public organizations have to rely on considerably softer measures of success.[56] Associated with the absence of appropriate measures of success is the (almost) permanent position of the civil servant. This makes it difficult for politically imposed managers to manipulate many of the threats and incentives that would be available in private organizations. Finally, there are often differences in the roles and motivations of many of the actors involved in the process of control, differing levels of long-term commitment to the organization, and different perspectives about the time in which change must be brought about.[57] All these factors make effective management of public organizations a particularly trying task.

The general purpose of hierarchical control is to promote uniformity of action by subordinates within the organization. One of the hallmarks and presumed benefits of bureaucratic organization is the elimination of personal discretion and caprice from the decisions taken by the organization. Unfortunately for those attempting to manage organizations, individuals like discretion and power, not so much to be able to deal capriciously with their clients as to have the opportunity to exercise some personal initiative. Further, they enjoy being able to establish personal relationships, i.e., those not strictly governed by the rules of the organization, with both superiors and subordinates. Many formal organizations tend to deny these opportunities to their members, with any number of adverse consequences both for individuals and for goal attainment within the organization. Leaving aside the consequences for individuals, let us look at the consequences for the organization.

One of the most important consequences is the isolation of strata within the organization.[58] Superior-subordinate relationships tend to become rigidified, with little opportunity for other than formal communication across strata. Each stratum becomes socially isolated from others, and each tends to develop its own norms of compliance with the directives of superiors. These norms are rarely in violation of the formal norms of the organization; in fact, there is a tendency to comply ritualistically with rules and directives while possibly subverting the real purposes of the organization. Thus complaints about bureaucratic red tape and inefficiency may largely result from the need of lower echelons in the organization to protect themselves from their superiors by complying with the letter of regulations and refusing to take any personal initiative outside those regulations that might subject them to later punishment. Their compliance is real, but paradoxically, by complying with the rules they may reduce the effectiveness and efficiency of the organization. This is another aspect of goal displacement, in that the rules become an end in themselves rather than a means to accomplishing the goals of the agency.

Associated with the isolation of strata is a tendency for organizations to develop faulty communication patterns. Within organizations, information is conceptualized as flowing upward, just as authority is conceptualized as flowing downward. There is a tendency, however, because of the power of superiors over subordinates, for each stratum within the organization to be somewhat less than candid when it communicates with its superiors.[59] In fact, there is a tendency systematically to distort the information passed upward to place the best possible construction on events, especially in light of what subordinates think their superiors want to hear. This is in part a function of the general organizational problem of each level having to synthesize and pass on only the relevant information to superiors, in order to prevent an overload of information as one goes up the organizational ladder. Many characteristics of formal bureaucratic structures tend to exacerbate this problem by the introduction of systematic distortion of information. Interestingly, superiors (having reached their position, one would hope, because of a certain amount of cleverness) tend to attempt to take into account the systematic distortion they believe has been introduced, and thus read reports skeptically and with an eye to what they think are the alternatives.[60] Unless the superior is more clever than he has any right to be, however, this attempt to counteract bias may actually introduce another distortion to the information. As this double distortion proceeds upward through several steps of the hierarchical ladder, one can obtain some conception of the distortion and misinformation that many modern organizations must contend with in making decisions.

The distortion of information as its passes through hierarchies is especially important in modern public bureaucracies when we consider the types of individuals who tend to occupy positions at each level of the hierachy. As Thompson argued some years ago, one characteristic of modern organizations is the concentration of technical expertise at the bottom of the hierarchy and the concentration of decision at the top.[61] In other words, we can expect the information passed up to decision makers to be systematically distorted; further, the decision makers might not have the ability to comprehend the technical content of the information even if it were passed on undistorted. The concentration of generalists in decision making in most public bureaucracies tends to exacerbate problems of hierarchical information flow, since they have little ability to absorb or develop information on their own.[62] Thus, if one were to make the most extreme case, one might say that decisions were being taken by people with inadequate and distorted information and that those individuals probably could not fruitfully utilize the proper information even if they had it. Even with a less extreme view, one can easily say that it is entirely possible that organizations have extreme difficulties in effectively processing information, especially `information with technical content, and consequently may lose the ability to "steer" themselves in policy formulation.

Given these problems of hierarchy and communication, what are the possibilities of creating effective organizations, especially effective public organizations? There is no simple answer, but there have been a number of suggestions for change. Some have involved altering the personalities of individuals—at least in their organizational roles —and modifying the dynamics of groups.[63] Others have concentrated on changing the approach of managers to the task of management.[64] One of the most innovative approaches to change is Landau's argument that it is essentially rational to be redundant and that the development of redundant channels of communication and control can be beneficial to an organization.[65] Redundancy was a tactic adopted by Franklin Roosevelt as President, to prevent the existing bureaus from sabotaging or delaying his New Deal Programs. The existence of dual hierarchies in Soviet administrative practice is perhaps an extreme version of redundancy intended to assure that there is a check on information and performance at all stages of the administrative process. To some degree the existence of ministerial *cabinets* in France and Belgium is a further use of redundant structures to check on the performance of administration. Downs further mentions the possibility of building in overlapping and redundant structures as a means of ensuring the flow of relatively unbiased information.[66] Interestingly, all these schemes involve the construction of organizations quite at odds with those that might be advocated by traditional students of management and public administration, for whom unity of command and the lack of overlapping functions were seen as two of the prime elements of proper organization.

Variations in Internal Organization

The problems of internal organization are general, and we should expect variation by both nation-state and the characteristics of the particular policy area being administered. Differences occur between those two broad categories of Western and non-Western systems, or developed and underdeveloped, if you prefer.[67] Despite their own variations, Western cultures are more accepting of impersonality, hierarchy, and bureaucracy than are non-Western cultures. Thus, we might expect the dysfunctions of bureaucracy outlined above to be more evident in non-Western cultures if attempts were made to enforce such a system. Attempts to depersonalize administration and policy through rules and procedure have been shown in a number of instances to be rather ineffective as a means of achieving ends in those systems.[68] The formal structures of most bureaucracies in the non-Western world conform quite closely with those of Western administration, in part as a function of colonial inheritance and in part because of the need to comply with certain formalities in order to receive aid from developed nations and international organizations. However, the actual operations of these structures tend to be quite different from the form, with nonbureaucratic criteria tending to supersede the rules, procedures, and hierarchy of the formal structure. Some of the bureaucratic dysfunctions related to communication may be overcome by a reliance on communalism and nonbu-reaucratic criteria in recruitment, as may in fact some problems of rigidity with clients. What is given up is the entire justification for having bureaucratic structures in the first place, namely, a high level of uniform behavior and in client treatment. The latter values are by no means perfectly attained in Western bureaucratic systems, but an attempt is made.

Western nations appear to show substantial variation in their prospects for effective bureaucracy. These have been discussed to some extent when discussing the "administrative cultures" of these countries.[69] What is important is the extent to which cultural differences tend to ease or exacerbate dysfunction in bureaucracy. One of the tendencies noted by Crozier in discussing these problems is the influence of general conceptions of authority and equality on the bureaucratic structure of organizations.[70] For example, he noted that perhaps as a function of generalized patterns of deference and acceptance of authority, the organizational structure of British ships tended to be substantially less complex and less dependent upon impersonal rules than those of American ships.[71] American crewmen, apparently socialized in more individualistic mores, were less willing to accept the personal authority of a superior, and formalized rules had to be devised to take the personal element out of rule enforcement. At the other end of the spectrum, societies in which authority is both accepted and revered, and where those in authoritative positions tend to view their roles somewhat paternalistically, can function with simple organizational structures and a relative absence of bureaucratic rules and still obtain high levels of uniformity in behavior. In their study of managerial attitudes cross-nationally, Haire, Ghiselli, and Porter found that there were several distinct blocs of Western nations in terms of their conceptions of the management role: Nordic, Anglo-American, and Latin-European.[72] The differences among these groups were rather subtle but pointed to important differences in attitudes toward managerial practice and authority even among Western nations.

There are also differences between types of organizations depending on the tasks they are intended to perform. Etzioni has provided one useful set of broad categories.[73] He classifies organizations according to the type of power that the organization seeks to use over its members and the type of compliance of the members. He classifies power as either coercive, remunerative, or normative. The compliance of organizational members may be either alternative, calculative, or moral. Although there may be mixed organizations, the three model types of organizations in this typology are coercive-alienative, remunerative-calculative, and normative-moral. Rather obviously, a normative-moral organization such as a church or even a highly committed public bureau is able to do its job effectively with a simpler organizational structure, fewer impersonal rules, and less dysfunctional activity than would other types of organization. On the other hand, such an organization would have more difficulty in modifying its goals and retaining its personnel than would an organization relying on remunerative power. Some public organizations of all three types exist, and managers, although they may not conceptualize it in exactly these terms, have to know how to employ the appropriate incentives with each type of organization.

Other schemes for classifying organizations depend more on the services provided by the organization. Blau and Scott use a classification of organizations based upon the criterion of *cui bono,* or who benefits.[74] Most public organizations fall into their category of commonweal organizations in that the public at large are the prime beneficiaries. Other public organizations would be service organizations in that the prime beneficiaries are the clients, e.g., social-service agencies. Again we can see that the dynamics of organizations whose intention it is to provide a service to the public at large, generally free and with no exclusion, will have different organizational problems than an organization whose intention is to serve only a limited number of individuals, based upon the particular needs of those individuals.[75] Moreover, the clients (consumers of services) for the commonweal organization tend to be considerably less dependent upon those organizations than do clients of service agents, so that for service organizations most conflicts emerge with the political representatives of the public at large over expense and responsibility.

Perrow along with Thompson and Tuden attempts to relate the characteristics of the problem of policy area to the type of decision making that is likely to occur.[76] Although both schemes (see figure 5.1) were intended to have universal applicability, they also have relevance to problems of public administrative agencies. In Thompson and Tuden's scheme, the same types of variation in the agreement on ends and the agreement on means occur among public agencies as they do more generally. The examples in figure 5.1 may not be universally agreed upon, but they should point out that, first, there is such variation, and second, that it will have consequences for public organizations. Likewise, the Perrow scheme, based largely on the

FIGURE 5.1

Typology of Policy Problems for Administration

| | | Preferences | |
		Agreement	Disagreement
Perception of Causation	Agreement	Programmed Decisions (public health)	Bargaining (incomes policy)
	Disagreement	Pragmatic (comprehensive education reform)	Inspiration (research and development)

SOURCES: Derived from James D. Thompson and Arthur Tuden, "Strategy, Structure, and Process of Organizational Decision," in *Comparative Studies in Administration* (Pittsburgh: University of Pittsburgh Administrative Science Center, 1959); Charles Perrow, *Organizational Analysis* (Belmont, Calif.: Wadsworth, 1970), pp. 80–91.

characteristics of technology and raw materials, has also been given examples from among public organizations, and the assumption is that organizations dealing with a stable (or stabilized) raw material, e.g., prisons, will have a vastly different type of organizational structure than will those dealing with essentially unknown materials, e.g., research and development agencies.[77] Of course, the characteristics of the individuals likely to be employed in such agencies and the tasks set out for them to do will also have an impact, but it does appear useful to look at the correspondence between organizations and the raw materials—most commonly human—with which they must deal.

SUMMARY

This chapter has provided a brief overview of the complex topic of the structure of public organizations. As such, it has been largely an introduction to the problems and questions that arise, rather than a set of definitive answers to those questions. Nevertheless, it should be clear that the design of administration is not an entirely technical exercise. There are a number of rather broad questions concerning the nature of the establishment as a whole that must be answered by political leaders or constitution writers rather than by the civil service. These answers may, in turn, greatly influence the overall effectiveness of the public establishment as well as the satisfaction of the public with that establishment. Beyond these questions, there are any number of problems with the internal organization of agencies and with the managing of an ongoing public enterprise. These must be considered in the light of the particular nation in question and the characteristics of the task involved. The basic task of organizational analysis, however, is to design organizations that enable occupants of the positions to at least have the possibility of providing effective services to the population. No organization chart or diagram of responsibilities can ensure this, so the task of the manager is largely to make it possible and perhaps even probable. The ultimate success or failure of the agency will remain with the individuals who inhabit it.

NOTES

1. See, for example, Dwight Waldo, "Public Administration," in *International Encyclopedia of the Social Sciences,* ed. Edward Shils (New York: Macmillan, 1968), pp. 145–56.
2. Herbert Simon, *Administrative Behavior* (New York: Macmillan, 1957), pp. 35–44.
3. Luther Gulick, "Notes on the Theory of Organization," in *Papers on the Science of Administration,* ed. Luther Gulick and L. F. Urwick (New York: Institute of Public Administration, 1937), pp. 3–50.
4. Ibid.; Schuyler Wallace, *Federal Departmentalism* (New York: Columbia University Press, 1941); George C. S. Benson, "Internal Administrative Organization," *Public Administration Review* 1, no. 4 (1941): 473–86.
5. Brian Chapman, *The Prefects and Provincial France* (London: Allen & Unwin, 1955), is now somewhat dated but still provides a useful description.
6. Robert Fried, *The Italian Prefects* (New Haven: Yale University Press, 1967).
7. Jean-Pierre Worms, "Le Préfet et ses notables," *Sociologie du Travail* 12, no. 3 (1966): 249–75.
8. Ibid., pp. 261 ff.
9. Some increase in the centralization of the system does appear to be occurring. See Kenneth Hanf, "Administrative Developments in East and West Germany: Stirrings of Reform," *Political Studies* 21, no. 1 (1973): 35–44.
10. Part of the political logic is, of course, to prevent the formation of a highly centralized political system, which might in turn be dominated by extremists.
11. See Sir David Milne, *The Scottish Office* (London: Allen & Unwin, 1957); James F. Kellas, *The Scottish Political System* (2nd ed.; Cambridge, England: Cambridge University Press, 1975), pp. 25–60.

12. See W. A. Robson, "The Missing Dimension of Government," *Political Quarterly* 42, no. 3 (1971): 233–46.
13. For a general discussion of this problem, see James W. Fesler, *Area and Administration* (n.p.: University of Alabama Press, 1949).
14. See J. Westerståhl, *Ett forskningsprogram: Den Kommunale Sjalvstyrelsen* (Stockholm: Almqvist & Wiksell, 1971).
15. See, for example, Elinor Ostrom, Roger B. Parks, and W. E. Oates, "Do We Really Want to Consolidate Urban Police Forces," *Public Administration Review* 30 (1973): 423–33.
16. See D. P. Bradford, R. A. Mott, and W. E. Oates, "The Rising Cost of Local Public Services: Some Evidence and Reflections," *National Tax Journal* 22, no. 2 (1969): 185–202.
17. Ostrom, Parks, and Oates, "Urban Police Forces."
18. Fesler, *Area and Administration*, p. 25.
19. This type of organization occurs in less extreme forms, as in the tendency to concentrate most legal services in a single legal agency, e.g., the Department of Justice.
20. Anthony Downs, *Inside Bureaucracy* (Boston: Little, Brown, 1967), pp. 211 ff.
21. The executive may not, however, see most conflicts and duplications since they are resolved at a lower level, which in turn reduces his control over the organization. An interesting discussion is provided in Robert Axelrod, *Conflict of Interest* (Chicago: Markham, 1969), pp. 121–43.
22. See chapter 7.
23. Peter Self, *Administrative Theories and Politics* (London: Allen & Unwin, 1972), p. 128.
24. Of course, the chancellor of the exchequer as head of the Treasury is somewhat more than just another minister, despite the alleged equality of the Cabinet. On the role of the Treasury in policy, see Hugh Heclo and Aaron Wildavsky, *The Private Government of Public Money* (Berkeley: University of California Press, 1974).
25. Self, *Administrative Theories*, pp. 133–34.
26. Ibid., p. 130; Sir Richard Clarke, "The Number and Size of Government Departments," *Political Quarterly* 43, no. 2 (1972): 169–86.
27. For an analysis of the concept, see William H. Starbuck, "Organizational Growth and Development," in *Handbook of Organizations*, ed. James G. March (Chicago: Rand McNally, 1965), pp. 496–98.
28. The job of some staff agencies is explicitly to impose some central control on line agencies, especially with regard to funding. This is especially true of a growing number of staff agencies engaged in cost-benefit analysis and program budgeting. See chapter 7. See also Aaron Wildavsky, "The Political Economy of Efficiency," *Public Administration Review* 26, no. 4 (1966): 292–310.
29. See Jeanne Siwek-Ponydesseau, "French Ministerial Staffs," in *The Mandarins of Western Europe*, ed. Mattei Dogan (New York: John Wiley, 1975), pp. 196–209.
30. Ezra Suleiman, *Power, Politics, and Bureaucracy in France* (Princeton: Princeton University Press, 1974), pp. 202–4.
31. Leo Moulin, "The Politicization of Administration in Belgium," in Dogan, *Mandarins*, pp. 163–84.
32. Ibid., p. 175.
33. Heclo and Wildavsky, *Public Money*, pp. 17–20.

34. See Nils Andréen et al., eds., *Svensk statsforvaltning i omdaning* (Stockholm: Almqvist & Wiksell, 1965); Pierre Vinde, *Hur sveriges styres* (Stockholm: Prisma, 1968).

35. Vinde, *Hur sveriges styres; The Swedish Civil Service* (Stockholm: Ministry of Finance, 1967), pp. 18–21.

36. See Francois Kesler, "Les anciens eleves de l'ecole Nationale d'Administration," *Revue francaise de science politique* 14, no. 2 (1964): 245–67.

37. Suleiman, *Power, Politics*, pp. 263–64.

38. Ibid., p. 271.

39. See for example, Arthur Maas, *Muddy Waters: The Army Corps of Engineers and the Nation's Rivers* (Cambridge, Mass.: Harvard University Press, 1951); Elizabeth B. Drew, "Dam Outrage: The Story of the Army Engineers," *Atlantic* 225 (1970): 51–62.

40. See chapter 6.

41. Henry J. Friendly, *The Federal Administrative Agencies* (Cambridge, Mass.: Harvard University Press, 1962); Theodore J. Lowi, *The End of Liberalism* (New York: Norton, 1969).

42. This is exacerbated when agencies or their components use different methodologies as in the instance of psychological or sociological caseworkers in social-service agencies.

43. This obviously impinges upon our earlier discussion of organization by area.

44. Herbert Kaufman, *The Forest Ranger: A Study in Administrative Behaviour* (Baltimore: Johns Hopkins University Press, 1967), pp. 176–83. This rapid transfer scheme also has the organizational benefit of building the concept of the service as a distinct organization and career.

45. Jean-Claude Theonig and E. Friedberg, *La creation des directions departmentales de l'equipment: phenomenes de corps et reforme administrative* (Paris: CNRS, 1970), pp. 39ff.; Grant McConnell, *Private Power and American Democracy* (New York: Knopf, 1970), pp. 216–19.

46. This seems to imply an acceptance of the dichotomy between politics and administration. This is to reflect the formal-legal dichotomy concerning the development of legislation and the political responsibility for policy.

47. See Richard Rose, *The Problem of Party Government* (London: Macmillan, 1974), pp. 417–21.

48. The classic statement of this pathology is Robert K. Merton, "The Unanticipated Consequences of Purposive Social Action," *American Sociological Review* 1, no. 4 (1936): 894–904; "Bureaucratic Structure and Personality," *Social Forces* 18, no. 4 (1940): 560–68.

49. Downs, *Inside Bureaucracy*, pp. 98–99.

50. Robert Presthus provides a thorough study of organizational socialization in private organizations in *The Organizational Society* (New York: Knopf, 1962); See also Downs, *Inside Bureaucracy*.

51. See, for example, Gilbert Steiner, *The State of Welfare* (Washington, D.C.: Brookings Institution, 1971), pp. 75–121; Frances Fox Piven and Richard A. Cloward, *Regulating the Poor* (London: Tavistock, 1972).

52. See, for example, D. B. Abernathy, "Bureaucracy and Economic Development in Africa," *Africa Review* 1, no. 1 (March 1971): 93–107.

53. David Sills, *The Volunteers* (Glencoe, Ill.: Free Press, 1957); Owen E. Pence, *The YMCA and Social Need* (New York: Association Press, 1939); Mayer N. Zald, *Organizational Change* (Chicago: University of Chicago Press, 1970).

54. See Dorwin Cartwright, "Influence, Leadership, Control," in *Handbook of Organizations*, ed. James G. March (Chicago: Rand McNally, 1965), pp. 1–47.

55. For a discussion of "search activity" in organizations, see Richard M. Cyert and James G. March, *The Behavioral Theory of the Firm* (Englewood Cliffs, N.J.: Prentice-Hall, 1963).

56. Some measures of "agency success" have to do with their success in budgeting, which functions as an analogue of the market for the public sector. See, for example, Ira Sharkansky, "Agency Requests, Gubernatorial Support, and Budget Success in State Legislatures," *American Political Science Review* 62, no. 4 (December 1968): 1220–31; Sharkansky and Augustus B. Turnbull III, "Budget-Making in Georgia and Wisconsin: A Test of a Model," *Midwest Journal of Political Science* 13, no. 4 (November 1969): 631–45.

57. Bruce Headey, *British Cabinet Ministers* (London: Allen & Unwin, 1974), 204–6.

58. Crozier's work on bureaucratic theory relies heavily on the concept of strata isolation. See Michel Crozier, *The Bureaucratic Phenomenon* (Chicago: University of Chicago Press, 1964), pp. 190–208.

59. See Gordon Tullock, *The Politics of Bureaucracy* (Washington, D.C.: Public Affairs Press, 1965), pp. 137–42; Downs, *Inside Bureaucracy*, pp. 112–31; Harold Wilensky, *Organizational Intelligence* (New York: Basic Books, 1967).

60. James G. March and Herbert A. Simon, *Organizations* (New York: John Wiley, 1958), pp. 164–66.

61. Victor Thompson, *Modern Organizations* (New York: Knopf, 1961).

62. Modern civil services, despite their important differences, tend to have a concentration of "generalists" at the top of the hierarchy.

63. See Daniel Katz and Robert L. Kahn, *The Social Psychology of Organizations* (New York: John Wiley, 1966), pp. 390–451.

64. Rensis Likert, *The Human Organization* (New York: McGraw-Hill, 1967).

65. Martin Landau, "On the Concept of the Self-Correcting Organization," *Public Administration Review* 33, no. 6 (1973): 533–42; "The Rationality of Redundancy," *Public Administration Review* 29 (1969): 346–58.

66. Downs, *Inside Bureaucracy*, pp. 119–20.

67. Mason Haire, Edwin E. Ghiselli, and Lyman W. Porter, *Managerial Thinking: An International Study* (New York: John Wiley, 1966).

68. See, for example, the articles in Joseph LaPalombara, ed., *Bureaucracy and Political Development* (Princeton: Princeton University Press, 1963).

69. See chapter 3.

70. Crozier, *Bureaucratic Phenomenon*, pp. 231–36.

71. Stephen Richardson, "Organizational Contrasts in British and American Ships," *Administrative Science Quarterly* 1, no. 2 (1956): 189–207.

72. Haire, Ghiselli, and Porter, *Managerial Thinking;* A. W. Clarke and S. McCabe, "Leadership Beliefs of Australian Managers," *Journal of Applied Psychology* 54, no. 1 (1970): 1–6; L. L. Cummings and Stuart M. Schmidt, "Managerial Attitudes of Greeks; The Role of Culture and Industrialization," *Administrative Science Quarterly* 17, no. 2 (1972): 265–72.

73. Amitai Etzioni, *A Comparative Analysis of Complex Organizations* (New York: Free Press, 1961), pp. 3–21.

74. Peter M. Blau and Richard M. Scott, *Formal Organizations* (San Francisco: Chandler, 1963), pp. 45–57.

75. For a discussion of incentives of bureaucrats in commonwealth agencies, see Timothy M. Hennessey and B. Guy Peters, "Postindustrialism and Public Policy" (Paper delivered at annual meeting of American Political Science Association, San Francisco, California, September 1975.)

76. Charles Perrow, *Organizational Analysis: A Sociological View* (Belmont,

Calif.: Wadsworth, 1970), pp. 80–91; James D. Thompson and Arthur Tuden, "Strategy, Structure, and Process of Organizational Decision," in *Comparative Studies in Administration* (Pittsburgh: University of Pittsburgh Administrative Science Center, 1959).

77. One of the classic studies of the organization of research remains Donald C. Pelz, "Some Social Factors Related to the Performance in a Research Organization," *Administrative Science Quarterly* 1, no. 3 (1956): 310–25.

POLITICS AND PUBLIC ADMINISTRATION:
Administration and Informal Political Actors

The preceding chapters were, in essence, the foundation for this and the following two chapters. We have by now discussed the relationship of public administration to its environment through an elaboration of the social and economic surroundings of administration, the cultural milieu in which administration functions, attempts of administration to recruit personnel from that environment, and the patterns of bureaucratic structure. In this chapter we begin to examine the relationship of politics to the conduct of administration and to the policy decisions made by administrators. The interaction of administration with both formal and informal political actors in the society obviously has an impact on the behavior of administrators and on their decisions. The extent of this influence, and the manner in which it is exerted, are the subjects of investigation in this chapter and those that follow.

Perhaps the best place to begin this discussion is by again noting the survival of the ancient administrative proverb that politics and administration are separate enterprises and that such a separation is valid both in the analysis of the institutions and behaviors of government and in the actual conduct of public business.[1] Although any number of authors have attempted to lay this proverb to rest, it has displayed amazing powers of survival and reappears in any number of settings in any number of political systems.[2] We must therefore assume that this proverb, if not entirely or even partially valid from an analytic perspective, serves some purpose for administrators and politicians. What does the artificial separation of these functions do that makes its survival so desirable for both actors? For administrators, this presumed separation of administration and politics allows them to engage in politics without the bother of being held accountable politically for the outcomes of their actions. Further, they can engage in policy making—presumably using technical or legal criteria for decision—without the interference of political actors who might otherwise make demands upon them for the modification of those policies.[3] Thus the actions of administrators may be regarded by politicians, the public, and even themselves as the result of the simple application of rational, legal, or technical criteria to questions of policy, which may make otherwise unacceptable decisions more palatable to the public.[4]

The separation of politics and administration also allows a certain latitude to politicians, which they might otherwise lack. In essence, the separation of these two types of institutional choices allows many of the difficult decisions of modern government to be made by individuals who will not have to face the public at a subsequent election.[5] Thus it may allow politics to shape or at least influence an important decision that will be announced by a "nonpolitical" institution that will not be held publicly accountable. Further, this conception that political and technical decision making can be separated in public life has allowed political reformers to remove many important public decisions as far as possible from the realm of "politics"—meaning largely corrupt, machine politics and other pejorative aspects of political life. This results in many important governmental functions being transferred from partisan political control to independent agencies, bureaucracies, and technocratic elites.[6] It is obviously assumed that the administrators who make decisions in these settings are in fact insulated from political pressures, and are able to make decisions *pro bono publico* because of that insulation. As we will show, however, these artificial separations of the political and administrative functions, instead of removing decisions from political influence, may actually subject them to different and more invidious types of political influences. These influences are believed to be more invidious because, having already been defined out of existence, they are difficult for the citizenry to identify and even more difficult to control.

Having still not completely exorcised the demon of the separation of political and administrative choice, we are now at least in a position to understand why the actors in the policy process may be willing to accept such a doctrine and why scholars may come to believe them. We will therefore go on to discuss the political environment of administrative decision as well as the political influences on those decisions. In so doing it is useful to distinguish several basic dimensions of the political activity of administrators. The first such dimension may be labeled "internal-external," or perhaps more appropriately "policy-survival." On this dimension we are attempting to distinguish between political activity within the agency, which seeks to take a

Policy-Survival

Formality		Internal	External
Formal		Administrator-Minister Relationship	Budgeting; Accountability
Informal		Administrative Lobbying	Public Support

FIGURE 6.1 Types of Bureaucratic Politics

variety of inputs from pressure groups, partisans, the political executive, and any number of other sources and develop a policy, from political activity directed toward the maintenance and growth of the organization. These two forms of politics are rarely so neatly separated in real life, and each contributes to the successful accomplishment of other goals. However, we can usefully distinguish these two for analytic purposes and discuss the types of influences likely to be brought and the major loci of political conflict for each.

The second dimension of administrative politics is one of officialdom, or formality. Administrators interact both with other governmental officials (legislators, the political executive, other administrators, representatives of subnational governments) and with unofficial political actors (largely the representatives of pressure groups). Again, these interactions are not always clearly separable, for officials often carry with them a continuing commitment to the cause of particular interests, and pressure groups may function in quasi-official capacities. However, it is useful to make such a distinction for analytic reasons because the style of the interaction, its legitimacy, and its probable influences on policy will vary as a function of the type of actor involved as well as a function of the type of agency activity involved.

The two dimensions of political activity by public administration, along with examples of each category of activity, are presented in figure 6.1. We show four categories based upon a cross-classification of the two dimensions. Thus, we will be looking at administrative politicized actions that have a characteristic of being both formal and informal, and directed more toward policy formation or survival. Our example of internal (policy)-formal administrative politics is the relationship between an upper-echelon civil servant and the cabinet minister he is designated to serve.[7] Increasingly, the ministers charged with extensive political chores in addition to managing a large bureaucratic organization cannot be reasonably expected to have a sufficient grasp of the issues involved or of the information available for many policy decisions; such decisions will therefore be produced through either consultation with, or delegation to, the senior administrative officials.[8] Consequently, interactions of this type have become one of the dominant features of the policy-making process and must be better understood in order to predict the outcomes of the policy process in contemporary political systems.

External-formal administrative politics are perhaps best seen in two ways. The first is the process of public budgeting in which administrative agencies have to seek their continued and expanded funding from other institutions of government.[9] A number of authors note that this is perhaps the most crucial locus of administrative politics because of its pivotal role in the future programs of the agency.[10] It is certainly a political activity that is the focus of an enormous amount of effort on the part of the agencies and one that has received considerable attention in the popular and scholarly literature.[11] It also involves the mobilization of considerable political support for the agency if it expects to be successful in obtaining its desired funding, and consequently is an activity that will involve considerable informal politics as well. The second important type of external-formal politics is the politics of public accountability through which other formal bodies may seek to curb the autonomy of the public bureaucracy. Given the importance of this type of politics in contemporary politics, we have saved this topic for a discussion in a chapter of its own.[12]

Internal-informal administrative politics is probably best characterized by the relationship of pressure groups and administration in the formation of policy. In virtually all political systems attempts are made by interest (or pressure) groups to influence public decisions.[13] The openness of the administration to these influences and the success of groups in obtaining the policies they seek are again a function of a number of institutional, political, and cultural factors that require further discussion and elaboration. However, except in the most totalitarian society, there is generally considerable opportunity for group action and for group influence on the process of policy formulation in bureaucracy.

Finally, external-informal administrative politics are best characterized by relationships between interest groups and administration in the attempts of administrators to develop public support for their programs and the continued success of the agency in the budgetary process. LaPalombara discusses these types of relationships as *clientela* relationships, and a number of authors have demonstrated the effects of the need for a clientele on the activities of administration.[14] As noted, this type of activity is inextricably bound with the ability of pressure groups to influence policy and the ability of agencies to survive in a competitive environment.

Now that we have some general picture of the scope and variety of administrative politics, we begin our more intensive discussion of the politics of administration by examining the informal side of these interactions—that is, the relationship between administration and pressure groups, political parties, and other unofficial political groups seeking to influence the course of public policy or whom the administrators rely upon in justifying their future programs and funding. Our discussion of the relationships of political parties to administration is substantially briefer than that of pressure groups. This is in large part due to the fact that the major influence of party appears to be manifested through official mechanisms, i.e., when members of the party occupy formal positions of leadership. Since, almost by definition, political parties are principally motivated by the opportunity to hold public office rather than the opportunity to influence policy through lobbying activities, it makes more sense to look at the official rather than the unofficial side of partisan activities.

BUREAUCRACY AND PRESSURE GROUPS

We must suppose that the conflict between the demands of pressure groups and the role of bureaucracy in decision making is, in most societies, one of the most basic in government. On the one hand there is an institution of government, representing the authority of the state, impartiality, and even a judicial temperament. On the other side of the conflict are groups that, by their very nature, represent only specialized narrow interests seeking some preferential treatment from government. This type of division of the role of the state and the role of interests is perceived differently in different political cultures.

FIGURE 6.2

Types of Interaction Between Pressure Groups and Bureaucracy

Characteristics

Types	Scope	Influence	Style	Impact
Legitimate	Broad	Great	Bargaining	Redistribution/Self-regulation
Clientela	Narrow	Moderate	Symbiosis	Self-regulation/Distribution
Parantela	Narrow	Moderate	Kinship	Regulation/Distribution
Illegitimate	Variable	None/Great	Confrontation	None/Redistribution

The conflict may not be as intense in Norway as in, say, France, but interestingly, this conflict has been sufficiently ameliorated in most societies so that the two sets of organization—administration and pressure groups—are able not only to coexist but even to cooperate effectively.[15] Further, it is especially interesting that societies that have tended to have the most positive conception of the public bureaucracy—Germany, the Netherlands, and the Scandinavian countries—have been more successful in accommodating to the roles of pressure groups in policy making than have political systems that have a less exalted conception of their civil servants.[16] In fact, a relatively positive evaluation of the civil service may be required to allow the civil servants any latitude in dealing with the pressure groups and in making accommodations to their demands.[17]

Given the apparent conflict in the roles of these two sets of political actors and institutions, how are they able to cooperate so well and so often in making public policy? The simplest and best explanation is that they need each other. Administrators need the political support and influence of pressure groups in their external relationships with other political institutions, and they further need the information supplied by pressure groups in making and defending policy. On the other side of the exchange, pressure groups need access to political decision making and influence over the decisions taken. This need of both parties for the resources of the other can provide a general answer to the finding of frequent cooperation between bureaucracies and pressure groups. We are left with the more formidable task of describing how the two partners in this exchange interact, and what the effects are of different patterns of interaction.

We may again fruitfully begin the discussion by presenting a classification of types of interactions between pressure groups and bureaucracies, along with the presumed characteristics and effects of each type. This is presented in figure 6.2. This classificatory scheme places the interaction between bureaucrats and pressure groups into four broad categories. This constitutes an informal continuum from situations in which pressure-group influence on policy is regarded as illegitimate to those where it is regarded as legitimate and necessary. These four categories are themselves rather broad and may contain some substantial variation, but it is still useful to use such a classificatory scheme to begin to understand the broad differences in relationships between these actors.

Legitimate Interactions

The first category of interactions between bureaucrats and pressure groups actions is labeled "legitimate." This denotes that in some political systems, not only are pressure groups an accepted fact of political life, but they are also legally and officially involved in the process of making and administering public policy. The major examples of this type are found in West Germany, the Low Countries and Scandinavia, but a number of other countries have adopted legitimate roles for pressure groups in more limited forms. More specifically, we can look at two forms of official or legitimate pressure-group involvement in administrative activity: required consultation and direct administration of public programs on behalf of the government.

REQUIRED CONSULTATION. The required-consultation mechanism for legitimating pressure-group involvement in policy making is, as the name implies, the result of a variety of rules that require administrative bodies preparing new regulations to consult with the relevant pressure groups for their opinions and to solicit advice and information from them. In some cases this is done in the preparation of legislation to be sent to a legislative body for enactment; in other cases it is used for regulations that the administrative body can issue as a result of delegated legislative authority. In either case, required consultation permits an interest group direct access to the making of administrative policies.

One method of assuring such input is through the use of *remiss* petitions in Sweden and Norway.[18] In both these countries, when policy modifications are being considered, the administrative agencies are required to ask for *remiss* from interest groups. These documents state the views of the group as well as some of the information that the group considers relevant to the case. Originally, the device was used only for pressure groups directly affected by the new set of regulations (e.g., agricultural groups affected by new regulations from an agricultural marketing board). More recently, the system has been extended to include virtually any organized group that wishes to submit an opinion.[19] While such a system provides no guarantee that the advice of the group will be heeded, it does ensure access to the relevant decision makers. Further, since it is customary for the *remisser* to be passed on with any proposed legislation, the system also provides some assurance that those who must finally pass legislation are also informed of interest-group opinion. In West Germany, public agencies seeking to write new legislation or regulations are required by law to seek advice from interested pressure groups. In Germany, the array of pressure groups consulted on any one issue is not generally so wide as in the Scandinavian countries, but the mechanism does allow direct and legitimate input of information and opinions.[20]

While the *remiss* system relies on formal written communications for the pressure groups to make their views known, other methods of required consultation use more personal methods. Most notable in this regard is the use of advisory committees in Norwegian administration.[21] On each committee a variety of administrative and interest-group personnel is charged with advising the respective administrative body on the proper course of public policy. These committees then provide a forum for the interest group to present their evidence and make a case for their particular views. Interestingly, however, most representatives on these committees do not view their role as that of an advocate of a particular position, but rather as more of a technical expert and manager.[22] This role conception is obviously useful in facilitating compromise on even difficult questions of policy. Sweden and Denmark have not yet gone as far in institutionalizing this form of pressure-group involvement, but they do have a number of less formal contacts for the purpose of advice, especially when an interest group may feel particularly disadvantaged by a policy. Similarly, in Germany, interest groups are represented on advisory boards for the ministries as a matter of legal right. While these advisory boards exist in a number of political systems—France is said to have some 1,400 of them and Switzerland rapidly creates and dissolves them—what distinguishes West Germany and Scandinavia is the official sanction given to the role of the groups in the process of making policy.[23] As Kvavik notes, these systems move the role of pressure-group influence from that of input to that of withinput; that is, in non-Eastonian language, the political system recognizes pressure groups as an integral part of the decision-making process and therefore accords them some of the same status accorded to other official participants in the policy process.[24] In Germany this may be viewed as a continuation of some of the traditional corporate conceptions of the state, but in all systems this type of influence provides an important alternative to the usual liberal means of representation through elections and legislatures.[25] Moreover, with the rapid growth of administrative policy making, it may soon surpass the liberal means in its impact on public policy.

IMPLEMENTATION.   The second major form of legitimate interest-group involvement in administration is the use of the groups as agents of implementation for public policies. Interest groups serve as quasi-official arms of the political system in implementing some programs about which they are assumed to have expert knowledge and skills. Again, this means of group involvement is particularly apparent in Scandinavia and also frequently occurs in the Low Countries.[26] One of the most common areas in which administration of this type occurs is agriculture, where either commodity groups or local farmers' organizations administer regulations or acreage allotments or contractual relationships with the government. In Sweden the implementation of many portions of the labor law is left to the individual groups most affected by the law.[27] Similarly, in the Netherlands much of that country's complex system of economic regulation is administered by boards composed largely of interest-group representatives charged with the "self-policing" of a particular industry in order to maintain the delicate economic balance within the country.[28] In each case, the government essentially allows interest groups to engage in activities in the name of the public with only indirect "political" control over their actions. They tend to be somewhat restrained by having competing interests represented on the same administrative boards, but this is obviously a manner in which interest groups can have a quite direct impact on the shape of public policy and its execution.

Institutional pressure groups would appear to constitute a special class of legitimate pressure groups. By definition, these are members of an important social or political institution, or that institution itself, acting in the capacity of a pressure group seeking to influence the shape of public policy.[29] Some rather obvious examples are the church, the army, and the bureaucracy itself.[30] Local governments, even in unitary regimes, may also act as institutional groups.[31] These groups seek to obtain benefits for themselves or their members, and their actions are legitimated through the prestige of the institution or perhaps the threat of extreme actions in the case of the army in some societies. Thus, although their position may provide them legitimacy, they may actually be better conceptualized as a special class of *clientela* groups in that they have legitimate access when a number of competing groups may not, and tend to seek more special-interest outputs than tends to be true in legitimate pressure-group systems.[32]

In figure 6.2 we also present a variety of the characteristics of the interactions of administrators and pressure groups. As noted, the scope of interaction between pressure groups and administration in "legitimate" situations tends to be quite broad. A single pressure group may be consulted on a variety of policies, and virtually all policy areas may be the subject of inputs from interested parties. Also, the influence of the groups on policy may be expected to be great relative to other types of interaction patterns. The legitimacy of the groups, their frequency of interaction with administrators, and their official or quasi-official status all make it possible for groups to have an impact that they would not have elsewhere. In part this is a function of not having to expend organizational resources simply to gain access, and in part a function of the roles adopted by the interest-group participants in the process. These perceived roles contribute to the bargaining style of their interactions. As noted by Kvavik, the dominant-role type in these negotiations is the expert who supplies information and opinion but who does not serve merely as an advocate of his particularistic viewpoint.[33] This bargaining activity is described by Rokkan as follows:

The crucial decisions on economic policy are rarely taken in the parties or Parliament: the central area is the bargaining table where the government authorities meet directly with the trade union leaders, the representatives of the farmers, the smallholders, and the fishermen, and the delegates of the Employers' Association. These yearly rounds of negotiations have in fact come to mean more in the lives of rank-and-file citizens than have formal elections. In these processes of intensive interaction the parliamentary notions of one member, one vote and majority rule make little sense. Decisions are not made through the counting of heads, but through complex considerations of short-term and long-term advantages in alternative lines of compromise.[34]

When the influence of pressure groups must be more covert, this important bargaining mode of interaction is of necessity lost in the politics of gaining access, necessitating that few groups rather than many will be involved in any one decision.

Finally, the policy consequences of this interaction between pressure groups and administrators are generally confined to two types (phrased in terms of the Salisbury typology): redistribution and self-regulation.[35] That is, in situations in which administrators are capable of imposing the choices made by groups through a bargaining and negotiation process, the decisions taken are likely to take from one group and give to another. This means of policy making is, however, a relatively safe manner in which to adopt redistributive policy since it ensures the participation of both winners and losers as well as assuring the application of technical knowledge to the choice. These two characteristics—the technical knowledge of the participants and the presence of all competing sides—were in fact the criteria selected by respondents in Kvavik's sample as most important in legitimating their decisions.[36] Elvander likewise notes that in Sweden the inclusion of all competing groups is important for the smooth implementation of policies adopted by pressure-group representatives cooperating with the government.[37] In addition, Heisler and Kvavik point out that continued access to policy making may be a sufficient motivation in itself to produce compliance with the decisions taken, even in the face of adverse decisions in the short run.[38] In situations in which the elite may lack the cohesion and consensus necessary to implement a redistributive decision, these legitimate interactions between interest groups and administrators may result in policies of self-regulation.[39] In these cases organizations are allowed generally to manage their own affairs and thereby essentially manage a sector of public policy for the government. One example of this type of policy outcome is in the area of agriculture, where the conflict within the sector is relatively slight so that there may be little need for directly redistributive decisions, and where some policies—such as the allocation of acreage allotments—may have little effect on other groups.[40] Even here there is potential conflict, however, between agricultural groups who would want high subsidies and therefore high food prices and labor groups who would want low prices and therefore lower subsidies. The choice between redistributive and self-regulative policies may depend on the breadth of groups involved in any one decision as well as the integration of the elites making and enforcing the decisions. In other policy areas, one group may have such a monopoly of information and expertise that it is given the responsibility of self-regulation on the basis of that expertise. This has been especially true of medical and legal groups in the United States and is a prevalent finding for similar groups in a variety of other political systems.[41]

Clientela Relationships

The second type of interaction between interest groups and ad-ministration is one of the two major types discussed by LaPalom-bara. A *clientela* relationship is said to exist when

> . . . an interest group, for whatever reasons, succeeds in becom-ing in the eyes of a given administrative agency, the natural ex-pression and representative of a given social sector which, in turn, constitutes the natural target or reference point for the activity of the administrative agency.[42]

This type of interaction is characterized by a perceived legitimacy on the part of administrators of one group rather than a formal state-ment of the legitimacy of all or virtually all groups. The consequences of this difference are, however, quite important. In the first place, the scope of interaction of pressure groups and administration tends to be rather severely constrained. Each agency tends to select a single pressure group as *the* legitimate representative of its particular social sector and to avoid most other groups seeking to present information and advice. Thus, whereas in the "legitimate" arrangement men-tioned previously the agency might be able or required to consult a broad range of groups, in a *clientela* relationship they will entertain a quite narrow range of information and advice. This narrowing is especially evident when two or more groups seek to organize a single sector of the society but only one is accorded regular access to de-cision making. This tends to skew the sources of information, generally in the direction toward which the administrators tended in the first place. Suleiman, for example, notes that in France—and certainly elsewhere—legitimate groups tend to be those whose economic strength is undeniable and whose demands are in general accord with government policy.[43]

The second consequence of this form of interaction is that while the influence of one group may be increased, the overall influence of pressure groups on public policy will be lessened. Not having legitimacy in any formal sense obviously reduces the acceptability of special-interest influence on policy for the general public, and the ability of the bureaucracy to accept advice is also limited. Further, each pressure group must expand relatively more of its organizational resources on the pursuit of access so that less is available for the information and influence functions. Moreover, in this process of seeking access any conception of the "public interest"—even as an aggregate of pressure-group interests—tends to be lost and replaced with a set of private interests, each represented in government by a single agency.[44] Associated with the above is a need to keep the negotiations and interactions of interest groups and administrators private and informal, thereby removing them even further from public scrutiny and accountability. All these characteristics of the scope and manner of interaction indicate that the pressure-group universe will tend to be less broadly influential over policies, with virtually any influence that does occur having something of a taint of illegality among the general public.

The description of the interactions of interest groups and administration in *clientela* politics leads to the characterization of these relationships as symbiotic. As in biological symbiosis, this relationship implies a mutual dependence of the two participants. The administrative agency depends upon the pressure group for information, advice, prior clearance of policy decisions, and most importantly, for political support in its competition with other agencies for the scarce resources within government. The pressure groups, on the other hand, depend upon the agency for access to decision making and ultimately for favorable decisions on certain policy choices. For both sides the existence of a *clientela* relationship serves to regularize the political environment and to develop friendships in what might otherwise be a hostile political world. This form of pressure-group relationship with administration has been noted by LaPalombara in Italy, has been used by several authors as a means of describing much of the politics of policy in the United States, and would seem to be prevalent in a number of other political systems that have strong interest groups but where the interactions of these groups and the government is at the margin of acceptability.[45]

Finally, the policy consequences of the *clientela* arrangement are those of producing essentially self-regulative and distributive outcomes. LaPalombara notes that regulation is one of the defining characteristics of a *clientela* relationship, but goes on to note that the regulative activities undertaken are not necessarily those that would promote the "public interest." [46] Rather, they are activities that quite directly promote the interests of the regulated. This pattern of regulation has, as noted, been referred to as "self-regulation." Again, this tendency toward self-regulation appears endemic to administrative agencies and especially independent regulatory commissions in the United States. Lowi has argued that "interest group liberalism," or the appropriation of the power of the state for private ends is in fact the dominant characteristic of contemporary public policy in the United States.[47] McConnell notes that the "outstanding political fact about independent regulatory commissions is that they have in general become the protectors and promoters of the industries they have been established to regulate." [48] Evidence from other political systems, however, is that this phenomenon is not confined to the United States but is a more general feature of industrial societies. In a variety of settings the need for political support is sufficient to necessitate the replacement of regulation with clientelism and self-regulation. Administrators may lack the resources and the central political support to enforce programs of regulation in the face of opposition of powerful and well-organized groups, so that in essence they must gain support from those groups.

As well as self-regulation, *clientela* relationships also tend to be associated with distributional outcomes, which may be merely more tangible types of self-regulative programs.[49] In distributional policies, however, instead of being allowed to make one's own regulations, one is granted certain continuing benefits. In Lowi's terms, these benefits "create privilege, and it is a type of privilege which is particularly hard to bear or combat because it is touched with the symbolism of the state." [50] The continuation of *clientela* politics can ensure that each of the clients receives something of value from the government and that questions of redistribution and the need for adjustment of the relative benefits are rarely subjects for discussion.

This form of policy making is in part a function of the peculiar politics and economics of public bureaucracies. Despite the arguments made that regard bureaucracy and bureaucrats as an integrated and homogeneous force, seeking to take control of the political system (at a minimum), bureaucracies are generally highly fragmented and divided political institutions. By being so fragmented, they are forced into competition simply because there is rarely any effective central means of allocating resources with respect to the merits of programs or the needs of society.[51] Hence, the budgetary process becomes a competitive process in which agencies seek to maximize their budgets at the expense of other agencies. Part of this bureaucratic acquisitiveness may be a function of sincere commitments to policy objectives, but much of it appears to be a function of the rather fundamental need for bureaucratic organizations to grow and survive.[52]

The budgetary process then tends to force public bureaucracies to seek public support and make distributive accommodations in order to gain that support. This outcome is further magnified by the division among the other actors in the budgetary process and their needs for other types of benefits and accommodations. The clientelism that extends between the pressure group and the administration may extend to a type of clientelism between legislative committees and the administrative agencies they are ostensibly overseeing.[53] This is in part a function of the stability of the actors involved in the process, as in the United States Congress, but more generally is related to the joint need of administrators and legislators to serve a constituency. For example, legislators interested in agricultural matters tend to come from predominantly agricultural districts; any attempt to curtail the activities of an agricultural agency would not be well received in their constituencies, thereby threatening their chances for reelection.[54]

We find, then, that there will often be a tight intermeshing of interest groups, administration, and legislators, all of whom have something to gain by certain expenditures, producing patterns of policy similar to those predicted by Salisbury and Heinz in such situations: the parceling out of goods and services available through the public budget in a manner that will provide each organized sector with some portion of the benefits.[55]

Parantela Relationships

This is the second type of administrative–pressure-group relationship mentioned by LaPalombara in his discussion of Italian interest groups. A *parantela* relationship describes a situation of "kinship" or close fraternal ties between a pressure group and the government or dominant political party.[56] These relationships have been held to be most characteristic of preindustrial societies, but our discussion will show them occurring in a number of political systems in which there is a single dominant party or faction and in which pressure groups must gain access and legitimacy through their attachment to that particular party rather than through their ability effectively to represent a sector of the society.

Parantela relationships between pressure groups and bureaucracies involve an indirect linkage between those actors rather than the direct linkage discussed in the *clientela* relationship. The important added linkage is the political party—most commonly a hegemonic party—with which the pressure group must develop some feeling of consanguinity. In these cases, the pressure groups obtain access to administrative decision making through the willingness of the party to intercede in its behalf with the bureaucracy and therefore in essence to control bureaucratic policy making.

There must, therefore, be a domination of policy making by a political party, which is not usually associated with Western democratic systems but which is still present in those systems. LaPalombara, for example, found relationships of this type existing in Italy with the Christian Democratic party.[57] In France the Gaullists interceded with the notoriously aloof French bureaucracy in order to favor one pressure group over another in policy disputes. Williams and Harrison, for example, report an instance in which Debré (as premier) forced one minister of agriculture to resign and had him replaced with a more vigorous minister in order to counteract the slowness of the bureaucracy in implementing the program on one agricultural interest group—the CNJA.[58] While this issue was complicated by many issues internal to agricultural politics in France, the fundamental point of the imposition of party control over administration in order to favor one group is clear.[59] This type of interaction does occur in Western political systems, but it is more typical of a number of political systems—the Soviet nations, a majority of African single-party states, and many Latin American countries—in which one party or coalition is dominant. As in the case of France, it is found also where partisan competition may exist but where there has been a tendency for one party to dominate government— France in the Fifth Republic, Italy, India, and Mexico, and in more competitive regimes, e.g., the relationships between the Trades Union

Congress and the Labour party in the United Kingdom and between the AFL–CIO and the Democratic party in the United States.

The effects of *parantela* relationships tend to be quite pervasive. It is, in fact, one tendency of these political systems that the hegemonic party will seek to impose its control over as much of the society and economy as is possible. One principle means of doing this is the fostering of *parantela* relationships in a number of social sectors through the cooptation of existing interest groups or through the creation of new groups directly allied with the party. The above example from France is an example of the party taking the side of an existing interest group in its struggle with other groups seeking to represent the same social interests, while the Spanish regime's organization of the workers into official or semiofficial syndicates is an example of a party creating its own interest-group structure.[60] In either case, this is an effective means through which the party can extend its scope downward into the society to control the nature of the inputs being generated and regularize the behavior of that social sector in accordance with the dictates of the party. It also serves as a means of checking bureaucratic autonomy within that particular policy area.

The above would seem to imply that pressure groups involved in a *parantela* relationship are little more than the pawns of a dominant political party, and such an interpretation would be justifiable in many instances. Weiner, for example, writing of the relationship of the Congress party in India and its affiliated labor union writes:

The Indian National Trade Union Congress—in reality the labor wing of the Congress Party—is organized along these principles of political responsibility and supports the basic program of the present government. Its leaders proudly declare that their demands are in the national interest, not in behalf of sectional interests. Their first loyalties are to the Congress Party, then to the present government, to the nation, and last of all to the workers who belong to the union.[61]

While the Indian case is illustrative of many *parantela* relationships, it is by no means an entirely general finding. Even in the case of authoritarian Spain, Anderson can write:

. . . the conventional picture of unrepresentativeness and ineffectiveness of the syndicates can be greatly overdrawn. The government and the syndicates did not speak with one voice on public policy. The syndical leaders were expected by the system itself to play the role of militant spokesmen for labor. . . . In their language and style of militancy many of the syndical leaders were not unlike their counterparts in other Western nations. They were brokers, and they bargained for their clients, though in the last analysis they accepted the judgment of the constituted authorities.[62]

The recent behavior of the more militant members of the Trades Union Congress in Great Britain with respect to the policies of the Labour government has tended to show the logical extremes to which the independence of *parantela* partners is able to extend.[63] Thus the pressure groups in these arrangements are frequently capable of exerting substantial influence over the course of public policy, and for many of the same reasons that *clientela* pressure groups do. The symbiosis between a hegemonic party and a pressure group is certainly not as important as that between the *clientela* partners, but it is present. The pressure groups can be expected to have some impact on bureaucratic choice because of their special relationship with the dominant party. Further, both the party and the bureaucracy gain the benefit of the specialized knowledge of the group, thereby reducing their own direct costs for policy development and planning. Moreover, the party's direct costs of social control may be reduced by developing subsidiary organizations to perform functions that might otherwise have to be performed centrally.[64] The above-mentioned example of the relationship between the syndicates and the government in Spain is one example of this type of control, as is the relationship between communist parties and their unions in hegemonic and competitive situations.

The influences of *parantela* relationships are likely to be broad simply because the hegemonic parties will seek to spread their influence as widely as possible, using these contacts as one means. For example, when the internal organization of the Convention People's party in Ghana was sufficiently divided to prevent its being an effective means of social mobilization, Nkrumah placed greater emphasis on affiliated groups such as labor unions and cooperatives as a means of bringing about the types of economic and social changes that his regime desired, including greater supervision of local administration.[65]

To some degree the policies adopted by the participants in *paran-*

tela relationships are a function of the ideology and program of the hegemonic party and as such may vary from programs of the far left to the far right ideologically. In general, however, there is a tendency toward distributive programs. By this we mean there is a tendency toward distributing various goods and services among the faithful and having certain groups develop claims on certain public goods and services as the appropriate representatives of certain social sectors. In this sense, the party is acting as something of a "canteen" for its adherents and for official groups by essentially subsidizing their existence in the marketplace of pressure groups—and thereby essentially depriving any competing, or potentially competing, groups.[66] Thus, in some ways, the *parantela* arrangement may approach the idea of the corporate state in which societal sectors are represented as such rather than as individuals, and receive policy benefits as members of the corporate entity rather than as a matter of individual right. Moreover, *parantela* relationships tend to be antithetical to the conception of modern politics about the universalism of the distribution of economic, social, and political benefits. Such benefits— even the most basic political benefits of the rights of organization and participation—are in *parantela* systems most definitely the function of having the proper political affiliations, and the influence that any group may expect to have over the outcomes of the decision-making process will be a function of this consanguinity.

A second effect of *parantela* relationships is also obviously regulative. This is true not only of the attempts of the party to regulate the outputs of the bureaucracy through regulating the advice that they receive, but more broadly to regulate the society as a whole through the use of intermediary groups. These intermediary groups not only structure inputs but also may serve as means of implementing the programs of the regime. The *parantela* relationships then serve as two-way streets, and information—and to a lesser extent power— can flow in both directions. The extent to which power can flow upward is, however, ultimately determined by the willingness of the dominant political party to entertain modifications and challenges.

Illegitimate Group Processes

The final category of interactions between administrators and pressure groups is labeled "illegitimate." This denotes a variety of situations in which the interaction of pressure groups with bureaucracy may be defined as outside the pale of normal political actions, but they

occur anyway. This may be a function of the political system as a
whole, which may attempt to suppress pluralism, or it may be a
function of the nature of particular groups, which are defined as being illegitimate as representatives of the social sector that they pur-
port to represent. In the first three types of interactions discussed,
some or all pressure groups were accepted as legitimate spokesmen
for some social sector or another. In the case of the illegitimate
pressure groups, neither the system as a whole nor individual administrators are willing to accept the legitimacy of the inputs of certain interest groups.

As might be expected, influence from pressure groups of this
type is not the normal pattern of policy making. They tend to be
indicative of some rather fundamental failures of the policy-making
system in satisfying demands of one or more sectors of the society.
Thus these individuals feel constrained to go outside the bounds of
"normal" politics to seek what they want from the political system.
We may, therefore, be talking in large part about the behavior of
"anomic" pressure groups in their attempts to exert influence through
protest, demonstrations, and violence. We need not, however, confine
this discussion entirely to violent groups, for there are a number of
situations in which pressure groups declared as illegitimate in *parantela* or *clientela* arrangements may still seek influence and may
occasionally actually exert some influence on policies. The latter instances are rare. As one of LaPalombara's respondents noted on this
topic:

> I know of no policy within the Ministry of Industry and Com-
> merce that says that there are certain groups in Italian society
> whose representatives will not at least be received. It is true that
> once this is done we will assign different importance or give
> varying weight to the proposals made to us by such groups, but
> they are free to approach us.[67]

Suleiman notes that in France groups defined as *groupes de pression* (in contrast to the acceptable "professional" groups) may be
received by the administrators but are unlikely to be able to produce
the results they desire.[68] The illegitimate groups continue, however,
to play by the administrator's rules and politely present their petitions,
probably knowing that their probability of success is nearly zero. We
may ask why these groups continue in these seemingly irrational
behaviors. There is the odd chance that they may actually have an

influence. More commonly, however, they persist simply because this is what their members expect them to do. This is the reason the members pay their dues, or give their allegiance, to the group, and the leaders have to carry through.[69]

The interaction between illegitimate pressure groups and administrators tends to produce high levels of frustration and alienation for those groups. This type of rather arbitrary categorization of pressure groups can be shown to take place even in political systems generally receptive, if not partial, to group influences. The extent of frustration is therefore likely to be even more intense in political systems that suppress rather than simply ignore the activities of groups declared to be illegitimate.

We can better understand the characterization of the influences of these groups as coming essentially from extralegal activities—through some sort of conflict with the system—and their influence as at best episodic. Likewise, the impacts of their activities on public policy are extremely difficult to predict, if they occur at all. Despite these limitations, it is important to understand that these influences may occasionally be productive of important changes. The French student movement of May 1968 and its associated activities have been used as an example of virtually every political phenomenon known to man, but that should not restrain us from pointing out that this is one example of an essentially illegitimate pressure group having a substantial impact on a regime and on the shape of public policy in the future.[70] The American students and the Vietnam war is another example, while in some Latin American countries the argument can be made that to accomplish almost any type of policy change requires the type of fundamental challenge to the system that can be offered by illegitimate groups.

When these groups are successful, the impacts of their activities tend to be redistributive, if for no other reason than they may force the system to recognize a set of demands that it could previously declare as being outside its concern. Most illegitimate pressure groups seek to transform the existing political system and its output distribution sufficiently so that one would hypothesize that such effects as were forthcoming from their activities would be in the direction of a redistribution of privilege, be it political, social, or economic.

To summarize what we have said about the interactions of pressure groups and administration, we should point to several of the more significant differences among these classes of interactions. First, the activities of illegitimate pressure groups are clearly the most distinctive. The other three patterns accord some legitimacy to the activities and influence of one or more groups, so that there are accepted patterns of interaction between the groups and the bureaucracy. In the case of illegitimate groups, such interaction—at least if it is to have any effect on policy outcomes—occurs almost by definition only in times of crisis. Thus the three legitimate patterns imply a certain stability and institutionalization of influence while the illegitimate pattern implies episodic influence or no influence at all.

Second, the legitimate pattern of interaction is the only one of the four in which there is little or no politics of access. In this arrangement, access exists for virtually any group that seeks it—even those that almost certainly would be declared illegitimate in other settings. By removing access from politics, such an interaction pattern may in fact make the pluralist's dream of a self-regulating universe of pressure groups making public policy a possibility if not a reality.[71] As long as access remains a scarce and a regulated commodity, the possibility of finding the "public interest" among a set of conflicting pressure groups is remote if not nonexistent. Having legitimate interactions of pressure groups with administration—and perhaps more importantly open interactions of pressure groups with each other in advising the administrators—by no means assures that such a mystical entity as the "public interest" will emerge, but it is more likely to appear when interests are forced to bargain than in a case in which each interest is able to capture its own portion of the administrative structure. This capture tends to convert public policy into private policy. Likewise, unless one considers the hegemonic political party as an accurate representation of the interests of the population, the control of pressure groups and bureaucracy by such a party is also likely to produce distortions of outputs from what would emerge from a bargaining table, especially when many interests may be defined out of existence by the dominant party. To put this in the terms of our original typology of interactions, serious distortions of policy from what would emerge from a simple bargaining process among competing groups are likely to occur when the politics of policy-making cannot be removed from the politics of organizational survival.

We should also note that we have not been able clearly to argue that any particular pattern of interaction characterizes any one nation or another, although the examples tend to point to some rather important patterns. In the first place, political systems with hegemonic political parties, be they ostensibly democratic or not, tend toward *parantela* relationships between interest groups and administrators, if for no other reason than that the hegemonic party is able to use these relationships as one means of social control and regulation. Second, legitimate interactions tend to be characteristic of the Northern European countries, which have had long histories of the involvement of organized groups in social and political life, and whose leaders have perceived a need to manage potentially divisive conflicts within the society, either ethnic or socioeconomic in origin.[72] Third, *clientela* arrangements tend to be quite common in any number of societies, especially when there is a fragmentation of interests and a lack of overall coordinating mechanisms in the political system (e.g., a dominant political party or movement) that can regulate the competition among interest groups or among the competing agencies within the bureaucracy. Finally, illegitimate interest groups may arise in virtually any setting but tend to be most important in settings where they are least likely, i.e., societies that seek to suppress interest groups or at least a wide variety of interest groups. That is to say, these groups are most important in settings where they serve as a fundamental challenge to the regime. This means that their day-to-day interactions with administrators will be unfruitful if they occur at all, but that they may produce substantial transformations of a political system.

Just as there is little pattern as to type of interest-group–bureaucratic interaction by political system, there is also little pattern by type of interest or policy area. There is some tendency for interest groups that can be clearly defined geographically to be able to establish clientele relationships with administration, perhaps because of the ability to mobilize political support easily. The most obvious example of this pattern is agriculture, which has been notoriously successful in clientele relationships in a number of political systems. Likewise, interest groups that may be vertically integrated with political parties—frequently labor unions and labor parties—may develop *parantela* relationships, even within the context of competitive political systems.[73] Finally, groups that may be regarded as outcasts in normal social affairs, or that are not regarded as having differentiated political viewpoints by the dominant community—racial minorities, students, women—may tend to act through illegitimate relationships with bureaucracies, if they are able to form any relationship at all.

BUREAUCRACY AND POLITICAL PARTIES

We will restrict our remarks on the relationship of political parties and bureaucracy until we begin the discussion of the interaction of formal political institutions and the bureaucracy. In most contemporary political systems, the direct impact of partisan concerns on bureaucracy has been consciously limited by a number of structural and procedural devices. The most important of these, of course, is the institutionalization of the merit system for appointment and retention of administrators so that parties can no longer force large-scale changes of administrative personnel when there is a change in governing parties. While patronage arrangements certainly do exist, they are generally regarded in Western countries as evidence of corruption and mismanagement. A number of non-Western countries, despite the tutelage of their former colonial countries, have continued or reinstituted nonmerit systems of appointment to administrative posts—even the most routine and trivial of posts. This is justified largely on the need for national unity and mobilization in the face of the difficulties of development. In such situations, loyalty to the nation—or more exactly to the current regime—is considered more important than the possession of certain scores on objective tests or the possession of requisite diplomas. This practice is by no means universal in the non-Western world, but a number of one-party regimes tend to recruit their bureaucracies in this fashion. As Nkrumah said in relationship to administration in Ghana:

> It is our intention to tighten up the regulations and to wipe out the disloyal elements of the civil service, even if by so doing we suffer some temporary dislocation of the service. For disloyal civil servants are no better than saboteurs.[74]

Also, in French-speaking Africa a number of one-party regimes have attempted to use partisan control to replace "selfish individualism" with "patriotic socialism." [75]

The most obvious example of the use of partisan control over the state bureaucracy occurs in the communist countries. The most pervasive method of control is the use of dual hierarchies simultaneously to administer public policy and to check for the political orthodoxy of the administrators and their behavior. Such a system of duplication appears redundant and inefficient to Western analysts of organizations, but it is deemed crucial in a system where political orthodoxy is so important. As with the non-Western systems of the underdeveloped world, partisan control and the use of the bureaucracy as a mechanism for fundamental social and economic change seem to go hand in hand. Where political neutrality is not really acceptable, much less valued, then many of the Western dogmas concerning nonpartisan, merit appointment simply are not feasible as criteria in evaluating recruitment and executive actions of administrators.

SUMMARY

We have developed a means of classifying and analyzing the politics of bureaucracy. Beginning with the notion that it is not useful to separate the political from the administrative in either real life or analysis, we have attempted to provide some means of better understanding how administration becomes involved with politics and political actors. This chapter has dealt primarily with administrative involvement with pressure groups, showing the extent to which these two political actors depend upon each other in their attempts to shape public policy and to survive in what might otherwise be an extremely hostile political environment. In three of the four patterns of interaction discussed, some type of legitimating relationship was developed so that a stable pattern of interaction between group and bureaucracy could be used in policy formation—the internal aspect of bureaucratic politics. These relationships could, in turn, directly (through clientelism) or indirectly (through *parantela* and legitimate interactions) produce some support for the programs and the continued existence of the specific bureaucratic agency involved. These are then two political actors who need each other in order to carry out their respective purposes in as efficient a manner as possible. Both operate on the fringes of political respectability and need friends in their battles. The symbiosis that tends to develop between bureaucracy and pressure group is readily explicable in terms of these needs for legitimation and support. The major question that remains is whether this symbiotic relationship is to be accepted—as with the legitimate groups—or forced further into the gray areas of politics.

We turn now to bureaucratic politics that is more directly concerned with power and policy rather than access. These are the politics of dealing with other formal institutions of government. Each of these actors has access to the arena of political conflict, and their position in that arena is more secure than that of the bureaucracy. Here, then, the bureaucracy must engage in substantially different types of political behaviors both to preserve its autonomy as an organization and to have an impact on public policy.

NOTES

1. Woodrow Wilson is often given credit for propounding this doctrine of separation. See his "The Study of Administration," *Political Science Quarterly* 2 (June 1887): 209–13. This doctrine was continued by writers such as Willoughby and Pfiffner. The attack was led by Paul Appleby in *Policy and Administration* (University: University of Alabama Press, 1949).

2. Several recent studies of administrative elites discuss the degree of politicization of the administrator. See Robert D. Putnam, "The Political Attitudes of Senior Civil Servants in Western Europe," *British Journal of Political Science* 3, no. 3 (July 1973): 257–90. Thomas J. Anton, Claes Linde and Anders Mellbourn, "Bureaucrats in Politics: A Profile of the Swedish Administrative Elite," *Canadian Public Administration* 16, no. 4 (Winter 1973): 627–51; Ezra N. Suleiman, *Politics, Power and Bureaucracy in France* (Princeton: Princeton University Press, 1974); Samuel Eldersveld, Sonja Hubee-Boonzaaijer, and Jan Kooiman, "Elite Perceptions of the Political Process in the Netherlands, Looked at in Comparative Perspective," in *The Mandarins of Western Europe*, ed. Mattei Dogan (New York: Halsted, 1975), pp. 129–61.

3. Putnam refers to this conception as that of the "classical bureaucrat." See Putnam, "Senior Civil Servants," p. 259.

4. A discussion of this in the context of the vale of cost-benefit analysis is supplied by Peter Self, *Econocrats and the Policy Process* (London: Macmillan, 1975).

5. These problems as they relate to the democratic theory are discussed in Emmette S. Redford, *Democracy in the Administrative State* (New York: Oxford University Press, 1969).

6. This is related to one of the paradoxes of modern society: as the political system becomes more decisive for the society, politics becomes less important. See Timothy M. Hennessey and B. Guy Peters, "Political Paradoxes in Postindustrialism: A Political Economy Perspective," *Policy Studies Journal* 3, no. 3 (Spring 1975): 233–40.

7. See, for example, Bruce Heady, *British Cabinet Ministers* (London: Allen & Unwin, 1975).

8. For a discussion of the problems of cabinet ministers in Britain, see Richard Rose, *The Problem of Party Government* (London: Macmillan, 1974), pp. 402–9; see also Ernest Marples, "A Dog's Life in the Ministry," in *Policy-Making in Britain*, ed. Richard Rose (London: Macmillan, 1969), pp. 115–32; Headey, *British Cabinet Ministers*.

9. There is a growing body of literature on the process of public budgeting in

ADMINISTRATION AND INFORMAL POLITICAL ACTORS 163

a number of political systems. For example, Hugh Heclo and Aaron Wildavsky, *The Private Government of Public Money* (Berkeley: University of California Press, 1974): Guy Lord, *The French Budgetary Process* (Berkeley: University of California Press, 1973); Nils Elvander, The *Svensk Skattepolitik 1945–1970: En studie i partiers och organisationers Funktioner* (Stockholm: Almqvist & Wiksell, 1972); Naomi Caiden and Aaron Wildavsky, *Planning and Budgeting in Poor Countries* (New York: John Wiley, 1974); David Coombes et al., *The Power of the Purse* (London: Allen & Unwin, 1976); John Higley, Karl Erik Brofoss, and Knut Groholt, "Top Civil Servants and National Budgets in Norway," in Dogan, *Mandarins.*

10. Aaron Wildavsky, *The Politics of the Budgetary Process* (2nd ed.; Boston: Little, Brown, 1974), pp. 1–5; William Niskanen, "Nonmarket Decision-Making: The Peculiar Economics of Bureaucracy," *American Economic Review* 58, no. 2 (May 1968): 293–305.

11. See note 9.

12. See chapter 8.

13. Compared to other parts of the political process, however, there have been rather few comparative studies of pressure groups. See Henry W. Ehrmann, *Interest Groups on Four Continents* (Pittsburgh: University of Pittsburgh Press, 1958); Gabriel A. Almond, "A Comparative Study of Interest Groups and the Political Process," *American Political Science Review* 52, no. 2 (March 1958): 270–82; Joseph LaPalombara, "The Utility and Limitations of Interest Group Theory in Non-American Field Situations," *Journal of Politics* 22, no. 1 (February 1960): 29–49; Robert V. Presthus, *Elites in the Policy Process* (London: Cambridge University Press, 1974).

14. Joseph LaPalombara, *Interest Groups in Italian Politics* (Princeton: Princeton University Press, 1963), pp. 252–305.

15. Jean Meynaud, *Nouvelles etudes sur les groupes de pression en France* (Paris: Colin, 1962), pp. 384 ff.

16. The relative influence of groups across cultures is difficult to measure accurately, but certainly the subjective analyses of most observers points to this relationship. See Phillipe Schmitter, "Still the Century of Corporatism," *Review of Politics* 36 (1974): 85–131.

17. This is well demonstrated in Anton, Linde and Mellbourn, "Bureaucrats in Politics."

18. Nils Elvander, *Interesseorganisationerna i dagens Sverige* (Lund: CWK Gleerup, 1966); J. Moren, *Organisasjonere og forvaltningen* (Bergen: Norges Handelhoyskole, 1958).

19. Elvander, *Interesseorganisationerna*, pp. 198–200.

20. Lewis Edinger, *Politics in Germany* (Boston: Little, Brown, 1968), pp. 208–9.

21. Robert B. Kvavik, "Interest Groups in a Cooptive Political System: The Case of Norway," in *Politics in Europe*, ed. Martin O. Heisler (New York: David McKay, 1974), pp. 93–116.

22. Ibid., pp. 110–15.

23. Yves Weber, *L'Administration Consultative* (Paris: Librarie General du Droit et Jurisprudence, 1968), p. 3; G. Mignot and P. d'Orsay, *La Machine Administrative* (Paris: PUF, 1972).

24. Kvavik, "Interest Groups," pp. 102–5.

25. See, for example, James H. Wolfe, "Corporatism in German Political Life: Functional Representation in the GDR and Bavaria," in Heisler, *Politics in Europe,* pp. 323–40.

26. Martin O. Heisler and Robert B. Kvavik, "Patterns of European Politics: The 'European Polity' Model," in Heisler, *Politics in Europe*, pp. 63–70; Wolfe, "German Corporatism"; Ralph H. Bowen, *German Theories of the Corporative State* (New York: McGraw-Hill, 1947), pp. 4–5.

27. Frank G. Castles, "The Political Functions of Organized Groups: The Swedish Case," *Political Studies* 21, no. 1 (March 1973): 33; Bo Carlson, *Trade Unions in Sweden* (Stockholm: Tidens, 1969), pp. 125–28.

28. James Goodyear Abert, *Economic Policy and Planning in the Netherlands* (New Haven: Yale University Press, 1969), pp. 55–67; B. M. Teldersstichtung, *The Public Industrial Organization in the Netherlands* (The Hague: Martinus Nijhoff, 1957).

29. Gabriel A. Almond and G. Bingham Powell, *Comparative Politics: A Developmental Approach* (Boston: Little, Brown, 1966), pp. 77–78.

30. See, for example, Richard A. Webster, *Christian Democracy in Italy* (London: Hollis & Cautes, 1961); Karl Schmitt, *The Roman Catholic Church in Modern Latin America* (New York: Knopf, 1972); John S. Ambler, *The French Army in Politics* (Columbus: Ohio State University Press, 1966); John J. Johnson, *The Role of the Military in Underdeveloped Countries* (Princeton: Princeton University Press, 1962).

31. See, for example, Howard A. Scarrow, "Policy Pressures by British Local Government: The Case of Regulation in the 'Public Interest,'" *Comparative Politics* 4, no. 1 (October 1971): 1–28; Jean-Pierre Worms, "Le Prefet et ses notables," *Sociologie du travail* 7 (July–September 1966): 249–76.

32. Scarrow, "Policy Pressures," pp. 15–19.

33. Kvavik, "Interest Groups," 111–12.

34. Stein Rokkan, "Norway: Numerical Democracy and Corporate Pluralism," in *Political Oppositions in Western Democracies*, ed. Robert A. Dahl (New Haven: Yale University Press, 1966), p. 107.

35. Robert H. Salisbury and John Heinz, "The Analysis of Public Policy: A Search for Theories and Roles," in *Political Science and Public Policy*, ed. Austin Ranney (Chicago: Markham, 1968), pp. 164–74; and John Heinz, "A Theory of Policy Analysis and Some Preliminary Applications," in *Policy Analysis in Political Science*, ed. Ira Sharkansky (Chicago: Markham, 1970), pp. 39–60.

36. Kvavik, "Interest Groups," p. 113.

37. Nils Elvander, *Interessorganisationer;* Lars Foyer, "Former för Kontakt och Samverken Mellan Staten och Organisationera," *Statens Offentliga Utredningar 1961* (Stockholm, 1961).

38. Heisler and Kvavik, "European Polity Model."

39. See L. J. Sharpe, "American Democracy Reconsidered," *British Journal of Political Science* 3 (January–April 1973): 1–28, 129–67, for a discussion in the American context.

40. A brief discussion is provided in Salisbury and Heinz, "Analysis of Public Policy," pp. 55–59.

41. See, for example, Theodore R. Marmor and David Thomas, "Doctors, Politics, and Pay Disputes," *British Journal of Political Science* 2 (1972): 426–37.

42. LaPalombara, *Interest Group Politics*, p. 262.

43. Suleiman, *Power, Politics*, pp. 338–39.

44. Alessandro Pizzorno contrasts the Anglo-Saxon and continental European traditions in this regard. See "Amoral Familialism and Historical Marginality," in *European Politics: A Reader*, ed. Richard Rose and Mattei Dogan (Boston: Little, Brown, 1971), pp. 90–92.

45. Theodore Lowi, *The End of Liberalism* (New York: Norton, 1969); Grant

McConnell, *Private Power and American Democracy* (New York: Knopf, 1966).

46. LaPalombara, *Interest Group Politics*, pp. 272–74.
47. Lowi, *End of Liberalism.*
48. McConnell, *Private Power*, p. 287.
49. Salisbury, "Public Policy."
50. Theodore Lowi, "The Public Philosophy: Interest Group Liberalism," *American Political Science Review* 61, no. 1 (March 1967): 19.
51. See, for example, William Niskanen, *Bureaucracy and Representative Government* (Chicago: Aldine/Atherton, 1971); Gordon Tullock, *The Politics of Bureaucracy* (Washington, D.C.: Public Affairs Press, 1965); Albert Breton, *The Economic Theory of Representative Government* (Chicago: Aldine, 1974), chaps. 9–10.
52. William Niskanen, "Nonmarket Decision-Making."
53. Within the context of American politics, Fenno finds that the Executive—both political and administrative—tends to have a significant influence on policy, and that clientele groups have little direct impact. See Richard F. Fenno, Jr., *Congressmen in Committee* (Boston: Little, Brown, 1973), pp. 43–45.
54. Richard Fenno, *The Power of the Purse* (Boston: Little, Brown, 1966), pp. 141–43, disagrees with this analysis.
55. Salisbury and Heinz, "Analysis of Public Policy," p. 48.
56. LaPalombara, *Interest Group Politics*, pp. 306–7.
57. Ibid., pp. 308–15.
58. Philip M. Williams and Martin Harrison, *Politics and Society in deGaulle's Republic* (Garden City, N.Y.: Doubleday, 1972), pp. 339–42.
59. See F. H. Virieu, *La Fin d'une Agriculture* (Paris: Colmann Levy, 1967).
60. Charles W. Anderson, *The Political Economy of Modern Spain* (Madison: University of Wisconsin Press, 1970), pp. 30–34.
61. Myron Weiner, *The Politics of Scarcity* (Chicago: University of Chicago Press, 1962), p. 78.
62. Anderson, *Political Economy of Modern Spain*, p. 69.
63. The Wilson government's need to request voluntary compliance for the unions in his "social contract" indicates the extent to which these two partners hold divergent views and the degree of independence of each. Likewise, the threats by the unions over recent expenditure cuts increased the differences between these "partners."
64. This then has many similarities to the legitimate pressure-group system with its use of groups to implement policy.
65. David Apter, *Ghana in Transition* (Princeton: Princeton University Press, 1963), pp. 340–44.
66. For the concept of the "canteen" in administrative behavior, see Fred Riggs, *Administration in Developing Countries: The Theory of Prismatic Society* (Boston: Houghton Mifflin, 1964), pp. 105–9.
67. LaPalombara, *Interest Group Politics*, p. 265.
68. Suleiman, *Power, Politics*, pp. 340–46.
69. See Robert Salisbury, "An Exchange Theory of Interest Groups," *Midwest Journal of Political Science* 23 (1969): 1–32.
70. The literature on the "Events" is by now huge, but John Gretton, *Students and Workers, An Analytical Account of Dissent in France, May–June, 1968* (London: MacDonald, 1969), remains one of the better accounts.
71. Sharpe, "American Democracy," especially pp. 21–23, 135–44.
72. Heisler and Kvavik, "European Polity Model."

73. The most obvious example is the special relationship between labor union federations and Labor or Social Democratic parties in Europe.
74. Kwame Nkrumah, *I Speak of Freedom: A Statement of African Ideology* (New York: Praeger, 1961), p. 173.
75. Aristide R. Zolberg, *Creating Political Order* (Chicago: Rand McNally, 1966), p. 121.

THE POLITICS OF BUREAUCRACY:
Bureaucracy and
Formal Political Actors

The previous chapter discussed the political relationship of bureaucracy to "informal" political actors such as pressure groups and political parties. We now turn our attention to the political relationships of the bureaucracy to formal institutional actors in government. In these relationships—labeled "formal-internal" and "formal-external" in our typology—the relative legitimacy of the bureaucracy is changed. When dealing with pressure groups the bureaucracy represents the majesty of the state; when dealing with legislatures, prime ministers, Presidents, and the courts the bureaucracy becomes an extraconstitutional interloper in the affairs of government. Thus, as with pressure groups in our previous analysis, the bureaucracy must either seek to have its actions legitimated formally or be capable of bargaining successfully for influence over decisions. It must also bargain for funds to continue its existence and operations. Although we would not want to carry the analogy too far, these options might correspond to the legitimate and *clientela* options available to pressure groups in their dealings with bureaucracy.[1]

The task of the bureaucracy in gaining access to decisions is rarely as taxing as that of the pressure groups; if anything, the tendency has been for the more representative and legitimate political institutions to throw power at the bureaucracy rather than resist its pleas for influence. These representative institutions are incapable of formally abdicating powers (even if they might want to), but they must bargain to get the assistance in policy making and implementation that only the bureaucracy can provide. This shifting of power relationships involves a delicate political process and some attention to public opinion. The public still regards their elected officials in legislatures and executives as responsible for the conduct of public business, and these institutions must therefore continue the form if not the substance of policy making in their interactions with the public bureaucracy.[2] Both sides in this exchange of power, influence, and money have a great deal to lose by a clumsy handling of the process, and a political "game" of conflict and compromise results.

Given this potential for either conflict or collaboration between the public bureaucracy and political institutions, what cards does each player hold in the game? The answers to these questions occupy the majority of this chapter. We organize this discussion by first looking at the resources that each actor has at its disposal and then looking at the means through which these resources are employed.

THE RESOURCES OF POLITICAL INSTITUTIONS

Perhaps the ultimate weapon at the disposal of political institutions is their *legitimacy*. Associated with legitimacy is the formal and constitutional authority to do the things that government is intended to do. Few constitutions even mention bureaucracies, much less vest any formal powers of decision making in them. Therefore, whether by delegation, funding, or acquiescence, bureaucratic actions must be legitimated by constitutionally prescribed actors. More often than not this legitimation comes through inaction and acquiescence rather than through formal action, but it still involves a transfer of authority.

Almost as important as the formal power and authority to perform tasks is the wherewithal to do them: money. The second major power held by political institutions, then, is the *power of the purse*.[3] In order to survive, prosper, and grow, agencies require money and must be able to influence political institutions to provide them that money. The budgetary process—or the politics of survival, as we referred to it earlier—is one of the crucial points of interaction in bureaucratic politics. The bureaucracy seeks money and the autonomy to spend it, while the political institutions seek control of their funds and to ensure accountability as to how it will be spent. The importance of the budget for both sets of actors has led to the development of a number of techniques on both sides to attempt to counteract the powers of the other.

Third, and certainly related to the first two items, is something that we might call *latitude*, or *autonomy for the agency*. In general, agencies seek to acquire as much latitude as they can. This refers primarily to latitude to make policy; they might seek a blanket grant of authority in an area of policy. It also may refer to budgeting; they might seek some latitude in the way in which funds must be spent.

On the other hand, the power to grant such latitude is a powerful weapon for the political institutions to gain concessions of information. It is their constitutional role to regulate policy and the implementation of policy. Moreover, they must be responsible politically for what happens to the country, and they want to control policy if they are to be held responsible for it. Thus, as well as bargaining over money, agencies and political institutions must also bargain over the degree of autonomy to be granted, the responsibility for funds and accounting, and the procedures for delegating authority.

The powers of political institutions mentioned to this point are largely formal and legal. These institutions have substantial political resources as well, if for no other reason than they are—to some degree—representative of the public. We may argue exactly how representative the institutions are along several dimensions, but they are generally the most representative institutions available.[4] As such they are able to mobilize political strength through their relationship to the public, political parties, and interest groups. The public will rarely rise up as a mass in righteous anger, but the politicians are quite capable of making it seem that way.[5] By any number of means —investigation, publicity, electoral campaigns, speeches, debates, etc. —the political institutions may be capable of pitting the "people" against the bureaucrats. Given the nature of bureaucracy, there is little the people are capable of doing even in their aroused state, but the bureaucracy can ignore public opinion only for so long. Moreover, the arousal of public opinion may make it considerably easier for the political institutions to employ the formal powers at their disposal. We must not forget that these are political institutions with an important relationship to the public, so that, as well as recounting their formal powers in combating the bureaucracy, we must be cognizant of this special relationship to the people.

THE RESOURCES OF THE BUREAUCRACY

On the other side of this conflict and consensus game are the cards held by the bureaucratic agencies. First among these are the resources of *information and expertise*. To the extent that government has at its disposal information, this information is concentrated in bureaucratic agencies. Going along with that information is the technical expertise to understand and interpret it. This relative monopoly of information can be translated into power in several ways. The most blatant is the argument that since they (the agency) know more about the subject, they should be given control over it. In other words, they are likely to do a better job (technically) of making policy in a certain issue area than would the relatively ignorant political executive and legislature. If that argument fails, as it often does, and the politicians are sufficiently audacious to attempt to make policy themselves, then the major source of information for formulating those policies will still be the bureaucracy.[6] This means that the bureaucracy is in a situation in which it can at least implicitly trade information for influence over policy, and indeed information may be produced selectively to make one type of decision a virtual inevitability. In the same vein, Bartlett has referred to legislatures "subsidizing" bureaus in order to get information about their operations, i.e., trading information for money.[7]

A second power at the disposal of the bureaucracy is their *power of decision.* Despite the "metaphysical pathos" about the red tape and inefficiency of bureaucracy (especially public bureaucracy), compared to many political institutions—especially legislative institutions—they seem a model of efficiency.[8] Having few procedural rules concerning free discussion, voting, and the like, bureaucracies are in a position to act more rapidly than legislatures on many issues. They also do not have to be as sensitive to the political pressures that may be coming from constituents in making their decisions. Political executives may share the advantage of rapid decision in situations where they are independent of the legislature, e.g., the French and American presidencies, but they are more commonly bound in democratic systems by a reliance on legislative action and approval.

Third, just as political institutions have their *political supporters,* so do bureaucratic institutions. In our previous chapter we discussed the relationship between bureaucracy and interest groups. In two of the four types of interactions there is a definite political linkage between an interest group and an agency. The bureaucracy has the ability to mobilize these political supporters in making claims for funding or for policy autonomy. The political support of other political institutions tends to be less policy specific than that of the agencies, and the agency can consequently mobilize a more interested and vocal group of supporters on an issue than would be likely for any legislative group that sought to oppose them.[9] This is especially true given the internal difficulties of decision within the legislature. This issue-specific political support can be of special importance because of the fragmented nature of decision making in many legislative bodies, with committees or other specialized bodies having a substantial influence over policy and funding. The agency is able to mobilize support before the appropriate committee, who may not have the interest or latitude to consider alternative uses for funds, and develop the case that indeed there is a large demand for the agency's services. The bargain struck with the client group, allowing access and influence, is generally consummated in front of a legislative committee.[10]

Having discussed the political powers of the bureaucracy, we now proceed to discuss the advantages they have by being *apolitical*. This may appear to be a contradiction, but it is an important means of understanding how bureaucracies are able to compete successfully for influence and power in decision making. Bureaucracies have the advantage of being formally divorced from partisan politics. Civil servants do not have to stand for election, are not faced with constituency pressures or pressures for conformity from their own party, and have been effectively neutered politically in most societies.[11] This isolation from partisan politics allows them to argue that not only are they expert in what they do, but also that their decision will not be affected by the need to placate voters. This partisan impartiality goes hand in hand with the expertise of the bureaucracy, to make a strong argument that their decisions will be superior on technical grounds to those that would be taken by political institutions. As noted, this appeal to the alleged impartiality of the bureaucracy has been most important in justifying the existence of independent regulatory bodies, but it is also a viable argument for virtually any form of bureaucratic organization.[12]

This "depoliticized" characteristic of bureaucracy makes bureaucratic decision making especially apropos for international and supranational organizations. Politics, especially politics centered around national loyalties, may threaten the continued existence of the organization and would certainly delay development of many policies. In these organizations it is common for the administrative branch to be the major decision-making body and in supranational organizations the driving force for integration.[13] They can do so simply because they can claim to be apolitical and not representative of any nation.

We have said that the bureaucracy is "allegedly" impartial in making its decisions. This is in part because the agencies themselves frequently have an *agency ideology* concerning policy.[14] This may be considered a fifth resource at the disposal of the bureaucracy. The ideologies referred to here are rarely if ever sweeping statements concerning the nature of the political world, but rather a conception of what should be done in a specific policy area and how it should be done. These ideologies tend to be policy specific and related to the task to be performed by the agency. They also tend to be rather impervious to the argument and evidence of outside "nonexperts" and to be self-serving for the agency. One of the classic examples of such an agency ideology is the doctrine of strategic bombing held by the United States Air Force. This doctrine, stated simply, is that the best means (if not the *only* means) of bringing an enemy to its knees is through strategically bombing its means of war production. This is alleged to have brought about the demise of Germany and Japan in the Second World War, and these cases are cited as proof of the doctrine. Such evidence as does exist on the effects of the bombing, however, indicates that if anything, production of war matériel increased during the bombing rather than decreased.[15] The air force—for obvious reasons—persists in its claim that bombing is the answer to the problems of war.

There are a number of other examples of the rigidity of military bureaucracies to ideologies of this sort, but some of the same behavior can be found in social and economic bureaucracies as well. Even though most social agencies at least pay lip service to the idea that most social problems are multidimensional, they tend to see them and act on them largely in terms of their own expertise, to try to capture clients rather than sending them on to seek other types of help, and to argue for increased funding in terms of the ability to solve social problems through their particular program. The numerous problems of agency coordination in social services is one indication of the reliance on agency ideologies about policy and solutions to problems.[16] Again, as with the air force, the motivations for such behavior are apparent, but it does not make this any less a sort of ideological behavior.

To return to the central point of this discussion of bureaucratic ideologies, we can see that the existence of such an ideology is important for the success of the agency in dealing with political institutions. Political actors rarely have a ready reply to such policy-specific ideologies. They labor under a number of disadvantages in competing with the bureaucrats, not the least of which is a frequent lack of any specific policy ideas. Many political leaders, when put into a ministerial role or cabinet role, simply don't have the background in the policy area to contribute much in the way of policy direction, and the demands of the job often prevent them from developing such direction.[17] The civil servants who work within the department —even the generalists at relatively high levels—rarely have such difficulties and are quite capable of providing a direction for the department's program. Most often this happens to be the direction in which they are already traveling.[18] In this case, the knowledge of simply approximately where they want to go in terms of policy places the bureaucrats at a distinct advantage in dealing with a politician who is only there for a short time, has relatively little information, and is not at all sure of what needs to be done.

Finally, the bureaucracy has the advantage of *permanence and stability*. It is difficult to fire a civil servant and may even be difficult to have one transferred. Civil servants can always adopt a strategy of waiting and delay. Ministers come and go, but the basic work of civil servants can be unaltered simply because the ministers rarely have time to learn what has to be changed or to put such a program into effect.

BUREAUCRATIC GOVERNMENT

The above catalog of the relative powers at the disposal of the two sides in this struggle for power has seemed to place most of the trumps in the hands of the bureaucrats. This is so true that many analysts have come to speak in terms of government by bureaucracy, or by "technocracy." [19] The catalog of the relative strengths of the institutions is partially influenced by the interests of this volume and its author, but even a more impartial analysis of the situation would have to accept the argument that bureaucracies have by now acquired considerable political clout, even to the point of coming to dominate policy making in many modern political systems. Have we come to the point where a new elite structure based on information, technical expertise, position, and policy ideas has come to determine who gets what, when, where, and why?

Our answer to this question is ambiguous and would depend in part on whether one thought in terms of an integrated bureaucratic elite producing policies, having common values, and essentially conspiring to remove authority from more responsible political decision makers; or whether one thought in terms of a number of independent policy elites whose powers were confined to one specific policy area and who were frequently in conflict with other similarly placed elites. If we wish to speak about an integrated bureaucratic power elite— as some rather apprehensively have—running a nation from a computer-equipped ivory tower, then we believe that no such creature actually exists, and Rose's characterization of government emerging from "directionless consensus" may be appropriate.[20] Perhaps even more than other potential elite bodies, e.g., aristocratic, corporate-capitalist, or partisan, a bureaucratic elite has less to integrate it. As noted, the backgrounds and educations of the bureaucracy tend to be similar, but its interests are rarely integrated and more likely competitive. Moreover, despite the shift from the "Weberian" to the "political" bureaucrat, the involvement of the bureaucracy in government is still apparently reluctant and hesitant.[21] The traditional normative structure around the bureaucracy that has been internalized by many civil servants is frequently one of separation of politics and administration. This does not mean that administrators will not "play politics" with respect to their own programs and budgets, but rather that they rarely become involved in macroscopic policy debates. Thus, although capable of supplying direction at the level of the agency, there is little to suggest that the bureaucracy as an entity has either the willingness or the integrated set of priorities that would allow it to direct society and the economy. One interesting contrast to this generalization would appear to be supplied by the USSR, or the USSR, Inc. as some writers have described it.[22] Here macro-policy is essentially a bureaucratic business, and much of the output of policy can be explained by the politics and program of the bureaucracy.

If we do not accept the existence of an integrated technocracy capable of guiding most political systems, we must accept the existence of a number of powerful technocracies having substantial power over more delineated policy areas. This case has been discussed in part when speaking of the resources at the disposal of agencies, but it is an important continuation of the argument that bureaucratic interests are more often in conflict than in collusion. Agencies may be analyzed quite fruitfully from the perspective of market competition over scarce goods and services—essentially the public budget.[23] Thus bureaucratic elites may regard each other in much the same way as business competitors do. Also, within each large department the interactions of agencies and bureaus may resemble the behavior of components of corporations. These public agencies, however, lack a free market for their products and are forced to compete for their share of the public budget for continued existence. In general, we can expect agencies to attempt to get as large a share of the budgetary pie as possible and at the same time seek to maximize their own independence from political control. This will of necessity involve conflict with other agencies, given a relatively fixed budget in any one year. Also, with regard to policy autonomy there will be conflict between agencies seeking to expand in order to be better able to survive and compete for increased budgetary allocations. Thus, by virtue of expertise, competition, and lack of overriding interests, bureaucracies tend to become dominant in one area, tend to resist encroachment within that area, and tend to seek to expand into the policy area occupied by other agencies.

One issue on which the bureaucracy acts as an entity is on the perquisites of the civil service. This is perhaps most noticeable with respect to salaries. With the formation of associations and unions of civil servants, this has significant implications for the political and economic systems. In particular, the demands of civil servants for pay increases can be cited as a significant contribution to price inflation in many advanced systems.[24] Moreover, these demands tend to place public employees in competition with private employees for available increases in resources. Given the lack of any ready measure of productivity in the public sector and the close proximity of civil servants to those deciding on their levels of pay, the tendency has been to grant pay increases in the public sector and to pay for them through printing more money.[25]

The competition between agencies is rarely absolute or even overt. To some degree all bureaus have a stake in getting more money, but they may not seek to expand their share of the total budget. The competition over the increases may not be worth the extra investment of organizational resources, may be an uncertain event, and may consequently result in strategies designed to ensure a "fair share" of the budget will come to the agency. Or the agencies may engage in competition over policy only when the central concerns of the agency are challenged, and may even cooperate in more peripheral concerns.[26] What will emerge from this discussion is a model of bureaucratic politics approaching a satisficing model. The agencies are in competition, but this competition is limited by the costs of that competition to the preservation of the relative position of the agency and its control over central policy concerns. Thus, to the extent that the bureaucracy as a whole has any unified policy concerns, they will frequently be over the preservation of the status quo. Even in more extreme versions of the bureaucratic politics model, the prime value to be maximized is security, and it would appear that this can be well achieved in a system of limited competition and well-delineated policy spheres.

Even within this more limited conception of the nature of bureaucratic politics, there will be variation among agencies and nations in the ability of agencies to play the game of politics and to control policy areas. For agencies, we can expect differences by the level of technological sophistication of the policy area, the level of politicization, the tenure of the organization, and the internal integration of the organization. First, the greater the technical content of a program, the more we would expect it to be controlled by bureaucratic rather than political officials. Politicians, given the handicaps under which they frequently labor, will probably not be able to intervene effectively in conflicts over highly scientific or technical policies. If they did, they might invite adverse popular sentiment for intervening in an affair about which they had little knowledge and which would be better left to the experts. Finally, there are likely to be fewer "counter experts" to offer advice contrary to that offered by the official experts in highly scientific policy areas, so that even if an attempt were made to alter the stream of advice coming to the politician in charge, it would be difficult to find competing testimony. In this case "technical" may be conceptualized also as "professional," so that when there is a large and reasonably integrated profession advocating some policy—usually through the appropriate agency—it becomes difficult for the politician to oppose it. The limiting case here may be the military, where the agency's employees are the professionals, and where the number of counter experts is limited.

Second, as an issue becomes politicized, i.e., becomes a matter of direct public concern, the ability of the bureaucracy to dominate solutions to the problem becomes lessened. Even issues of a technical nature, when injected into the view of the public (and the politicians), may require nonbureaucratic resolution. Examples of this are the recent concerns over the safety standards applied to atomic reactors in the United States and the environmental safety of oil drilling in the North Sea off Scotland and Norway.[27] These are both technical questions that had previously been left to the relevant experts. But the concern of environmental and labor groups in both countries has been forcing political as well as administrative action. The current worldwide economic slowdown also has been forcing greater popular consideration of economic policies, and subsequent loss of the ability of the economic bureaucrats in the Treasuries and central banks to dominate this policy area completely.

Third, the tenure of the organization tends to affect the degree to which policies are controlled by the bureaucracy. Agencies that have been in operation tend to develop not only routines for handling the making of policy but also some political credits with their ostensible political masters. In other words, if an agency has been in business a long time, it will tend to have colonized a policy area more thoroughly than a new agency and be more likely to be successful in getting what it wants in the budgetary process. This makes it difficult for any political leader to disturb the smooth flow of paper within the agency or strenuously oppose the granting of a fair share to the agency. Organizational inertia is a powerful explanation of the stability of much public policy in the face of changes of conditions and governments. It further makes it necessary to develop new organizations when seeking to alter the direction of policy significantly. Bureaucratic reorganization may be in part a show for the public and for professional public administrators, but it may also be crucial to shifting the existing organizations out of their operating ruts and into some new policy directions.

Fourth, the degree of integration within the organization will affect its success in bureaucratic politics. The more integrated an agency is, the more likely it is to be able to dominate a policy field. The corps structure of some organizations assists in integrating the advice given to political leaders and stiffens the organizational resistance to the imposition of external priorities. The military bureaucracy is perhaps the most obvious example of such internal homogeneity of values and motivations, but other organizations with either a strong internal socialization (the Forest Service or the British Treasury) or a common professional background (legal agencies or social-work agencies) may also be able to operate on their own values rather than on values imposed externally.[28]

Finally, the type of goods being produced by an agency influences its ability to be successful in bureaucratic politics. In general, the closer the goods being produced are to goods that can be produced in the private market, the greater will be the ability of external agents to question the internal operations of the agency. Thus, agencies that supply "public goods" are more resistant to external control of their policies than are agencies that supply quasi-public or private goods.[29] Further, agencies have a strong incentive to direct their own programs in directions divorced from market forces, to attempt to remove any pricing mechanism from their programs, and to emphasize the "public" nature of what they do. Political institutions have a strong incentive to attempt to price or control access to the services provided by agencies so that they may be better able to assess the contribution that the agency's program is making to the "public interest."

The differences among nations with respect to the success of the public bureaucracy in politics involve a number of factors, among them such things as the characteristics of the respective actors—legislatures, executives, and bureaucracies—in the policy-making system; the level of social, economic, and political development; the development of certain policy-making techniques such as program budgeting; and last but not least the nature of the constitutional and legal structures of the nation. We could develop a vast number of hypotheses about the influences of each of these factors, but such a list and its discussion might severely disrupt any narrative qualities this chapter has. One particularly crucial national difference, however, may be the career structures and aspirations of officials. Many of the models of bureaucratic aggrandizement may simply describe an *American* way of living in a formal organization. It is less than clear, for example, that British civil servants see their security or careers dependent upon their success in the budgetary process. In fact, to the degree that such success may potentially be achieved by stratagems and ploys such as are at times employed by U.S. agencies, it may actually limit future success.[30] Therefore, we next discuss some techniques that each of the actors in this political game can use in order to get their way in the budgetary and policy-formulation processes.

STRATEGIES IN BUREAUCRATIC POLITICS

The preceding discussion has been something of a static recounting of the weapons available to each of the combatants in this conflict over power and money. This section is intended as a more dynamic recounting of the manners in which those weapons are employed. This is a partial list of the strategies available, and concentrates on events in the last few years in order to show the evolution of bureaucratic politics, especially the increasing political strength of the bureaucracy.

Bureaucratic Ploys

We begin with a set of devices, stratagems, and structures that greatly assist the bureaucracy in gaining its ends of the control over policy and stable if not expanding budgetary commitments. In most cases these ploys are related to the ability of the bureaucracy to mobilize information and expertise, and secondarily to the ability to mobilize bias in the form of pressure-group support for programs. These ploys largely involve the removal of policy from consideration by political officials and placing it in the hands of presumably neutral, expert, and objective administrators. As admirable as this may sound in theory—at least to those who advocate "rational" policy making in government—it represents a movement away from the ability of elected or even selected leaders to control government and supply the quality and quantity of goods and services demanded by the public.

PLANNING. The first and perhaps most important of the strategies of expanding bureaucratic influence is public planning. This device began as a means of controlling the economy but has been extended to a variety of social and economic spheres such as land use, transportation, urban areas, and even social services.[31] Indications are that planning is becoming increasingly indicative as opposed to advisory, so that much economic and social policy for many nations is being determined by bureaucratic planning bodies. Moreover, even in those societies that are not centrally planned and coordinated, each individual agency is developing its own planning capacity.

The need and justification for planning is obvious from a number of perspectives. In the first place, planning involves the systematic application of knowledge to important areas of human concern and allows some long-range manipulation of the state of the economy and society. Likewise, it can make the nature of the economy more amenable to the desires of the public, and by removing many decisions from the marketplace allow for investment in areas that, while socially desirable, may not be particularly profitable in a private market. By removing to some extent macro-economic policy from the political agenda, the device may successfully defuse many important political conflicts, especially where politics is heavily influenced by segmental disputes within the society. As Abert says of economic planning in the Netherlands, ". . . the technical process of economic planning is accorded a position of major influence [because of] the lack of a political consensus that might resolve economic issues through the electoral process." [32] Thus, the tendency toward adopting planning as a means of making long-range policy tends to remove some aspect of public policy from the partisanship and divisiveness of politics and transport it to the rarefied atmosphere of "rational" decision making.

It should be clear that planning is a very strong weapon for the

bureaucratic politician. It places the regulation of the national economy or some other aspect of national policy in his hands. If planning
is accepted as the "proper" means of making policy for the nation,
then the proper policy becomes the one that the planners advocate,
and the burden of proof falls on those who advocate anything else.
This may be especially true of policy areas other than the economy
where the effects of the policy decisions are not as apparent through
such things as inflation and unemployment, and where the requirement of capital investment means that the effects will be years in
the future.[33]

A second item in favor of bureaucracy planning, especially economic planning, is that it is difficult for the average layman—or
politician—to understand. Much current economic planning is done
using such devices as mathematically sophisticated econometric models processed by computer and dependent upon large quantities of
economic theory. Few members of the political community have the
skills, or are willing to invest the time required to acquire the skills,
to understand fully the reasoning behind these planning methods or
the assumptions on which they are built. The politicians are at the
mercy of the planners in having the programs and their implications
explained to them.[34] Some political systems have gone even farther in
having the plan go into effect unless actively blocked by the political
institutions.[35] Given that this would be a difficult and time-consuming
activity with very little probable payoff to a politician, since his constituents probably wouldn't understand it anyway, this active block-
ing will rarely be undertaken.

A third item favoring the bureaucracy and the planners is the
integration of the plan. Almost by definition, planning offers something of an integrated and comprehensive view of some aspect of social or economic life and an integrated set of policies for achieving
certain ends in that policy area. As such, any attempt by political
institutions to modify the plan can be opposed as upsetting the whole
plan. As Shonfield put it:

> . . . if parliament is to play an effective part in the business of
> national planning—and if it does not the outlook for the future
> of democracy is bleak—then members of parliament will also
> have to recognize some theoretical, as well as practical limitations
> on the exercise of their collective sovereignty. These theoretical
> limitations apply to the whole procedure of introducing a parlia-

mentary amendment to a set of planning proposals, whose merit
is their intellectual coherence and self-consistency. If any significant element in them is changed, the whole structure must be
adapted to accommodate the alteration.[36]

He goes on to argue that such adaptability is crucial on the part of
the planners, but the presence of an integrated plan makes it difficult
for any political organization to make the types of alterations and
modifications at which they are perhaps most adept. The burden
of proof would again appear to fall on those who want to change the
plan rather than those who want to accept it.

Following from the above, it is difficult for political institutions to
attack the efficacy of the planning process as a means of allocating
resources. Certainly some plans are more successful than others, but
with the exception of a few societies that approach being totally
planned, there are always sufficient areas of independence so that
plan failures can be blamed on those nonplanned sectors of the
economy, or on oil prices, or on drought. This not only can be used as
a means to argue for more public control of the marketplace, but
also prevents the public and its representatives from measuring bureaucratic or planning output in the same way they might measure
the output of other governmental programs such as garbage collection or water supply. Planning is thus one of the public goods mentioned previously that often defy accurate pricing.

In this discussion we should be careful not to assume that planners
and the rest of the bureaucratic establishment are necessarily homogeneous. In many cases, in fact, there is significant friction between
the traditional bureaucracy and newer planning agencies.[37] As with
the conflict between line and staff, the presence of planning agencies
threatens line agencies, and planning tends to direct resources away
from pet projects of line agencies. However, the planning process
must be seen as directing political control and authority away from
the "political" institutions and toward bureaucratic (especially when
each agency or department does its own planning) or technocratic
agencies.

Planning constitutes a major weapon in the hands of the bureaucracy, both at agency and societal levels. It provides a technical means
of reinforcing and quantifying the positions of the bureaucracy and
at the same time removes many important and sensitive matters from
the hands of partisan decision makers. Planners can argue that their

decisions will be objectively superior to those reached by partisan institutions, that they can impose a longer time perspective on the problem than the politicians, and that they can prevent special-interest considerations from determining policy. Despite these to some degree commendable attributes of planning, the major effect that we must be concerned about here is to remove those decisions from the hands of politically responsible officials and place them into the hands of bureaucratic elites.

PPBS.   The acronym PPBS refers to *Planning-Programming-Budgeting System*.[38] This is a second and probably more pervasive means of institutionalizing the technical expertise of the bureaucracy in the policy-making process. Again, as with planning, this is undertaken with the admirable intention of improving the objective quality of public decisions and of relating budgeting more directly to the final products of public programs. Interestingly, if anything, these reformed systems of budgeting (including such variants as "zero-base" budgeting) were designed to break the stranglehold of the bureaucracy on the budget through incrementalism. Their effect, however, would appear to have been actually to strengthen the position of the agency in relationship to parliaments or political executives.

The essential idea of PPBS is that instead of allocating the agency budget in terms of line items such as personnel, equipment, supplies, and the like, funds should be allocated to programs. For example, in a Highways Department we might allocate funds to highway construction, highway maintenance, right-of-way acquisition, etc. McNamara's programs budget for the Department of Defense had nine programs ranging from strategic deterrence to sealift.[39] Exact definitions of programs vary considerably in terms of their complexity and level of abstraction, but in all cases the idea of program budgeting is to be able to assess the unit costs of government production better, to plan the allocation of funds more effectively, and to be able to control public expenditures. If program budgeting were to work effectively, then the integration of financial with program management would produce "more bang for the buck" in each area of public policy. Few people in or out of government would argue with these stated intentions, but in practice the expectations concerning PPBS have not been fulfilled; if anything, it has been a tool for administrators to use in justifying their programs. In fact, it has been argued that PPBS could as easily serve the interests of a budget-maximizing bureaucrat as it serves the interests of budget-minimizing politicians.[40]

In the first place, program budgeting requires considerably more information about the activities of the agencies than is required for traditional line-item budgeting. Where is that information to come from? Clearly it must come from the agencies themselves. Assuming that the agencies do not directly fib about the operations of their agencies, this still gives them a substantial impact over the outcomes of budgeting. Program budgeting requires a considerable investment of time and money to do effectively, so programs as well as agencies are selected for more intensive analysis in any one year. It has become the practice in several nations to allow agencies to select the programs to be reviewed with the effect that those programs with the greatest potential for growth are reviewed.[41] Frequently, centralized budget agencies—if they exist—lack sufficient staff to scrutinize the activities of agencies fully, or to collect independent information. The bureaucracy may therefore not be effectively restrained by this device in its search for secure funding.

A second point is that program budgeting forces some decentralization of control within the bureaucracy. One effect of the programming process is to allow each bureau chief considerably more latitude than would be allowed under a line-item budget.[42] Instead of funds being allocated for items such as personnel, equipment, etc., they would be allocated for doing a job. The bureau chief would be allowed latitude in how he used the funds. For example, if he found that he could build roads cheaper by using less sophisticated machinery and more hand labor, a bureau chief would be able to do so. While this may, and should, have the effect of producing better policy outputs at a lower or equal cost, the *political* effect is to make it more difficult to impose central control on the operations of the bureaus and agencies.

Third, few political bodies are likely to be willing or able to invest the time and money required to undertake their own program review of agencies. They rarely have the staff to compete with those of the agencies, so that the competition for control becomes a conflict between a "computer and slide rule." [43] Even if legislatures or even political executives were to respond favorably to the imposition of such management techniques—and the evidence is largely that they have not—they might still be at a severe disadvantage in attempting to understand and alter the outputs of program budgeting by the agencies and centralized budgeting agencies.

Finally, program budgeting frequently fails in the design of programs in meaningful and operational terms. What, for example, is a program for government in the area of education? Is it to have students sitting in classes, is it to have them receive diplomas, to pass standardized tests at certain levels, or is it imparting the ability for the students to earn a living? Any one of the above might be argued as the appropriate measure of educational output for budgetary purposes, and education is in some ways easier than other areas of government. What is the proper means of evaluating deterrence programs in defense budgets? Given these difficulties, the definitions of programs have varied from precise indicators of output to very vague statements of objectives. These difficulties have further decreased the feeling that PPBS is a useful device for government and consequently have increasingly isolated budget makers from the rest of the political process. This can only have the effect of increasing bureaucratic control over the outputs of the process, if for no other reason than the program budgeters may themselves need clients in order to survive. The most obvious clients, as in so many cases, are the very people they were intended to control.

Despite these difficulties, program budgeting has been introduced in a large number of countries. This has been especially evident in the Third World, at the instigation of the United Nations.[44] This diffusion does not appear to be so much a part of a grand design of the world's bureaucrats to take over the management of government as a function of the rather obvious intellectual appeal of the technique. Those who are genuinely concerned about the improvement of governmental performance want to get the most effect out of each dollar or rupee spent, and program budgeting appears to offer a magic solution to that problem. But, like many magic solutions to the problems of government imposed externally, the outputs are usually as good as the inputs of money and time and expertise. Few governments—if any—have apparently been willing to invest in the technique in a way that would allow it to fulfill its promise, and it may more frequently have the opposite effect. This is likely to be especially true because PPBS, like planning, requires "information, knowledge, political stability . . . undreamed of in their existence." It is a technique that may "maximize every known disability and minimize any possible advantage of poor countries." [45] Thus, in fairness, one can say that although the technique certainly is a promising one, the misapplication or underapplication of it generates a distinct set of administrative and political problems.

TECHNICAL BUDGETING.   Related to both planning and program budgeting is what we might call "technical budgeting." By this we refer to a tendency to assign the budgetary function to a special body having highly developed technical skills and little if any political responsibility. Another variant of budgeting with some of the same implications is a tendency to develop middle-range budgetary forecasting, with projected budgets made for five- to seven-year periods.[46] The formulation of the national budget in Norway is perhaps the best example of technical budgeting. The budget is formulated by a group of civil servants and technicians using a quite complex model of the Norwegian economy.[47] These "technocrats" develop a draft budget that is then scrutinized by a select committee of civil servants and the government, is reformulated, and is finally passed. This procedure gives to one set of civil servants rather obviously great powers over the formulation of the Norwegian budget. As Higley et al. argue:

> It is in the nature of the process that the choices of the civil servants who collect and analyze the mass of data from which the national budget is constructed are of fundamental importance to the outcome. It is so because the civil servants have a virtual monopoly of the technical knowledge necessary to the process and because the process gives the initiative to them throughout. . . . Moreover, many of the communications from the civil service to the government take the adversary form: civil servants tell the government how the national budget should be composed. Thus, not only are they in control of the general framework in which decisions are made, but they also define the important questions, influence the directions of the politicians' attention, and argue for their proposed solutions with the help of esoteric knowledge that is difficult to refute.[48]

The authors point out that elected ministers can and do have an impact on the final shape of the budget, but the choices they make are likely to be small relative to the overall content of the budget, and these choices will tend to be within the general parameters already established. Planning the reformulation of one aspect of the budget will tend to require a reformulation of the entire document, and the substitutions of the judgment of ministers and politicians for that

of experts. This is quite a burden for politicians to bear in attempting
to retain control over policy.

The process of technical budgeting is perhaps most advanced in
Norway, but it occurs in many other countries. The task of budgeting
is by now too complex, and with the growth of Keynesian and post-
Keynesian economic concepts, too important to be left to amateurs.
The ways in which the bureaucracy can impose itself upon the formulation of the budget are rarely so explicitly technical as in Norway,
but civil servants can claim a level of expertise rarely matched by
politicians. For example, even in Britain with its tradition and ideal
of responsible political control of the budget, the Treasury has specialized knowledge about economic and public expenditure that allows it to claim a special impact on the budget.[49] It would appear
that most of the budget is worked out by "partisan mutual adjustment" between civil servants in the spending ministries and civil
servants from the Treasury, with the politicians intervening mainly
in situations that could not be resolved at lower levels. In France, the
budget division of the Ministry of Finance

> not only tries to influence the general policy of the government
> during the period of global preparation of the budget, but it also
> takes advantage of the period of detailed preparation to scrutin-
> ize, approve, or disapprove every detailed new measure proposed
> by the spending ministries.[50]

Thus the simple fact that a ministry or division deals constantly with
problems of budgeting and expenditure control tends to supply them
with, if not specialized knowledge on particular policies, at least a
general knowledge of public finance, which can be translated into
control over policy.

Here again, as with the conflict between planners and line bureaucrats, we find that the "bureaucracy" as a whole rarely marches
to the same drummer. There is an almost inherent conflict between
the spending ministries and the financial ministry. They are all bureaucrats in the generic sense but show here a lack of any common
interest that might make them a unified body controlling public policy. We might be better able to understand the outcome of what
happens in budgeting in terms of the *conflicts* of these agencies.
This would in fact be the conflict of differing types of expertise:
one of policy areas and one of economic effects. In any case, despite
who may win that conflict, the political institutions of legislatures

and presidents may be excluded from it. The anticipated reactions of the actors may be influenced by the threat of the imposition of political authority, but in day-to-day operations, it is a bureaucratic war.

INCREMENTALISM. Following from the above discussion of budgeting, a number of procedural and financial factors tend to preserve the "fair share" of agencies in the budgeting process and to reduce conflict even with the financial ministries. Most consideration of budgets has to do with increases in expenditure rather than ongoing expenditure, and in most cases neither the agencies, the financial ministry, nor the political institutions have the interest or ability to alter the ongoing expenditure. Further, many levels of expenditure, particularly in federal arrangements, depend upon the actions of other governments, so that to some degree these expenditures are uncontrollable.[51] Thus a tendency to accept incremental solutions to the problem of budgeting tends to reduce time in analysis and preserve the fair share of each agency.

This tendency toward incrementalism comes about in a number of ways. The simplest is through the inability or unwillingness of financial ministries or political institutions to ask agencies to justify their "base," or the previous year's expenditure. To some degree it is logical to assume that this was in fact done the previous year. Moreover, it seems more rational from the point of view of the small amount of time and energy available to politicians to scrutinize most closely the "camel's nose" as it seeks to get in under the tent.[52] The tendency toward incrementalism is institutionalized in France where the parliament is by law unable to consider attacking the base of the agency and can consider only the changes proposed by the government—these are almost invariably additions rather than deletions.[53] The result here, as is true in any incremental arrangement, is that the security of the agency—that most precious of quantities to the good bureaucrat—is preserved.

ADVISORY BODIES. Another useful device for the bureaucracy in gaining control over policy areas is the use of advisory bodies or committees in the formulation of policy. We have previously discussed bodies of this type that are attached to ministries, but they also provide a useful means of understanding something of the influence of administration on policy. It is, in fact, in part because of the pressure-group connection that these bodies can become so successful in assisting bureaucratic power. In the societies where the use

of advisory bodies is so important in making policy—principally
Scandinavia and the Low Countries—the imprimateur of pressure
groups is important in legitimating policy. Since these advisory boards
are attached to the ministries and thereby interact largely with civil
servants, there is the possibility of substantial reciprocal influence
over policy. Further, many of the members of the advisory bodies
are themselves members of the civil service. For example, in Norway, one study showed that in 1966, 272 civil servants held 623
positions in 351 (of 954) advisory committees.[54] In France, although
the numerical membership of civil servants in ministerial advisory
boards is generally not large, they tend to hold the more important
positions of chairman and *rapporteur*, so that what the committee
advises is at least interpreted by the civil service before dissemination.[55] Thus the civil service can be expected to have a significant
influence over the findings of ministerial advisory boards, and these
boards often have a crucial role in determining the final outcome of
policy. Board or committee findings tend to have the approval of both
pressure groups and the civil service, have substantial informational
backing, and therefore become quite difficult for anyone to oppose
politically. Thus the vertical integration of many pressure groups into
the ministries, and the general ability of the ministries to dominate
one policy area, makes the formulation of much public policy in
practice—if not officially—the product of negotiation between representatives of pressure groups and the civil service.[56]

A second type of advisory committee tends to be independent of
any particular ministry although it may be working on a problem
clearly identified with the concerns of the ministry. Again, we have
discussed bodies such as Royal Commissions, Presidential Task Forces,
and the like when discussing pressure-group impact on policy.[57]
These advisory bodies tend to have substantial bureaucratic input as
well, and if anything, the influence of the bureaucracy has been increasing in recent years.[58] This growing influence has been in part
a function of the growing technical expertise of the bureaucracy
in a variety of policy areas and in part a recognition of the need to
obtain cooperation from the civil service if the program is to be effective once adopted.[59]

It should be obvious that, whoever benefits directly by the use of
such advisory bodies, it is not the political actors who will be ultimately held responsible for their actions and policies. These political
actors gain in the short run by having a sensitive issue defused, but
in the long run the likely effects are to increase bureaucratic in-

fluence over the policy. Further, the issues likely to be sent to commissions of this type are the truly sensitive ones that cannot be resolved easily by political actors. Thus, if we are willing to admit that most routine decisions are largely determined administratively, and now we see that many extremely broad and sensitive decisions are increasingly influenced by bureaucracy, the roles of the political institutions are being diminished rather dramatically. They do not have the time nor staff to handle most decisions, and they lack the consensus to handle most major decisions, leaving them with the task of setting broad policy guidelines on issues where there is already a certain amount of consensus. This may be an extreme statement, but the evidence to this point in the analysis would seem to support it.

The listing of the various ploys and strategies available to the bureaucracy, and in fact often unwittingly placed in their hands, gives some idea of the way in which their expertise, internal organization, and position in the structures of government can be translated into effective political power. The devices listed above have relied largely on the expertise and information available to the bureaucracy and consequently have assumed the lack of same on the part of the political institutions. In this next section we look at the ways in which the political institutions have sought to counterattack against growing bureaucratic influence on policy.

Politicians' Ploys

Given the imposing list of formal powers that the political institutions have been said to have, it may seem strange that they would need to search out new means of asserting their power and their control over policy and the budget. However, the skills and expertise of the bureaucracy (at least in relative terms) and the largely antiquated structure of many political institutions have made such a search necessary.

SPECIAL BUDGETARY INSTITUTIONS. One of the first things that the political institutions must seek to recover is some effective control over the public budget. In order to do so, several forms of specialized budgetary institutions have been devised. The most common is something on the order of the Office of Management and Budget (OMB) in the United States.[60] The idea of these bodies is to develop an expert institution responsible directly to the political executive rather than to the bureaucracy. Most budgeting systems require a review of agency requests by other civil servants in a Ministry of Finance, Treasury, or some other similar body, but few provide for an office so directly responsible to a political actor or institution. It is expected that the existence of such a body will allow the executive to be able to have an independent watchdog on expenditures and to have a policy staff directly concerned with expenditures and policy. A vigorous bureaucratic agency such as the British Treasury or the Swedish Ministry of Finance may be able to provide something of the same type of control, but the linkage to the chief political executive may not always be so clear. This lack of linkage will often result in deliberations between civil servants over policy rather than the imposition of executive guidelines.

Unfortunately, little is actually known about the ability of OMB to control expenditures effectively either in the aggregate or in an allocative sense. Such accounts of the ability of the agency to impose presidential goals are that the success is partial, and as is often true, the weakness tends to be rather far down the bureaucratic hierarchy. In this case it is with the individual budget examiners attached to the agency. Their job is to keep a close eye on the spending of the agency and to work with the agency in the preparation of expenditure requests for the coming fiscal year. It is often easy for a budget examiner to become a captive of the agency he is supposed to control.[61] He sees considerably more of the people whose budget he is supposed to watch than he does of those for whom he is ostensibly controlling it and may tend to adopt their view of policy priorities rather than that of the budget bureau. On the other hand, the informal norms concerning careers in OMB have been that it pays to cut budgets, and only those with records of cutting budgets successfully are likely to advance within the organization.

Although OMB may be far from totally successful in imposing its (and the President's) will on the budgetary process, it is at a distinct advantage compared to the task allotted to many chief executives in seeking to control their budgets. As noted, most countries use essentially a bureaucratic agency as a means of performing the budget examining functions—the Treasury in Britain and the Ministry of Finance in most countries. Despite the norms of these organizations, they remain essentially civil-service organizations and as such may not willingly accept the goals of an executive attempting to improve his political future. In addition, many parliamentary political systems tend to be apprehensive about a prime minister attempting to control the budget from his office rather than through the collectivity of the Cabinet, so that the internal negotiations over the budget may become so difficult that bureaucratic domination is inevitable. Even in West Germany where the chancellor is in a stronger position than most parliamentary executives, the chancellor's use of his position to impose priorities in budgeting is not well received, and much of the power devolves to the Ministry of Finance.[62] Thus, although independent executive budgeting agencies may be far from a perfect solution to controlling public expenditure and the powers of the bureaucracy, they are probably a better solution than has been found in many political systems.

Legislatures have also begun to evolve a number of specialized institutions for dealing with the problem of budgeting. The development of the Congressional Budget Office in the U.S. Congress, and its provision of a rather large and well-qualified staff, is one obvious example of a legislature attempting to regain some control over the level of public expenditure.[63] In this case, the conflict is obviously with both the bureaucracy and the Presidency. In Britain there have been attempts to revive the Public Accounts Committee as an effective policy as well as financial instrument of Parliament. While these efforts are certainly steps in the proper direction from the point of view of the legislatures, they are as yet unproved, and the general direction is actually more that of giving the legislature less of a role in the budgetary process.

ORGANIZATIONAL DIFFERENTIATION.   The formation of committees such as those noted above is a part of a general tendency toward organizational differentiation that is manifesting itself in many political institutions seeking to control public expenditure and public policy. In order to be able to counteract the specialization and differentiation of the bureaucracy, executives and legislatures have adopted some similar organizational tactics. In general, there has been a growth of the organization within the office of the chief executive, even in situations such as Britain where the individual power of the chief executive tends to be restricted by a number of conventions.[64] This tendency has been especially apparent in many single-party states faced with either opposition or a lack of enthusiasm in the bureaucracy. This has forced political leaders to develop their own means of monitoring the implementation of programs or of actually implementing them themselves.

The ability of many public organizations to differentiate is often limited by law, so the institutions will be at a severe disadvantage in attempting to compete with the bureaucracy. For example, in France, the National Assembly is constitutionally limited to six committees, which in turn greatly limits their ability to compete with a highly developed bureaucracy and political executive. Further, recent congressional actions have limited the ability of the American President to reorganize his office and expand its staff; again, some limitation of the differentiation, undertaken for political reasons, will have the effect of limited ability to manage effectively.

COUNTER-STAFFS.   One extremely important means which political leaders can employ in attempting to control the powers of the bureaucracy is the development of their own staffs and sources of information. This enables them to remove the bureaucratic bias in the information received. These independent sources of information may be institutionalized, as in the Executive Office of the President of the United States, or they may be the more casual use of outside consultants.[65] In either case, the stratagem involved is to break the hold that the bureaucracy has on expertise. It also enables the political leader to break the stranglehold that the bureaucracy often has on the initiation of policy.

The use of counter-staffs varies rather markedly across political systems and across policy areas. In the first place, there must be a source of counter-information, and until recently, this has not existed in policy areas such as atomic energy, space technology, or defense. Also, in most underdeveloped countries, the available scientific and technical ability of the country tends to be concentrated in the public bureaucracy, so there may simply be no other source of internal information. It is also more likely that counter-staffs and information— often by the ton—will be available on highly politicized issues, those that involve well-developed professional organizations, and those in which pressure groups have a direct interest. However, most of these issues are ones on which the average politician is also likely to have information or a strong ideological commitment; consequently, much of this information may be redundant.

One principal source of the use of counter-staffs is the problem of segmentalization and politicization in the society. In the first place, there may be conflict or at a minimum distrust between a minister who belonged to one segmental group in the society, e.g., Catholic, Francophone, or Ibo, and a civil servant of a competing segmental group. Politics itself may serve to generate segmental conflicts, and frequently political leaders of newer countries cannot trust their civil servants, who are either expatriates or were trained under the colonial regime. Even in more developed political systems, many incoming political leaders feel that they cannot trust the advice of civil servants left over from the previous Cabinet. This is especially true for ministers from leftist political parties, who tend to regard the civil service—perhaps properly—as a conservative institution.[66] This is not to say that civil servants would purposefully obstruct or sabotage a program—there is little evidence of that—but rather that perhaps unwittingly their implementation of programs and their granting of proper advice would not be as energetic as it might be.

The second form of politicization that affects the use of existing staffs by political leaders is the level of institutional politicization or the perceived conflict between different political institutions for control of policy in government. For example, in the United States, one of the major reasons for the development of large executive staffs by the President, and for the development of relatively large staffs by Congress, is the perception that these two branches of government are in conflict over the control of the policy-making machinery. In countries with long histories of strong bureaucratic control of policy— or at least perceived bureaucratic control of policy—there will be a similar perception of conflict with the bureaucracy. So, in France, the ministerial *cabinets* constitute a counter-staff attempting to combat the influence of the bureaucracy.[67] On the other hand, a society that is more integrated politically in both segmental and institutional terms—such as Britain—will develop relatively few staff personnel directly accountable to politicians.[68] The norms that the civil service is sufficiently trustworthy and sufficiently devoid of any ideological dispositions allow politicians to accept their advice even after long periods in Opposition. While there is little objective evidence of the impartiality of those civil servants, Britain is perhaps less well served in policy terms because of the belief. Although in comparison to most politicians, civil servants are experts, compared to the types of policy staffs developed in other countries, the British may remain "talented amateurs." [69] This results in much policy being determined by "muddling through" or by "directionless consensus."

CONTROL OF STAFF.   One principal weapon available to the civil service in any attempt to gain control over policy is its permanence. Politicians may come and go; the bureaucracy remains. This not only presents several long-term strategies to administrators who are not pleased with their current political "master," but it also presents those political masters with some quite difficult problems of controlling their civil servants. Counter-staffs are one solution to this problem, but there may also be solutions within the context of the civil service and personnel policy.

The most obvious means of allowing political control over their civil servants is enabling them to select their own, at least those who will be their immediate subordinates, and more importantly, their policy advisers. This can provide some of the advantages of the counter-staff without involving its redundancy and dual lines of authority. Given the limitations of most civil-service systems, this means that the choice must come within the confines of the available civil servants, but some systems such as France allow the minister to select among the available personnel for his *directeurs*.[70] The system in the United States is similar in its effect, but instead of having the immediate subordinates of political executives be civil servants, they are political appointees. They are therefore not protected by any statutory guarantees of tenure and can be shuffled at will. Thus, in the United States political appointees fill policy advisory and managerial posts that are filled by senior civil servants in other democratic political systems, allowing considerably more direct political supervision of implementation and more directly partisan policy advice.[71]

Most Latin American countries have not fully institutionalized the norms of civil service impartiality or tenure, so any changes in the government may also occasion changes in the civil service.[72] This may occur primarily at the upper echelons of the civil service, so the routine tasks of government continue to be performed much as they always have been, but this system does allow some flexibility for political leaders in seeking advice from civil servants. It is, of course, roundly condemned by advocates of "proper" public personnel procedures and may affect the behavior of bureaucrats who want to remain in office regardless of regime. However, for a political situation in which the policy differences are likely to be great, this sort of flexibility may be a crucial means of managing the senior civil service.

THE PARTY.   Another powerful option available to some political leaders is the existence of a strong political party or movement that can be used to ensure the compliance and control of the civil service. This mechanism is available most notably in the communist countries and in single-party states in the Third World. In these situations the existence of the party and its associated ideology perform a dual service in controlling policy initiatives by the public bureaucracy.

First, the party provides definite ideological and policy guidance, which an astute civil servant can either internalize or at least follow in making and advising on policy. Since the inception of an ideological regime is usually associated with a significant reshuffling of the civil service, most of those placed in positions of authority are likely to have internalized the ideology and program, but even in cases in which the existing civil service continues—often from the lack of any available alternative personnel—the existence of an ideology can provide them some ready guidance in what to propose and implement.

The second means through which the existence of a strong ideological party assists the ability of politicians to reduce bureaucratic initiative and dominance of policy making is that it provides a check on performance and usually a means of correcting unsuitable performance. In such political systems the party tends to be more involved in everyday life than in most democratic political systems, to check more thoroughly on bureaucratic actions, and to be more resentful of bureaucratic domination of policy than even democratic systems. Thus, for example, in the People's Republic of China, the party and ideology serve as a means of guiding and correcting bureaucratic policy, either through direct action or through self-criticism.[73] In the Soviet Union and in Eastern European countries, although it may be difficult at times to distinguish political from administrative personnel, the dual hierarchy of party and bureaucracy serve as mutual checks on policy formulation at each level of government. This does not necessarily mean that policy making in the Soviet Union is any less bureaucratic than elsewhere—to the extent that we mean bureaucratic policies as those divorced from control by market forces or public opinion—but only that the bureaucracy that does make policy is likely to be more sensitive to political cues than other bureaucracies. They will be generally more willing to comply with the demands of a political elite, and given the presence of an expressed ideology, they may also be more capable of finding what the leaders want to do. Thus, although the policies that ensue may be divorced from direct control by popular opinion, they may paradoxically be more responsive to some political forces than are policies made in democratic systems. The conflict between "Red" and "Expert" may not always be resolved in favor of "Red," but the divergence is rarely as great as occurs in less ideological regimes.

THE MILITARY.   The military may constitute a special case of the party or ideological governments. It is a special case largely because of the greater willingness to employ physical coercion to obtain its ends, among them the submission of the bureaucracy to the demands of politicians—in this case military politicians. As well as an ideology and a set of coordinating principles—or at times instead of them—the military may just have guns. It does not follow, however, that military governments must employ force to gain their ends in dealing with the bureaucracy. In the many cases in which the military and the bureaucracy are primarily conservative forces, they often willingly coalesce against forces of the left.[74] This pattern has been more common in Latin America, while the pattern of the military representing modernizing ideals in opposition to a conservative bureaucracy—frequently inherited from colonial days—has been more common in Africa.

SUMMARY AND CONCLUSIONS

This chapter has examined the problems facing political leaders seeking to control the policy-making role of the bureaucracy. We have shown the relatively great power and influence over policy that the bureaucracy appears to be accumulating, in part as a function of its own characteristics and in part as a function of the weaknesses in other competitive institutions. We have discussed a conception of bureaucratic politics dominated not so much by the search for every possible increment in budgets or policy purview, but rather by the search for stability and security within one particular policy area. Finally, the catalog of weapons at the disposal of the bureaucracy and its competitors would seem to argue that the bureaucracy may be in even a stronger position than has been supposed. Most important in this catalog was the control of information and expertise.

The conclusion that emerges from this analysis is that the public bureaucracy is in a quite strong position vis-à-vis other potential policy-making institutions. It has the expertise, the time, the stability, and the techniques required to be an effective policy maker in a modern age. What is required, however, is legitimacy and popular control. The legitimacy can perhaps be gained in part through effectiveness, and if largely bureaucratic processes of decision making are capable of producing results valued by the population, then the institutions are likely to be accepted as appropriate decision makers. They may lack formal legitimacy, but in terms of having operational legitimacy, they may become the appropriate collective allocators of values.

The question of popular control is perhaps more difficult. This has two possible interpretations. The first is the ability of the public to make its preferences known to the bureaucracy, through some yet unspecified means, and to have the bureaucracy make decisions consistent with those expressed preferences. If we extend the arguments presented in the chapter, then the general public must be seen as being in an even more difficult position in dealing with the bureaucracy than the political elite. The second possible meaning of popular control is the ability of the citizens to obtain redress of grievances for certain administrative actions that violate the rights—economic or civil—of individuals. This is more of an ex post facto control, for which a number of procedural devices have been developed and which have met with a variety of successes and failures. It is to these problems of popular and democratic control of administration that we now turn. We shift our attention from the broad determination of policy to the more microscopic determination of policy, largely with respect to single individuals. This also turns our attention back to a concern with the lower echelons of bureaucracy as those most likely to be held responsible for acts of malfeasance or nonfeasance.

NOTES

1. See chapter 6.
2. See chapter 3.
3. See, for example, David Coombes et al., *The Power of the Purse* (London: Allen & Unwin, 1976).
4. As pointed out previously, the public bureaucracy may be at least as representative of the population demographically as the political elite. See chapter 4.
5. The current debate over the size, salaries, and pensions of the civil service in the UK is perhaps a good example of this phenomenon.
6. See Guy Benvieniste, *The Politics of Expertise* (London: Croom Helm, 1973), pp. 123–26.
7. Randall Bartlett, *The Economic Foundations of Political Power* (New York: Free Press, 1973), pp. 63–64, 70–75.
8. Alvin W. Gouldner, "Metaphysical Pathos and the Theory of Bureaucracy," *American Political Science Review* 49 (1955): 496–507.
9. This support has been demonstrated in the preceding chapter when discussing the *clientela* and *parantela* systems.
10. This relationship between interest-group agency and committee has been referred to as the "iron triangle" in American policy making. It is especially important to note in this case that the committees are hardly impartial but

tend to represent constituencies vitally concerned with the policy area. See Charles O. Jones, "The Role of the Congressional Subcommittee," *Midwest Journal of Political Science* 6 (1962): 327–44.

11. A number of countries do not see any conflict between a civil-service position and political activity. So, for example, about one-fifth of the Bundestag in West Germany is composed of civil servants on leave.

12. This involves popular acceptance of the Weberian conception of administration. While inaccurate in most instances, this is a useful fiction for the administrators.

13. Leon N. Lindberg and Stuart A. Scheingold, *Europe's Would Be Polity* (Englewood Cliffs, N.J.: Prentice-Hall, 1970). A different view is provided by David Coombes, *Politics and Bureaucracy in the European Community* (London: Allen & Unwin, 1970).

14. For a general discussion, see Philip Selznick, *Leadership in Administration* (New York: Harper & Row, 1957), pp. 150–52; Harold Wilensky, *Organizational Intelligence* (New York: Basic Books, 1966); Samuel P. Huntington, *The Common Defense* (New York: Columbia University Press, 1961), pp. 384–409.

15. See Wilensky, *Organizational Intelligence*, pp. 24–34.

16. See James L. Sundquist, "Coordinating the War on Poverty," *Annals of the American Academy of Political And Social Sciences* 385 (1969): 41–49; Hugh Heclo, "The Frontiers of Social Policy," *Policy Studies* (forthcoming).

17. See Bruce Headey, *The British Cabinet Ministers: The Roles of Politicians in Executive Office* (London: Allen & Unwin, 1975), pp. 90–99.

18. See Richard Crossman, *The Diaries of a Cabinet Minister* (London: Hamish Hamilton and Jonathan Cape, 1975), 1:618.

19. Jean Meynaud, *Technocracy* (London: Faber & Faber, 1968); J. Ellul, *The Technological Society* (New York: Knopf, 1965); Charles A. Thrall, *Technology, Power and Social Change* (New York: Lexington, 1972).

20. Richard Rose, *The Problem of Party Government* (London: Macmillan, 1974), pp. 423–24.

21. Robert D. Putnam, "The Political Attitudes of Senior Civil Servants in Britain, Germany and Italy," *British Journal of Political Science* 3 (1973): 257–90.

22. See Jerry F. Hough, "The Bureaucratic Model and the Nature of the Soviet System," *Journal of Comparative Administration* 5 (1973): 136–67.

23. Anthony Downs, *Inside Bureaucracy* (Boston: Little, Brown, 1966); Gordon Tullock, *The Politics of Bureaucracy* (Washington, D.C.: Public Affairs Press, 1965); see also chapter 2.

24. Samuel P. Huntington, "Postindustrial Politics: How Benign Will It Be?" *Comparative Politics* 6 (1974): 181–82.

25. Ludwig Von Mises, *Bureaucracy* (New Haven: Yale University Press, 1962); Richard N. Billings and John Grierga, *Power to the Public Worker* (New York: Luce, 1974).

26. See Robert E. Goodin, "The Logic of Bureaucratic Back-Scratching," *Public Choice* 21 (1975): 53–68.

27. See, for examples, articles in the *New York Times*, 20 and 22 September 1975, 25 and 26 October 1975; R. Gillette, "Nuclear Critics Escalate War of Numbers," *Science* 189 (1975): 62; also, a series of articles in the *Times* (London) in November and December 1975 on safety in the North Sea.

28. The "military mind" if it does exist is almost a stereotype for such homogeneity. See also Herbert Kaufman, *The Forest Ranger* (Baltimore: Johns Hopkins University Press, 1960).

29. Timothy M. Hennessey and B. Guy Peters, "Postindustrialism and Public Policy" (Paper presented at annual meeting of the American Political Science Association, San Francisco, California, September 1975).

30. See Hugh Heclo and Aaron Wildavsky, *The Private Government of Public Money* (Berkeley: University of California Press, 1974), pp. 14–29.

31. Some idea of the breadth of modern planning is given in Jack Hayward and Michael Watson, eds., *Planning, Politics and Public Policy: The British, French and Italian Experience* (London: Cambridge University Press, 1975).

32. J. G. Abert, *Economic Policy and Planning in the Netherlands 1950–1965* (New Haven: Yale University Press, 1969), p. 39.

33. Even in the economy planning can be a means of obscuring the relationship between political choice and economic outcomes. In areas such as transportation or social policy the relationship is quite obscured.

34. John Higley, Karl Erik Brofoss, and Knut Groholt, "Top Civil Servants and the National Budget in Norway," in *The Mandarins of Western Europe*, ed. Mattei Dogan (New York: Halsted, 1975), pp. 252–74.

35. In practice this is not so undemocratic as it may appear because the process of consultation going into the preparation of the plan requires that everyone's views are known and, to some degree, taken into account in the final shape of the plan.

36. Andrew Shonfield, *Modern Capitalism* (London: Oxford University Press, 1965), p. 235.

37. See Michael Watson, "Planning in the Liberal-Democratic State," in Hayward and Watson, *Planning, Politics and Public Policy*, pp. 464–77.

38. The literature on PPBS is voluminous. A useful summary is provided in Jesse Burkhead and Jerry Miner, *Public Expenditure* (Chicago: Aldine, 1971), pp. 174–205. Also, Jacques Bravo, "La R.C.B. et Le Management de l'Etat," *Revue de Science Financere* 64 (1972): 289–356. (RCB is the French acronym for PPBS.)

39. Bureau of the Budget, *Special Analyses Budget of the United States* (Washington, D.C.: Government Printing Office, 1971), p. 273. Defense has been the one area of public policy which has been most commonly subjected to PPBS. See Keith Hartley, "Program Budgeting and the Economics of Defense," *Public Administration* 52 (1974): 55–72. Paolo Urio, "Rational Decision-making and National Defense in Switzerland," *Annuaire Suisse de Science Politique* 11 (1971): 25–42.

40. Hartley, "Program Budgeting," p. 69.

41. Heclo and Wildavsky, *Public Money*, p. 293.

42. Bravo, "La R.C.B.," pp. 339–42.

43. Rudolf Klein, "The Politics of PPBS," *Political Quarterly* 43 (1972): 280–81.

44. See, for example, United Nations Bureau of Technical Assistance Operations. *Report of the Inter-Regional Workshop on Problems of Budget Classification and Management in Developing Countries*, September 1967.

45. Naomi Caiden and Aaron Wildavsky, *Planning and Budgeting in Poor Countries* (New York: John Wiley, 1974), p. 293.

46. Karl Heinrich Friauf, "Parliamentary Control of the Budget in the Federal Republic of Germany," in Coombes, *Power of the Purse*, pp. 74–77; Frieder Naschold, "Probleme der mehrjahrigen Finanzplannung des Bundes," in *Praxis*, ed. V. Ronge and G. Schmieg (Munchen: Piper, 1971).

47. Higley, Brofoss, and Groholt, "Top Civil Servants."

48. Ibid., pp. 266–67.

49. Henry Roseveare, *The Treasury* (London: Allen Lane, 1969), provides an historical account of the development of these budgetary powers.

50. Guy Lord, *The French Budgetary Process* (Berkeley: University of California Press, 1974), p. 133.
51. Martha Derthick, *Uncontrollable Spending for Social Services Grants* (Washington, D.C.: Brookings Institution, 1975).
52. Heclo and Wildavsky, *Public Money*, pp. 47–48; Aaron Wildavsky, *The Politics of the Budgetary Process* (Boston: Little, Brown, 1966), pp. 111–13.
53. Lord, *French Budgetary Process*, pp. 29–33.
54. Higley, Brofoss, and Groholt, "Top Civil Servants," pp. 262–63.
55. Yves Weber, *L'Administration consultative* (Paris: Librarie General du Droit et Jurisprudence, 1968), p. 3.
56. See chapter 6.
57. Ibid.
58. See, for example, H. Meijer, "Bureaucracy and Policy Formation in Sweden," *Scandinavian Political Studies* 4 (1969): 103–16.
59. See Renate Mayntz and Fritz W. Scharpf, *Policy-Making in the German Federal Bureaucracy* (Amsterdam: Elsevier, 1975), pp. 92–93; Barbara Castle, "Mandarin Power," *Sunday Times*, 10 June 1973.
60. See, for example, Richard Rose, *Managing Presidential Objectives* (forthcoming).
61. In a similar finding in a different context see Caiden and Wildavsky, *Planning and Budgeting*, p. 110; Wildavsky, *Politics of the Budgetary Process*, p. 39. See also Heclo and Wildavsky, *Public Money*, pp. 118–28. See also James W. Davis and Randall B. Ripley, "The Bureau of the Budget and Executive Branch Agencies: A Note on Their Interaction," *Journal of Politics* 29 (1967): 749–69.
62. Mayntz and Scharpf, *Policy-Making in Germany*, pp. 38–45.
63. A good summary is provided in Malcolm E. Jewell and Samuel C. Patterson, *The Legislative Process in the United States* (2nd ed.; New York: Random House, 1973), pp. 249–77.
64. Hans Daalder, *Cabinet Reform in Britain, 1914–1963* (London: Oxford University Press, 1964).
65. See Thomas E. Cronin, "The Swelling of the Presidency," *Saturday Review of the Society* 1 (February 1973): 30–36; Norman C. Thomas and Hans W. Baade, eds., *The Institutionalized Presidency* (Dobbs Ferry, N.Y.: Oceana Publications, 1972). In contrast see Peter Hennessey, "The Cabinet Office," *Times* (London), 8 March 1976.
66. James Petras, *Politics and Social Forces in Chilean Development* (Berkeley: University of California Press, 1969).
67. Sisson refers to the Cabinet as the political "dynamite" for the ministers within the administration. C. H. Sisson, *The Spirit of British Administration and Some European Comparisons* (London: Faber & Faber, 1959), p. 10.
68. Headey, *British Cabinet Ministers*, pp. 110–31; S. Brittan, "The Irregulars," *Crossbow* (October-December 1966).
69. A good discussion is provided in R. G. S. Brown, *The Administrative Process in Britain* (London: Methuen, 1971), pp. 38–63.
70. Ezra N. Suleiman, *Politics, Power and Bureaucracy in France* (Princeton: Princeton University Press, 1974), pp. 137–54. This choice may be circumscribed, but it is still there.
71. See Richard Neustadt, "White House and Whitehall," *Public Interest* 2 (1966): 55–69.
72. F. Tannenbaum, "Politica y administracion publica en Latino-America," *Foro Internacional* 4 (1963): 243–59; J. C. Rey, "Burocracia y politica," *Revista de la Facultad de Derecho* (Caracas) 29 (1964): 83–100.

73. See Derek J. Waller, "Revolutionary Intellectuals and Managerial Modernizers," *Political Quarterly* 45 (1974): 5–12; A. D. Barnett, "Mechanisms for Party Control in the Government Bureaucracy in China," *Asian Survey* 6 (1966): 659–74.

74. Henry Bienen, "Public Order and the Military in Africa," in his *The Military Intervenes: Case Studies in Political Development* (New York: Russell Sage, 1968), pp. 35–69. In many cases the civil service and the officer corps are recruited from the same middle-class stratum and tend to represent the conservative values of that stratum, especially in Latin America.

THE POLITICS OF
ADMINISTRATIVE ACCOUNTABILITY

We have documented the growth of public administration and the increasing influence of administrative agencies on policy. These developments make the perennial political problem of the control of administration more important than ever. This problem may be phrased in terms of "control," "accountability," or "responsibility," but the basic problem remains: how do political leaders and the public persuade, cajole, or force administrative agencies to do their bidding?

Traditionally there have been two broad schools of thought regarding this question. The first has assumed that responsibility was "an inward sense of personal obligation"; the second assumed that the first was not enough, and some external forces must be employed in order to enforce responsible behavior.[1] The first approach to the problem assumes that civil servants have ethical values and professional standards that will guide them in the performance of their tasks. The second assumes that these values are not sufficient; there must be a means of punishing behavior not in accordance with stated law and legislative intent.

This chapter dwells heavily on methods of enforcing responsibility, in large part because governments have spent so much time in trying to devise methods of control. However, throughout, it must be remembered that civil servants are probably no better or worse ethically than individuals who work in the private sector. The major difference is that they work for the government, and in democratic government it is assumed that they work at least indirectly for all of us. Thus the problem of accountability is more acute in public agencies not because of the nature of the individuals employed and their lack of personal responsibility, but because of the nature of the jobs and the nature of the power vested in government. Even in liberal democracies, the state has a number of presumptive claims on individuals (such as arrests, taxes, and conscription), which threaten abuse. The problem is assuring the proper use of these claims.

Another factor that produces problems of control and responsibility is the vast growth of administrative involvement in government. Not only do public administrators execute the laws, but they consciously also make laws and even adjudicate laws. Much of the legislation coming out of the legislative organs of political systems these days is actually enabling legislation for the bureaucracy. It sets the broad outlines of policy but requires the bureaucracy to issue regulations to fill in the details.[2] If it were not for this, legislatures would be more bogged down than they already are. In the same way more adjudication is carried on in administrative tribunals than in the regular courts in many countries.[3] Although conducted by administrators, and often informally, these adjudications have the same impact as if done in a regular court.[4] Thus the problems of controlling administration have grown from simply (?) controlling the execution of policy to the more complex tasks of also controlling policy formulation and adjudication.

DIMENSIONS OF RESPONSIBILITY

In a discussion of accountability and control the basic dualism with which the man in the street—not to mention politicians and academic commentators—regards the bureaucracy is apparent.[5] On the one hand, bureaucracy is characterized as a Leviathan, a monolithic and virtually uncontrollable force eating away at personal liberties and economic resources. On the other hand, bureaucracy is a fool: a fragmented set of individuals so bound with red tape and rule books that they don't know what they are about at any one time, sending television sets to people who lack electricity and doing research on the optimal shape of toilet seats.[6] It is truly remarkable the degree to which these apparently contradictory viewpoints about bureaucracy can coexist in the thoughts and writings of the same commentators. Leaving inconsistencies aside, it is also important to note the extent to which these two perspectives on the problems of bureaucracy in modern government point to different problems and different requirements for accountability and control.

On a more personal level, there is also a dualism in reactions to bureaucracy, although this is rarely expressed by the same individuals. On the one hand, there are frequent complaints about bureaucracy and bureaucrats operating *ultra vires*, beyond the scope of their authority. Complaints about police brutality, the role of the FBI in domestic surveillance in the United States, Swedish tax collectors breaking into homes, and Danish welfare workers removing children from their parents are all complaints about bureaucracy operating in an apparently illegal or arbitrary manner. Bureaucrats have gone beyond the scope of their prescribed authority and are acting on the basis of personal values and "initiative." On the other hand, we frequently hear complaints from clients of public agencies concerning excessive adherence to rules and procedures. In these cases the clients—most commonly the clients of social-service agencies—feel that they are denied the type of assistance they need, or indeed deserve, because of strict adherence to procedures. This is a case of adherence to rules with a vengeance, so much so that the initial intention of the program may be lost.

The first two types of perceived problems with bureaucracy, the Leviathan and the fool, are essentially institutional problems, involving the activities of the bureaucracy as an entity. The second set of problems is more commonly associated with the behavior of individuals occupying positions within the hierarchy—usually at the bottom.[7] Two of the problems involve the use of excessive power or the evasion of legal safeguards, or conversely, the failure to go outside normal channels in seeking information, advice, or coordination. These four types of perceived problems of administrative accountability can be seen as the product of the interaction of two dimensions of control. One is the personal or institutional level at which the problem occurs, and the second is the degree of activity of the administrator in question (overactive or underactive). These two dimensions and the resulting four types of problems are shown in figure 8.1.

Other than as an intellectual exercise, the cross-classification of these two dimensions of administrative complaints should enable us to conceptualize better the politics of administrative accountability. On one dimension—the institutional-personal—the politics are those of the institutional conflict of the bureaucracy with other political institutions such as the legislature or the executive, as opposed to the politics of influencing the behavior of individual administrators who interact with clients. The institutional control may involve large-scale political conflict often of a quite intense nature, while individual control may involve only altering the attitudes or behavior of one individual. Obviously, different solutions are needed for the two types of problems. However, we must be aware of the possibility of in-

Action		Actor	
		Institution	Individual
Excessive		CIA Surveillance	Police Brutality
Too Little		"Red Tape"	Self-Protection by Bureaucrat

FIGURE 8.1 A Typology of Perceived Difficulties with Bureaucracy

dividual problems escalating to institutional crises, as illustrated by the role of the FBI and CIA in domestic surveillance and the relationship between actions of individual policemen and urban unrest in the last decade in the United States.

On the other dimension of accountability, the difference in politics appears to be the difference between institutionalizing and enforcing controls versus the politics of relaxing existing regulations. These actions are again somewhat contradictory, but both involve getting administrators to do what the public, the clients, and the political leaders want them to do. The former involves political action in writing legislation, and perhaps more importantly, political will in enforcing existing regulations. It may also involve the willingness on the part of individual citizens to invest large amounts of time and possibly money to combat what they consider to be injustices resulting from the administrative process.

The loosening of institutional rules of procedure is a more difficult process. To some degree it involves the legislation of discretionary powers for administrators, an action that clashes with the concern of control and accountability mentioned above, and also with many general constitutional statements concerning the responsibility of *political* actors for policy. Another dimension in loosening the bonds of the proverbial red tape is more personal and involves training for an understanding of clients and their problems. Finally, some changes may have to be within the individual administrator—and within the culture of the agency—and would involve an increased willingness to take responsibility for actions and willingness to use rules for the benefit of client rather than the protection of the civil servant. Each of these, especially the latter, is more easily said than done.

Another factor that must be taken into account in this prologue to the study of administrative accountability is that much of the problem is a function of that often-mentioned desire to separate administration from politics.[8] In this case, it is especially important that most Western societies and nations following their examples have sought to separate the tenure of administrators from political control, except in the most extreme cases, and even then only after a rather arduous process.[9] When there was a spoils system—not necessarily the good old days—many problems of administrative accountability we face today simply did not arise. The administrator was in office at the pleasure of a political official, and if the civil servant didn't do what was expected, the civil servant was out of a job. This system did not assure any more accountability to the public, and its difficulties have been well documented by reformers.[10] Few people would seriously advocate returning to a patronage system of allocating public jobs, but it is important to remember that the choice of a merit system for public management has a number of latent consequences for administrative accountability. The most important is the security, and to some degree the unresponsiveness, of the public employee. The goods and services produced by public service are not marketed, or if they are it is in a monopolistic situation. The failure to make a profit or break even isn't associated with the termination of public employment, so there is little to make the civil servant responsive to the wishes of markets, politicians, or the public. The job carries sufficient security so that after a suitable probationary period, the civil servant can be terminated only by a lengthy process proving positive malfeasance or nonfeasance. This discussion should not be taken to imply that public employees are inferior people morally, or that they are in their jobs only to make a secure living. Rather, it is to imply that the structure of incentives within most civil-service systems places more emphasis on security than on project completion or public responsiveness.[11] Thus, in an attempt to insulate civil servants from political pressures, reforms in the public service have gone far to insulate the civil service from *all* pressures, thus creating significant problems of accountability and control.

Now, with some idea of the dimensions of the problem of administrative accountability and control, we shall proceed to discuss the instruments by which accountability may be enforced. We do this by discussing the instruments available to each actor seeking to exercise control and attempt to evaluate these instruments within different contexts. In this discussion, we also link these instruments and their effectiveness back to these basic dimensions and the particular types of control over problems already outlined.

INSTRUMENTS OF ACCOUNTABILITY

The list of procedures, institutions, and actors that have been devised to attempt to control administration is by now very long and equally varied. We cannot hope to discuss each of them in this chapter, not even in one book. Therefore, we shall concentrate on those that seem to offer the most promise of being effective—either to us or to significant portions of public opinion. The one common thread that binds all these proposed solutions together is that they depend upon implementation by someone, and this is the weak link in the chain of control. Most of the methods to be discussed could be effective, but all rely on human implementation. We must therefore also seek to determine which methods have the lowest political costs for the implementers.

Organizational Methods

The simplest means of policing public administration is to allow the civil servants to police themselves. One means is that suggested by Friedrich—relying on the internalized values of the civil servants—and we shall return to that option later.[12] What we are interested in here is the use of organizational methods to enforce compliance among the members of the public bureaucracy with popular or legal sanctions. Thus, while each individual in the organization may not have accepted the standards proposed by Friedrich, are there still means by which the organization itself can control them? It should be pointed out that although ostensibly the simplest method of control, this may in fact involve the highest political costs simply because of the internal strife within the organization that it may create. Further, it may open up the agency to further attacks from other political institutions.

PUBLICITY.   Although it may be considered a method in itself, publicity is one organizational means of controlling the bureaucracy. It would tend to be particularly useful in dealing with individual actions both going beyond, or excessively adhering to, rules and procedures.

The characterization of this method as organizational may strike the reader as a bit odd, but the point is that publicity carries little or no direct sanction, but instead depends largely upon the organization to correct the errors brought to light. If the organization does not respond, then the legislative or legal methods can come into play. However, it is easier, cheaper, and quicker for the organization to respond. It reduces the external control on the organization and may preserve for it some latitude for action. It is the hope of those advocating publicity as a means of control that this will indeed happen.

Perhaps the administrative system most notable for the use of publicity is Sweden. Swedish public officials have been described as working within a "goldfish bowl," in that their actions are almost entirely open to public inspection.[13] Whenever an official reaches a decision, this decision must be justified in writing, and the written justification is recorded as a part of the file to be made available to the citizen(s) upon request. In addition, many forms collected by the government that in most societies would be regarded as confidential —such as income tax returns—are made public in Sweden.[14] This system is intended to make the administrative system and the political system as a whole more responsive to the people for the simple reason that if people know what decisions have been reached and why, they are better able to contest them. Further, openness to the press enables even greater dissemination of information. This openness also must have a deterrent effect on administrators; they will not do anything that cannot be well justified. Of course, there are means of circumventing the system. An officer in each ministry decides which materials are private or confidential, and although there is an appeal from that decision, in most cases it is final. Likewise, information that is sensitive can be sent through private communication rather than through public channels, and finally the press is frequently criticized for being insufficiently interested in pursuing matters that appear in the files.[15] Despite these problems, the system seems to be a step in the right direction for those wishing to control more fully the activities of the public bureaucracy.

The Swedish system is the most publicized of several systems relying upon information for control, but some steps have been taken in other systems to use information as a mechanism of control. Norway has adopted a system of publicity quite similar to that in Sweden.[16] In the United States the excesses of Watergate and some general increase in distrust of government have led to the passage of a number of "sunshine laws," allowing public access to records and to meetings of administrative bodies, especially those functioning in a quasi-legislative or quasi-judicial manner. Canadian administrative procedures have been modified to allow greater publicity of decisions and information. It is probably fair to say that a general increase in distrust of government and in political awareness of populations has been associated with increased pressure on government to open up its proceedings to the people and the press.

Publicity, as with many questions of administrative responsibility and accountability, is not a wholly positive value. While it is certainly important that the public have access to relevant information about administration, working in a goldfish bowl cannot be as efficient as working in private. Further, it tends to expose the activities of administrators to political pressures that might not be felt directly in a more closed system. The contrast with Great Britain comes to mind almost immediately. The tradition and practice of British administration has been that of almost total secrecy and privacy for administrators.[17] Although the press is tending to place pressure on this secrecy, as far as most of the public know—especially when it comes to policy decisions and advice—the bureaucrats are "faceless." Secrecy has been adopted quite simply to ensure that administrators as public servants will be isolated from short-term political pressures and be free to make decisions in what they consider to be the "public interest."[18] Recent decisions concerning the publication of the Crossman diaries and the institutionalization of a parliamentary ombudsman have opened even this system of administration to greater public scrutiny, but it remains very much more private than most. The point is that certain values can be maximized by a closed and private system of administration, just as certain things can be gained by having a very open system of administration. It is simply a matter of choice for the public and for political elites of what type of system they want and can have.

INTERNAL DISCIPLINE.   Internal discipline within public organizations is another potentially effective means of controlling administration without having to resort to the imposition of external political control. It is therefore a relatively "cheap" means of control in terms of time and total institutional energy. On the other hand, it assumes that there will be someone in a responsible position within the hierarchy who has values more in line with those assumed to be held by the public than those held by erring subordinates. Given our conception of the average public administrator as probably no better or no worse than the average citizen, the probabilities of finding such a person in the hierarchy are good. However, there are a number of impediments to any person exercising authority over subordinates guilty of other than the most obvious malfeasance in office.

First, the sanctions available within civil-service systems are not particularly strong, especially if the person involved is not a "climber" seeking advancement.[19] These problems are especially apparent when the individual whom the superior would like to sanction is guilty only of being overzealous in the application of rules rather than in circumventing rules. Further, the application of such sanctions as do exist requires long and often complex administrative hearings, with the scales apparently weighted in favor of the civil servant.[20] Police review boards, for example, generally include mostly other policemen who, despite their intentions of maintaining the integrity of the force, also well understand the problems of the individual policeman faced with a dangerous or compromising situation. Finally, unionization of public employees—both industrial and nonindustrial —has added to the difficulties in implementing internal controls.[21] Thus those sanctions that can be readily employed tend to be rather weak, and those with teeth are difficult to implement.

There are also powerful organizational reasons for failing to enforce sanctions against employees. As noted in earlier chapters, bureaucratic politics plays a major if not paramount role for many public administrators and their agencies.[22] They must compete for money, employees, and legislative time with all other agencies, and there is not a quicker way to reduce their potential success in this conflict over resources than to have a scandal. Although the agency can try to make the best of it by saying they were "cleaning their own house," it may still produce considerable difficulty for the agency at the next budget time.[23] In these days of tight public funds, the firing of an employee may mean the loss of a position. It thus becomes difficult for any public administrator, no matter how committed to proper administrative practice, to impose discipline upon an employee, especially when word of such discipline will leak out to concerned politicians.

Related to the above point is that administrators (one hopes) want to get things done and consequently do not want to employ excessive amounts of time and energy in prosecuting members of their own organizations. And, they generally get rated themselves on their ability to get the job done, not on the internal discipline of their organization. Therefore, those who are themselves "climbers" will tend to expend more effort on program execution than on organizational control. For many agencies—social-service agency or the police—this tendency is enhanced by the fact that the clients are neither of high status nor skilled politically, so their claims against the organization can be easily dismissed.

Another factor favoring nonenforcement of administrative regulations within an agency is that it is frequently necessary to circumvent regulations in order to get the job done. In the United States and other countries that have had recent major political scandals, this reasoning may sound dubious to many readers, but there are situations in which administrative rules and regulations are impediments to providing a service or getting a job done. Blau provides a classic example in the FBI agents who had to engage in an explicit violation of the rules requiring reporting an attempted bribe in order to perform their jobs well.[24] Many regulations associated with the granting of social services make it more difficult for the client to receive aid, and these must frequently be ignored by employees seeking to assist a client.

Finally, we must remember that the civil service constitutes a career just as does working in any other organization or profession. As such, there is a certain amount of camaraderie and *esprit de corps*, which makes strict adherence to internal discipline more difficult. Despite formal lines of authority, informal organizations may link individuals who are formally superior and subordinate as equals, thus making the imposition of discipline difficult. In situations where the civil service is regarded as a highly differentiated organization from the rest of society (France?), or within segments of the public bureaucracy that are themselves highly integrated (the police or the military), there is an unwillingness to bring discredit upon the service, so many internal matters may not be exposed.[25] Even in less differentiated positions there may well be a feeling that one should not criticize one's fellow civil servants unduly, if for no other reason than the tables may be turned.

Thus, as we said when beginning our discussion of administrative control, control depends not only on the existence of a set of institutions and procedures, but also on the willingness to employ those procedures. In the case of internal discipline, both are frequently lacking. The lack of will is rarely due to collusion or widespread immorality, but more commonly due simply to the politics of bureaucratic agencies and their needs to survive. Likewise, the methods available are at best awkward and cumbersome, and at worst absolutely unworkable.

Group and Public Pressures

Another means of exercising control of administration without resort to formal conflicts between institutions is through pressure-group activity and public opinion. We have already discussed something of the relationship between pressure groups and the bureaucracy, with the conclusion that pressure groups may frequently be the source of administrative failure to operate in the "public interest." [26] How do we now say that these same pressure groups may also serve as a check on administration? In the first place, although pressure groups may not in fact serve the public interest broadly defined, they do certainly serve a narrow clientele, and it is frequently that clientele which are most affected by the activities of a certain agency. Thus, by informing their members of the activities of the agency, they can in turn exercise some effective popular control. Of course, the end result of this is frequently legislation or administrative action favoring the special interest, but even this constitutes *some* responsiveness on the part of the agency.

Second, one of the most important political developments in recent years has been the organization of so-called public-interest pressure groups, organized and functioning much as any other pressure group but ostensibly representing no special interest. In the United States this movement has manifested itself through Common Cause and the whole consumer movement beginning with Ralph Nader.[27] Publicity and the publication of complaints against government are the weapons most frequently employed by these organizations, but they have also engaged in lobbying both legislators and administrative agencies. Finally, in the American context these organizations have been reasonably successful in the courts, while in the European nations the creation of a number of ministries and boards for consumer affairs has tended to absorb many complaints without resort to judicial means.[28]

Another especially interesting aspect of the use of organizations as a check on bureaucracy has been governmental fostering of organizations, almost to the extent of creating their own opposition. During the War on Poverty in the United States the doctrine of "maximum feasible participation" was designed to allow the residents of communities affected by these social programs to have some input into the making and implementation of policies.[29] The idea was to allow residents to gain political skills and simultaneously to prevent programs from becoming excessively bureaucratized and bound in red tape.[30] In Britain, the recent reorganization of the National Health Service has included the development of Community Health Councils designed to prevent domination of the service by specialist physicians and ensure greater regard for community wishes.[31] In many African countries undergoing political mobilization and social change, village councils or organizations have been developed, again with the intention of providing local input and serving as a check on bureaucratic excesses.[32] In all these cases, the governments have actively fostered organizations that would serve as oppositions to its own bureaucracy, an interesting if not always entirely successful approach to administrative accountability.

Another development has been the growth of client organizations for some public services. These have existed for some time for middle- and upper-class services, such as education, but the more interesting development is the growth of organizations of lower-status recipients of social benefits. These people had once been regarded by the community, and even by themselves, as having the right to express nothing but gratitude for receiving benefits. Now, however, they have become increasingly vocal in their demands for improved benefits and improved administration.[33] Also important in this regard has been the increasing political mobilization of the elderly, so that "gray power" can become effective in placing pressure on government for increased pensions and improved administration of pension programs. While these organizations clearly do not represent the broader public interest, they can be effective in placing pressures for improvements in social administration.

In evaluation, despite the obvious success of some groups, it is difficult to be very sanguine about their efficacy as a general solution to the problems of administrative control. Their effectiveness is limited by the same factors limiting the effectiveness of pressure groups more generally, mainly that they must work through second and third parties in order to have their suggestions or demands realized. Further, despite successes in the short run, many of the social groups who could benefit most by organizations of this type still lack the political and organizational skills required for continued success. Finally, consumer groups and consumer agencies may, in the long run, prove to be little different from other types of agencies and other types of pressure groups. They may come to represent a special interest, or more appropriately, a special approach to consumer problems, requiring yet another set of controls to control the controllers.

Political Methods of Control

If the methods of publicity, organization, and internal discipline within the organization do not prove effective in controlling administration—as indeed they may not—then a second level of control will have to be introduced. This control is through political institutions. The logic is that political institutions rightly regard themselves as the representatives of the people, even when they have not been directly elected. They rightly regard themselves as the source of the delegated powers that the bureaucracy may currently exercise and as having the right to withdraw those powers if they are abused. We have already discussed the conflict between the political institutions and the bureaucracy over policy.[34] Many points made there apply to this discussion as well. Rather than arguing over the ability of these two sets of institutions to control policy in a broad sense, here we shall be looking at their respective abilities to control decisions in more specific cases, even if only in an ex post facto manner. Many powers of the several institutions are the same, but we should now discuss the ways in which those powers can be brought to bear on specific cases of administration or maladministration.[35]

THE LEGISLATURE. Legislative institutions have come more to the forefront of the battle over administrative control in recent years. This is in part because the growing concern among voters has been translated into action by their elected representatives. Further, the sheer volume of administrative work now being performed has meant that there is more need for the legislature to exercise its oversight functions. This is especially true of the increasing volume of administrative rulings having the force of law and issued by powers delegated from the legislature. It is up to the legislature to try at least to keep track of these rulings, even if they cannot always control their content. Finally, the increasing executive dominance of policy making in legislatures has left harassing administration one of the few remaining ways in which the individual legislator can acquire wide publicity and national stature.

1. Funding. Funding programs is a principal means through which the legislature is able to exercise control over administration. Some problems of exercising policy control through funding have already been discussed at length. However, although the power of the purse

may be a blunt instrument in exercising broad policy control, it may be successful in dealing with a recalcitrant administrator or agency. Although we might hope that legislatures had something better to do with their collective time, the instances of committees and even whole legislatures spending substantial amounts of time on small problems of individual agencies, and even individual administrators, are legion, especially within the United States. Few other political systems have allowed legislative bodies such freedom in budgeting to enable them to delve into the financial and administrative details of agencies. At the subnational level, again within the United States, legislative involvement in administration via the budget is even more evident, to the point of removing people from office simply by refusing to appropriate money for the position they occupy. The punishment for improper administration is rarely so direct, but it does frequently occur by reducing the appropriations for the whole agency. These powers over budgeting give the American Congress and state legislatures significant powers over agencies that have been largely forfeited in parliamentary systems with stronger discipline.[36]

Another aspect of the power of the purse in checking administration is a much blunter instrument. This is the ability to pass private legislation to compensate individuals for the actions of public administrators. Most political systems provide some means of passing "private bills" to provide such compensation, but these provide no penalties for the offending civil servant, and require political leverage for the citizen in order to have his grievances redressed.

The funding control of legislatures over administration is potentially a vital and powerful force, but as with many legislative weapons, it is a difficult one to employ effectively. By their very nature legislative bodies tend to be cumbersome, and detailed consideration of administrative actions can occur only in the sensational or highly politicized cases, even in systems such as that of the United States, which pride themselves on the ability to use the budget as a means of control. Also, the increasing importance of macro-economic policy has meant that substantial control over the budget has passed from legislatures to executives and central banks.[37] Budgets have become too important (economically and politically) to allow legislatures to use them to punish the wicked and reward the just.

2. *Investigation.* Probably the most frequently cited power of the legislature to control administration is through investigations. These may range from simple questions and interpolations in legislative

sessions to full-scale committee investigations to the institutionalization of an officer to investigate for the legislature. All these devices
rely in part upon publicity as a means of righting a wrong, but they
can also be useful in writing new legislation and correcting defects in
old legislation.

The simplest form of legislative investigation is the parliamentary
question or interpolation. In virtually all parliamentary systems there
is some means for legislators to ask questions of government ministers.
While these may be about policy decisions made by the minister, they
may also pertain to questions of administration within the ministry.
This is especially true of systems in the British tradition where the
minister is considered responsible politically for all that goes on
within the ministry, even down to the behavior of lowly clerks. The
question hour can call attention to problems, embarrass the government, and alert an "attentive public" to current problems of administration. Other than producing broader political debate on the topic,
however, it can go no further. It depends upon the actions of the
government, administrators, and the public to be effective in bringing
about change.

Within the American context the most common form of legislative
investigation is the congressional committee, generally operating
through hearings.[38] The functional specialization of congressional
committees, and the further specialization into subcommittees, special, and select committees provides an extensive and well-qualified
array of investigative bodies. This investigative role in Congress came
into most prominence during the McCarthy period in the early 1950s
and more recently has been prominent in investigations over the role
of the CIA in internal affairs and the involvement of multinational
corporations in bribery abroad. While these hearings have made the
headlines, they are overshadowed in volume by a large number of ongoing investigations into virtually every policy area. The ostensible
purpose of these investigations is legislation, but in practice both the
airing of information and the ability to delve into administrative practices have impacts on the conduct of administration.

Although the committee system of Congress and its investigations
in the United States are most familiar, similar systems exist in other
political systems. Germany has an extensive array of legislative committees specialized along functional lines and involved in legislative
oversight.[39] The role of the Japanese Parliament investigation has been
highlighted by the recent scandal over Lockheed bribes.[40] The
United Kingdom has only three permanent committees concerned

with investigation and oversight, all of which are directly related to the traditional parliamentary concern over the control of the purse.[41] There is also a select committee that deals with delegated legislation, a particularly touchy subject in a system based upon parliamentary responsibility for policy.

We could go on enumerating slight differences in committee and investigatory arrangements, but the basic point is that legislatures investigate, they tend to do so through committees, and the investigations are generally related to exercising oversight within a specific policy field. These committees and their investigations have generally been one of the most effective legislative means of influencing the conduct of administration. The relationship between the committee and the agency tends to be an ongoing one, so the agency has a great deal to gain in the long run by cooperation. Further, the committees tend to be expert especially where members can and often do remain members of the same committee for a long time. Nevertheless, there is a danger of the committee and the agency becoming too friendly, much in the way described in reference to pressure groups.[42]

The final method of legislative investigation might be discussed as a separate topic, given the amount of interest that has been expressed in it. This is the institution of the ombudsman or its equivalent.[43] Although often presented as a magical cure for what ails administration and society, this method of control generally relies upon the legislature as a means of implementation. Although there are variations between countries, the powers of the ombudsman generally do not include the ability to issue binding judgments on administrators or to effect restitution for an aggrieved citizen. In general, the ombudsman can investigate, negotiate with civil servants, report to the legislature, or perhaps introduce legislation. The legislature is then expected to carry the case onward if some reason for further action is found. Most commonly, this will involve simply providing some redress for the citizen, but several systems allow the ombudsman to introduce more general suggestions concerning procedures to prevent future problems.[44]

The ombudsman has been most commonly associated with Scandinavian countries, but the institution has now been adopted in the United Kingdom, New Zealand, Israel, Japan, in West Germany for military affairs, Yugoslavia, and in modified forms in Poland and the Soviet Union.[45] Also, several states in the United States have also adopted the system.[46] Variations among systems are rather great, and little is to be gained from a detailed examination of those differences here. One major difference is the ability to act independently or not, with some officers such as the Parliamentary Commissioner in the United Kingdom requiring a request from a Member of Parliament before initiating action.[47] Another variation is the ability of the officer to initiate legislation or not, with the Finnish ombudsman, among others, having the ability to introduce legislation as a matter of right.[48] There is also the question of the coverage of policies, with some countries extending the system to cover prisoners and soldiers and others confining it to civil administration.[49]

On balance, the ombudsman system is difficult to evaluate. On the one hand, it provides a tribune for the people, with the advantage of being both inside and outside government.[50] Being inside, or more properly being an officially sanctioned gadfly, allows the ombudsman access, and requires that this person's findings and suggestions be taken seriously. On the other hand, being outside government makes the office appear to most people that they do in fact have an advocate who is free of most bureaucratic impediments, and who will therefore freely speak for the "people." [51] At the same time that the office is symbolically well placed, its success requires a number of steps to be gone through. Most importantly, citizens who may be most in need of services are quite unlikely to be aware of the office. It also depends upon the willingness of the legislature to follow through. This is in part dependent upon the stature of the individual holding the office, the degree of institutionalization of the office in the particular country, and legislative procedures in handling suggestions from the ombudsman.[52] It may also depend upon the type of results sought, whether compensation for individuals or punishment for administrators. The former may be easy to obtain, since sums of money sought are frequently minute, or privileges rather minor. Actions against individual administrators may be more difficult to obtain, may have destructive effects on morale in the civil service, and may in fact accentuate problems of rigidity within the public bureaucracy. Thus this system may be useful in redressing personal grievances but less successful as a means of bringing about significant procedural or policy changes within the public service.

3. *Constituency Service.* A third major means through which the legislature can influence the conduct of the civil service is what Americans refer to as "constituency service" [53] In Ireland it has been referred to as "going around persecuting civil servants." [54] The idea is

the same. The average citizen frequently feels powerless in the face of the bureaucracy and looks for some means of influencing that bureaucracy. One of the handiest such devices is the elected representative. After all, the citizen put this person in office, and the citizen should therefore be able to get the representative to do something for him. Thus, many legislators are expected to spend significant portions of their time solving problems that their constituents have had with the civil service. Perhaps the constituent did not get a pension check on time, or the veterans' death benefit is not paid as it should be, or a grant-in-aid for a local project is not approved. The legislator can become directly involved in attempting to find out what has happened, to get the problem corrected as quickly as possible. In practice, many legislators find this to be a significant portion of their jobs and an activity that is highly visible to constituents. While it may be a useful means of control, it often is also an inefficient means. It concentrates on particular cases, and the legislature may not have time to develop legislation to cover the more general problem. It also exhausts much of the credit that the legislators may have with the bureaucrats, by "persecuting" them over relatively petty issues. It is a method of control that is generally highly regarded by the recipients of its benefits, but that may in the long run perpetuate problems of control rather than solve them.

4. *Post-audit.* The final legislative power over administration to be discussed here is the post-audit of accounts.[55] We have already noted the powers of the legislature in the appropriations process, and the legislature also exercises an oversight function after the funds have been spent. In virtually all political systems the post-audit function is a legislative function. In the United States the General Accounting Office is a creature of the Congress, responsible for reporting to the Congress on the improper expenditure of public money by administrative agencies.[56] The Controller and Auditor General in the United Kingdom, the *Bundesrechnungshof* in Germany, the Italian *Corte di Conti*, and the vast majority of auditing agencies are required to report to the legislature.[57] One significant exception is the French *Cours des Comptes*, which is more directly linked to the bureaucracy through recruitment and staffing and to the President through organization and responsibility. It reports to the National Assembly, but serves primarily the President.

The idea of the post-audit is rather simple. The legislature appropriates money for specific purposes, and it must therefore be sure that the executive spends the money as appropriated. In some systems this is justified by the concept of the separation of powers, while in others it is simply to ensure that the public treasury is protected from undue demands. In either case, real spending is compared with authorized expenditure, and any discrepancies are noted. Depending on the system in question, individuals may be held responsible personally for any difference.

The post-audit system of legislative control of administration made a great deal of sense when the bookkeeping of government was a bit like your father's old ledger in the desk upstairs. It is still a valuable means of checking on what has happened, but less so as the finances of government become more complex both in terms of variety of things purchased and complexity of financial arrangements. Government programs can no longer be readily calculated on the basis of annual appropriations; building a dam or an aircraft carrier simply takes much too long. So funds appropriated in any one year may be kept "in the pipeline" and quite legally spent some years later. Also, the exact purposes for which the funds were originally allocated may have become obsolete or the cost of performing a function may become (remarkably) cheaper, so that some of the funds in the pipeline may become almost discretionary. The Pentagon once calculated that, although Congress might cut off funds for the Vietnam war, they still had sufficient funds authorized in that proverbial pipeline to keep the thing going for some months.[58] Not only does the pipeline present a problem to auditors, so do many reserve financial powers granted governments.

As noted, the budget is now a much too important part of economic policy and economic stability to allow it to be shackled entirely by decisions taken by the legislature some months in advance of execution. Therefore, many political systems allow the government considerable latitude in shifting not only the types of expenditure made, but even the aggregate total in order to attempt to overcome economic problems.[59] This is further affected by the uncontrollable nature of many expenditures dependent upon fluctuations in the economy (e.g., unemployment benefits) and the greater latitude given public managers under reforms such as PPBS.[60] All in all, modern governmental finance makes the job of the auditor difficult and makes the job of the legislator in understanding the findings of the auditor equally difficult. Except in cases of *clear* misappropriation, if any exist any longer, the legislature must deal with a number of gray areas of law and policy, making control that much more difficult.

5. *Summary.* The instruments of administrative control available to legislative bodies then, while important, suffer from many of the difficulties mentioned when discussing the relative strengths of the legislature and the bureaucracy in making public policy. These powers depend upon the concerted action of the legislature, which is not always forthcoming. Further, even if it is forthcoming, it is more likely to be far removed in time from the actual commission or omission of the offending administrative action. Likewise, it is increasingly difficult for legislatures to keep pace with the quantity of things required to be done in modern governments, making delegated legislative powers of the administrative agencies even more crucial to the conduct of government. Finally, the political power base of the legislator is not generally enhanced by performing the time-consuming, painstaking, and generally dull job of keeping track of agencies and their actions. Even if it were, the influence of partisan loyalty on decisions might prevent full exercise of oversight. Except for the occasional case that can be used to make publicity and political hay, much of this oversight work is unlikely to aid a legislator's career either with his constituents or his own party. There are, however, two major sources of legislative strength in exercising control. First, the major defense is an internal value structure within the legislature—possessed to some degree by certain committees in the American Congress and the German *Bundestag*—which places a high value on keeping track of the bureaucracy.[61] These norms are difficult to enforce and do little for the legislator who is not reelected, but they are crucial to effective control. The second is, as policy-making powers pass to bureaucrats and to the political executive, the legislature's role may become increasingly that of watchdog. More time and energy may be available for the job of pursuing problems and persecuting the perpetrators.

THE EXECUTIVE.   In examining the organization chart of government, the political executive would appear to be in the best position to exercise control over the performance of the public bureaucracy. The lines of authority and control are all right there on the organizational chart; all that is required is the exercise of that authority. Or so it looks when we look solely at the formal structures. In practice, the operation of executive authority over the bureaucracy is susbtantially more difficult. The existence of the civil-service system and other aspects of public personnel management frequently prevent political executives from getting the service and advice of the administrators that they might most like to employ. This is confounded by the feeling of many legislative bodies—perhaps quite accurate—that the best way of controlling an executive is to control the executive latitude in dealing with and leading the bureaucracy. Thus the ability of the executive to control the bureaucracy—which frequently operates as an almost entirely separate branch of government—is seriously curtailed.

In the absence of the ability of the executive to hire, promote, move, and fire whomever he wants, a number of other, less blatant controls come into play. Some of those operating through the budgetary process have already been mentioned, although more drastic executive fiscal powers such as impoundment may be used to place controls on the bureaucracy. These controls in many ways may constitute a meat axe rather than a sharp knife and consequently cannot be readily employed. They offer little if any means of dealing with recalcitrant individuals or just plain rigidity in administration.

1. *Personnel Powers.* The powers of the executive in dealing with the bureaucracy are variable across political systems. The major variations come in the ability to appoint and remove officials, the ability to shuffle employees around among agencies and on and off personal staffs, and the ability to use executive authority to bring about reorganization of government. As for the ability to appoint, some variations have already been noted. The ability of an American President to appoint about 2,000 people in the executive branch, to remove most of them without approval of the Senate, and to appoint his own personal staff are important powers even though restrained by many customs and procedural checks.[62] It becomes especially significant when compared with the British prime minister whose appointment powers are virtually nonexistent and whose ministers have only a limited choice over the permanent secretary who will serve them in office. This may also be contrasted with the ability of the French, Belgian, and German ministers to select whomever they want as the *chef du direction* or its equivalent.[63] Likewise, many underdeveloped countries—especially those of Latin America—have developed the form without the substance of civil-service arrangements so that an incoming government has a fairly wide choice of its senior civil servants

and advisers.[64] Totalitarian or authoritarian systems have more extensive controls over personnel; those who may be considered politically unreliable can be easily removed, demoted, or reappointed.[65]

2. *Investigation.* The executive also has the ability to conduct investigations of administrative activities. These investigations may be initiated by legislative actions, as when the results of a question in Parliament prove sufficiently embarrassing to provoke an executive response. Investigations are commonly done internally, and in fact many executive departments have their own divisions associated with continuous inspection and review. The military is perhaps most notable in this regard, with institutions such as the Inspector General serving as an internal check on the administration and efficiency of the services. Likewise, the use of inspectorates is a quite common feature of the administrative system of France and of administrative systems derivative from the French tradition.[66] While their work is not entirely investigative, it certainly does involve some snooping into proper administration of the laws, especially financial laws. Finally, many political executives, meaning here mainly individuals at the ministerial or Cabinet level, may initiate their own investigations of problems and procedures simply because they are concerned about the functioning of their department. However, just as was true for agencies, there are strong incentives for a "spending minister" to keep any irregularities in administration very quiet indeed.

Investigations of administration may also be initiated by higher executives—such as presidents and prime ministers—and will then frequently involve very broad perspectives on administration. In the American context, the Brownlow Commission and the two Hoover Commissions were examples of executive initiatives directed at thorough reviews of the structures and procedures of administration.[67] In the United Kingdom, commissions such as Fulton and Plowden have also involved extensive investigations into the basic structures and procedures of administration, with advocacy of sweeping reforms.[68] Other executive initiatives in investigating the work of public administration may be less sweeping and tend to be initiated by scandal or crisis. Even in societies with long histories of respect for the bureaucracy and of good administration, major scandals frequently generate large-scale investigations of adminstration.[69]

3. *Reorganization.* One important power granted to executives is the power to reorganize government. This power is not totally execu-

tive, with legislatures having at times equal or coordinate powers, but the executive is frequently able to use the power to good effect. While the legislature may change the shape of the organization chart and then go away to see what happens, the executive gets the opportunity to work with the new structure created. So, an executive such as Franklin Roosevelt was able to effect extensive reorganizations and use those reorganizations for his own purposes in office.[70] At other times, the results of reorganization may not be those anticipated, as with the numerous reorganizations of the British government in the 1960s and '70s.[71] However, the executive still gets the opportunity to try and make them work.

Reorganization can be used to place a mortmain on the activities of future executives and can therefore serve as a check on administration for some time in the future. Reorganizations—if that is not too weak a word—such as nationalization of industry make it difficult for any future executives to reverse the economic policies of one particular administration. It is simply too difficult to nationalize and reprivatize industry after every election, so once done, nationalization tends to persist. Likewise, when activities of government are "hived off" and depoliticized, it becomes difficult for subsequent executives to alter their structure, or in many cases incumbents of positions, without the appearance of being excessively partisan in handling policy.[72] Thus, "hiving off" may actually be "blanketing in."

Reorganization may also be important for establishing executive control. Many subnational governments, and some national governments, have gone to great lengths to depoliticize, hive-off, and judicialize important political decisions. The existence of numerous appointive commissions, boards, institutes, etc., many of which are self-perpetuating or have sufficient long tenures of office to prevent a political executive from having much real control over their composition, severely dilutes the ability of an executive to carry out control. He becomes, much as Neustadt's President, a bargainer but not a commander.[73] The justifications for the existence of independent bodies is well known, but the latent consequences must also be considered. As executives have come to be blamed, if not praised, for virtually everything that occurs within their governments, they want to be able to control what actually does happen and consequently would want to bring as many functions as possible under their purview. This does not ensure their success in exercising control, but it does given them a structural base with which to try. Even when agencies are under the control of the executive, reorganization can be used to attempt to make them conform more with the program of the executive, as the moving of the functions of the Office of Economic Opportunity under more conventional agencies can illustrate.[74] Again, there is no guarantee of success, but only of the opportunity.

4. *Fiscal Powers.* Finally, the executive may seek to control administration through fiscal powers. In most political systems the budget is an executive function and an executive document. Legislatures may certainly be involved in the final determination, but in a parliamentary system this is frequently little more than a rubber stamp. Thus the executive has the opportunity to reward friends and punish enemies in a tangible fashion. On the other hand, the actual impact of many fiscal powers of the executive are often limited.

First, the fiscal powers are not often sensitive or flexible. It is difficult to punish one administrator, or at times even one agency, through the fiscal powers.[75] This might involve reduction or elimination of appropriations of a larger administrative unit, which may be exactly the policy area in which the executive wanted more rather than less activity. Further, even if the powers were more sensitive, the political base of the agency may be such that the executive could not realistically afford to cut appropriations.

An executive is also limited in his ability to control many of the actors in the budgetary process. A prime minister in Britain, for example, may find it somewhat difficult to control the actions of the Treasury, just as it is difficult for other executives to control the actions of economic and fiscal planners or central banks.[76] In general, ministers of finance and their counterparts have gained substantial institutional powers over the budget, so that it may be difficult or impossible for a chief executive to intervene in the process personally, especially when this is seen to be politically motivated.[77] Further, the expertise of financial ministries may make such political imposition unwise. The chief executive may certainly have political influence over the actions of the finance minister, but frequently that cannot be translated into control of the budget, so the ability of a chief executive to use the fiscal powers will depend upon his ability to command the loyalty and obedience of the financial officer.

5. *Summary.* The powers of the executive in dealing with the bureaucracy, despite the formal positions in the organizational chart of government, are somewhat constrained. Just as with internal discipline within administration, many tactics that would be useful in enforcing accountability would involve some political risk to the execu-

tive. Further, many reforms in the nineteenth and twentieth centuries have removed many of the options available to executives in controlling their organizations. Thus, the executive is left with a number of powers, but these are blunted by difficulty in distinguishing between whole agencies, individual administrators, and even effects on clients. The executive remains in a strong position to negotiate with the bureaucracy for compliance on policy and on procedure but is rarely in a position to command their obedience.

THE JUDICIARY. The final set of institutional checks on the accountability of the civil service is the legal system. Virtually all political systems provide a means of citizens' challenging the actions of administrators and at times the policy choices made by government through administration. There are, however, a number of important variations in these judicial powers, which become important for an understanding of judicial control of administration.

The first major difference among Western and Western-derivative systems of law is between those systems having a separate system of administrative courts and those relying on the regular courts. This difference is not entirely clear-cut, however. Even systems of law using the regular courts for administrative matters (such as the United States, the United Kingdom, and many former British colonies) have large numbers of administrative hearings conducted in separate administrative tribunals within the administration itself.[78] These, in volume terms at least, greatly surpass the number of cases in the regular courts. Further, these systems tend to have separate bodies of administrative law, dealing with such matters as proper administrative procedure, the rights and duties of administrators, and the like.

Finally, even in countries using the regular courts, there may be some special courts that handle purely administrative matters, especially taxation. These three caveats aside, there is a difference between countries such as the United Kingdom, Denmark, and Norway, which use regular courts, and France, Germany, and Sweden (among others), which use administrative courts to handle administrative matters. To reach the regular courts, a case must generally have some importance as a matter of general law—in the United States it may frequently involve a constitutional question or denial of guaranteed rights such as due process or equal protection. This simply makes it more difficult to bring cases than in systems that are more used to dealing with strictly administrative malfeasance.

The general format of administrative courts is illustrated by the French mode, with a series of administrative courts roughly paralleling the organization of the regular courts. These end in the *section de contineaux* of the Conseil d'État.[79] The individuals serving as judges in these courts are generally themselves former administrators or at least trained as administrators in the ENA. As such, they bring special knowledge to their roles as adjudicators. It also raises the problem of their potentially being partial to the side of the administrator in a conflict. These courts have the right to both quash administrative actions and provide redress for individuals harmed by administrative actions—this redress may at times be recovered from the offending administrator. They can also provide punishment for the offending civil servant, even to the point of having him dismissed from service.

While the legal protections available in administrative law are certainly important, they too present a number of significant difficulties for the average citizen seeking to receive relief from what he considers an improper administrative act. The proceedings are legal, even in systems having separate administrative courts, and therefore involve specialized knowledge of procedure and form, which only a lawyer can provide. Thus the expense of acquiring a lawyer—even if compensated later as it is in some systems if the citizen wins the case—can present an impediment to most citizens. Likewise, the need to have a justifiable complaint against the administrator, as opposed to simply a complaint about rudeness or delay that did not produce any real economic or personal harm, limits this as a device for control of mundane but still irritating bits of maladministration.

Finally, administrative law operates as a check after the fact. It can generally only redress harms or quash actions; only rarely can it command the administration to perform actions. As such, it remains a negative check on bureaucracy. Thus, despite the general importance of the existence of administrative law as a control on administration, the check is limited by the complexity of most procedures, the slowness of the proceedings (the Conseil d'État currently has a backlog of several years), and the negative nature of the remedies available.

Normative Restraints

The final means of enforcing administrative accountability—that advocated by Friedrich—is normative control.[80] By this we mean the development of mechanisms within the bureaucracy and within individual bureaucrats that can serve as a guide to administration "in the public interest." This is certainly the cheapest form of control we might obtain, and in the end the most efficient in that it can *prevent* grievances rather than merely correcting them ex post facto. Even if all the institutional mechanisms for control outlined were more effective than we tend to think they are, the lack of commitment to public service—or more properly an active commitment to private service—could prevent them from working just through the sheer magnitude of the problem. And if such a commitment to the public service is generally held—as indeed we believe it is—the need to employ institutional mechanisms would be rather slight, and any of them could do the job. The current state of administrative practice would seem to approximate more closely the latter situation than the former one of rampant bureaucratic malfeasance, even given the number of complaints that do arise against bureaucracy. If we look at the volume of complaints relative to the number of decisions and actions taken, it seems that most civil service systems do, on the average, a decent job. We still need institutional mechanisms for the deviant cases, but these fortunately remain the unusual rather than the typical.

It should be pointed out that all administrative systems need not have—nor do they have—the same values concerning the accountability of public officials. Ilchman speaks of the need for role congruence between the expectations of the population and the behavior of administrators.[81] The ideas of universalism and equality that are prized so highly in Western societies—and that form the basis of many complaints against bureaucracy—would find few supporters in non-Western countries. In fact, an administrator seeking to employ such values in decision making would encounter some of the same difficulties as an administrator in Western countries attempting to make decisions primarily on the basis of family or clan membership. In other words, the problems of accountability vary, just as do the cultures of administration, with the basic consideration being that administrators do what is expected of them by the citizens.

Other than singing songs of praise to good administrative values, what can be done to promote accountability through normative constraints? In the short run probably very little. As noted, most political systems have a rather well established conception of their bureaucracy, and in most systems this conception is not generally positive.[82] It is perhaps becoming less favorable due to increases in the size and cost of the public bureaucracy. Thus the projection of good administrative values cannot come from the larger society, so it must be generated internally. This is relatively easy to do among the elite branches of the civil service, which have strong *esprit de corps*, a feeling of responsibility for the guidance of society, and already favored positions in society.[83] It is considerably more difficult among the run-of-the-mill public employees, who have little to distinguish themselves from private employees upon whom great demands of public service and loyalty are not made. Again, we do not think that those who opt for public service are any better or worse than those who opt for private employment; the major difference is the demands and expectations of the job. If an employee of a private firm does not give the customer satisfaction, there is recourse to future consumer behavior. If a public employee fails to provide satisfaction, it may literally become a federal case.

The vast improvements in public salaries and benefits, condemned on many accounts, may also serve a useful function in terms of internalized controls in bureaucracy. The higher salary levels make the public service a safe and rewarding place of employment, but they also provide some tangible reward for the demands of the office. Higher salaries may also recruit more people of great talent to the public service, people who were deterred by the relatively low compensation previously.

The causal factor in some of the increases in public salaries— unions of public employees—may also play a valuable role in raising morale and standards in the public service. Unions can make the job of the civil servant more of a profession, just as higher salaries attract more qualified people. This is especially important in societies such as the United States or Australia where the civil service has not been highly regarded and has not enjoyed the high status it commands in Western Europe.[84] One possible side effect, however, is to make the public service too much of a profession, and further isolate it from the society at large.

Normative control, then, is the ultimate control on bureaucracy. It is cheap, reliable, and operates before the grievance rather than simply providing compensation afterward. Most societies are indeed fortunate that they have such high levels of this form of control already in operation so that the institutional mechanisms painfully outlined above have to be employed relatively infrequently.

THE LIMITS OF CONTROL

We have to this point been discussing the average, garden-variety problems of administrative accountability and control. There are, however, a number of more specialized problems and considerations that also deserve attention. In these cases, public control and accountability reach their limits and are often exceeded. Nevertheless, these problems are not that unusual any longer and require some extensive thought to be brought into line with our normal thinking about responsible bureaucracy.

The Professions

One of the most commonly mentioned problems straining administrative control is the existence of professional employees within the public bureaucracy. Almost by definition, a professional has the type of internalized value structure concerning relationships with clients that we were advocating for civil servants earlier. The problem is that these professional values often conflict with the values of the agency for which they work. One common case is the scientist who works for a government research office. One norm of the scientific profession is the free flow of information and ideas.[85] Such free flow of ideas, when working for the government on secret materials, just would not be tolerated. In the same manner, a physician working for a public agency continues to believe in his or her primary responsibility to the patient, which may come into conflict with recordkeeping demands or requirements of standard treatment in the public organization. The list of similar conflicts could be extended, but the basic point is made. Professionals may have values that conflict fundamentally with the requirements of their public jobs. The public sector needs to employ professionals, so some accommodation of values must be made, perhaps on both sides. This is, however, one important instance in which the normal procedures of control and accountability may simply not be applicable.

Nationalized Industries

When government goes into business it also presents new problems of control and accountability.[86] In some ways public corporations appear to present fewer problems of control. After all, they have a statement of profit or loss (usually the latter) so that one can see at a glance just how well they are managed. In practice it is really not as easy as all that. In the first place, making a profit is but one goal, and perhaps not a very important goal, for a public corporation. If the function was profitable, and profit was all we cared about, the industry might just as well have been left private. In the case of public transportation, the goals of providing cheap transportation, rapid transportation, reducing the numbers of automobiles on the roads, spreading out peak hours of traffic, redevelopment of declining areas, etc., may all conflict with the goal of making a profit. Thus, evaluation of the management of a public corporation may involve considerably more than simply looking at the balance sheet at the end of the year.

Second, there is almost invariably a difficulty in controlling public corporations that have been "hived off" from direct political control.[87] The most common structural arrangement for such corporations is to have an independent or semiindependent board of management. They are thus removed from direct lines of executive authority. While these lines of authority are no panacea for the problems of control, they at least provide a connection with government. A nationalized industry or public corporation is generally supposed to be independent of such control, presumably so that it can make economic rather than political judgments about its progress. This leaves the corporation in the position of obviously being a political entity but with only limited connection with political leadership and guidance. It is perhaps as awkward a position for the managers as it is for the public.

Unions

In addition to the positive benefits that unions of public employees can have for the public service, we must also look at some problems of control that they engender. As well as the protection afforded public employees by civil-service regulations, many are now provided additional protection through unions. Likewise, many industrial employees who were minimally protected by civil-service procedures are now more fully protected by unions. While these developments are perfectly understandable in modern societies, they make the job of the public manager much more difficult. There is the procedural problem of conforming to both civil service and union regulations on hiring, firing, and transferring employees. It is simply that much more difficult to manipulate staff the way the manager might like. In addition, employees must now be dealt with as a bloc, with threats of strikes even against vital services such as police and fire and sanitation. Unlike strikes in most industrial firms, there is no way of doing without those services for more than a short period of time, so public managers and political officials are forced to provide a settlement acceptable to the unions. Although these jobs may be, as in the case of sanitation workers, of very low status, their importance to the community may be such that they will be in a comparable bargaining position to physicians in the public service. So not only does the political system lose control over its employees, it also loses control over its own budget.

Political Structure

The political structure of the country can also present significant difficulties in controlling the administration of public policy. Federalism is perhaps the most notable structure inhibiting control. The arrangements of federalism need not be as extreme as those of West Germany, which has most programs of the control government administered by the constituent *Länder,* but even the less extreme versions of the structure require some administration of programs by administrators not directly responsible to the policy makers.[88] For example, in the United States most federal social-welfare law is executed by employees of state and local governments, as is most federal education law. This means simply that the control of the federal government is reduced and is left primarily with the rather blunt power of withdrawing federal money from the program.

A variant of structure that also inhibits control of administration is the separation of policy-making and executing agencies, as in Sweden.[89] The ministries are held responsible for the formulation of policy, while the boards are held responsible for the execution of those policies. Again, there is a separation that can only make it more difficult to control what actually happens with a policy rather than simply what the policy is on paper.

Culture

We have already outlined variations in culture affecting the success or failure of bureaucratic means of policy execution.[90] We should perhaps remember those variations in the light of what we have been talking about in terms of control of administration. The basic point is that some political systems and cultures lack the normative commitment to public morality and proper administration we have just said was so important for control of administration. Many, in fact, regard the Western model of bureaucracy as alien and almost immoral. The possession of a bureaucrat's job is not an evidence of public trust or responsibility, but rather an opportunity for the individual and the family. It is the individual who fails to provide handsomely for the family, rather than the individual who does, who will be regarded as immoral in such cultural settings. While Western (or nontraditional) values have certainly spread, they still are not universal, so we must be cognizant when speaking of administrative control of the very different cultural settings in which the problem may occur.

Nonadministration

Finally, nonadministration, just like nonpolicy, is difficult to control. It is much more difficult to control something that does not happen than something that is done improperly. In other words, it is considerably harder to get the bureaucracy to do something than it is to stop it from doing something it shouldn't be doing. This is an obvious restatement of the two dimensions of activity with which we began this chapter. There are few positive checks to force individuals or agencies to make decisions, while there are a number of procedures for stopping them, or for obtaining compensation for an improper decision. Even the political executive, who is presumed to be able to command action, may not be able to command in practice, but may only bargain with the myriad of actors all of whom are somewhat involved in executing policy. Even a President vitally concerned about the presence of missiles in Cuba or urban problems in Oakland, or a minister of education concerned about educational reform, cannot command action.[91] The bureaucracy apparently has its own ways of doing things, which means that they will not necessarily be done when executives of government want them done. If presidents and prime ministers have these problems, what about us poor average blokes? The answer is that we have to rely first on the general acceptance of the ideas of "good government" by most of the people whom we employ in the public service, and second, we have to be willing to go to the trouble of using the available political methods when those internal norms do not work as we think they should.

SUMMARY AND CONCLUSIONS

The basic conclusions of this chapter are actually summed up in the preceding sentence. The control of administration, even in the currently swollen state of government and bureaucracy, seems to

depend on two rather personal characteristics of people. The first is
the internalized sense of their proper role on the part of civil servants. This sense of civic responsibility, duty, or even honor may vary
across cultures, even within the narrow range of Western governments, but the basic ideas of responsiveness to demands, responsibility to political leaders, and accountability for actions are found in
virtually all systems. They may not always be put into effect, but the
values are generally understood. We have said before that most civil
servants appear to accept these values and generally try to put them
into operation. If it were not for this widespread acceptance of those
values, all the institutional mechanisms of control we have outlined
would be buried in the sheer volume of maladministration.

The second component of a properly functioning system of administrative accountability and control is the population served by the
civil service. In practice, most methods of accountability depend
upon individual or group actions to press demands before the mechanisms can go into operation. Thus, responsibility and accountability
implies a pair of actors—there must be someone to be responsible to.
Even institutional mechanisms within political institutions such as
legislatures would be ineffective if politicians found that the population did not care. There would be little or no incentive to expend
energy and time. In short, there is simply no means of ensuring
proper administration for an apathetic, cynical population.

If we return to the several dimensions of accountability and control
with which we began this discussion, we can see that the two are
quite well covered by the mechanisms outlined. First, there are a
number of checks on bureaucratic institutions but relatively fewer
checks on individuals, in large part due to their insulation by the organization. It is sometimes difficult for political institutions to deal
with individuals without dealing with an entire organization. Thus,
in order to keep the wheels of government turning, many personal
actions may yet go unpunished. Likewise, there are any number of
procedures for dealing with sins of commission but relatively few for
dealing with sins of ommission, or simply excessive rigidity. In many
cases the "nonadministrators" are technically correct in terms of the
rule book but manage to undermine the intent of programs by their
adherence to the letter of the law.

It is clear from earlier chapters that the role of public bureaucracy
in making public policy is on the increase. Therefore, the questions of
accountability and control become even more crucial as bureaucracy
grows in power. Trends in government and society would appear to

make control both easier and more difficult for future generations of citizens and politicians. On the one hand, the spread of mass education and the media makes it easier for the population to be informed about the actions of bureaucracy. A number of legal changes in the requirements for publicity in a number of countries is making information more widely available. Mass education may also mean that the public bureaucracy will be drawn from a broader spectrum of the population and therefore have both greater empathy with the problems of citizens and a better understanding of the public's conception of bureaucracy. Finally, recent events in a number of countries—the United States, Japan, West Germany, and the Netherlands are examples—have led their populations to be concerned about what happens in government and to be more willing to question the activities of public officials. If such healthy skepticism does not develop into cynicism and a rejection of the political system as immoral and essentially unjust, then it can help to promote effective popular control over bureaucratic behavior.

At the same time, there are several developments promoting greater insulation from control for the bureaucracy. In addition to the increasing size of bureaucracy and the complexity of the tasks they undertake, the increasing affluence of most Western populations has been associated with an increasing demand for publicly provided goods. There may therefore be a feeling that goods and services produced through the political process may be superior to those privately provided, and therefore less questioning of the actual costs and benefits of public programs. In addition, a number of personnel practices in the public service may tend to insulate the bureaucracy further. In particular, the growth of public-employee unions may limit the ability of managers to control personnel. Finally, there appears to be an increasing tendency to hive-off and depoliticize public services. This is in part a reaction to the popular revulsion over politics mentioned above, but it may also be due to the increasing involvement in services with some market characteristics. In either case, depoliticization is in most cases simply a formula for bureaucratic power.

In sum, the pressures for greater accountability seem stronger than those for greater insulation. We may expect greater public concern and involvement in public affairs. How effective this will be will ultimately depend upon the willingness of the population to persist in pressing their demands and using the mechanisms available to them. There is the danger that short-run failures may produce enduring cynicism and a long-term "tuning out" of the population from the affairs of government. The numerous institutional mechanisms discussed here are available to aid in the search for responsibility, but in the long run responsibility in government can come only from the interplay of responsible officials and citizens.

NOTES

1. See Carl J. Friedrich, "Public Policy and the Nature of Administrative Responsibility," in *Public Policy*, ed. Friedrich and Mason (Cambridge, Mass.: Harvard University Press, 1940); Herbert Finer, "Administrative Responsibility in Democratic Government," *Public Administration Review* 1 (1941): 335–50.
2. A useful summary for the United States is W. W. Boyer, *Bureaucracy on Trial* (Indianapolis: Bobbs-Merrill, 1967).
3. Some indication of the volume is given in R. G. S. Brown, *The Management of Welfare* (London: Fontana, 1975), pp. 104–6. Also, Committee on Tribunals (Franks Committee), *Report, Cmnd. 218* (London: HMSO, 1957). Also, in the United States, the Social Security Administration now handles over 4 millon cases each year.
4. Even on appeal, the facts found in the administrative hearing are generally the facts of the case (in the U.S.), with decisions being overturned on points of law.
5. Anthony Downs, *Inside Bureaucracy* (Boston: Little, Brown, 1966), pp. 132–33.
6. The latter case is one in which, although the welfare officers are operating within their legal authority, their actions so violate many people's conceptions of the role of the bureaucracy that they have brought the place of the welfare system into question.
7. See chapters 1 and 5.
8. Dwight Waldo, *The Administrative State* (New York: Knopf, 1948). United States Civil Service Commission, *History of the Federal Civil Service* (Washington, D.C.: Government Printing Office, 1941).
9. One important exception is West Germany, where senior civil servants are indeed identified politically and where, as the "purges" of 1969 showed, changes in governments may also involve changes in civil servants. See N. Lehmann and Renate Mayntz, *Personal im öffentlichen Dienst* (Baden-Baden: Nomas Verlag, 1973), chap. 11.
10. For reviews, see Henry Parris, *Constitutional Bureaucracy* (London: Allen & Unwin, 1968); Ari Hoogenboom, *Outlawing the Spoils* (Urbana, Ill.: University of Illinois Press, 1968).
11. We gave some indication of the structure of incentives in chapter 4, with the basic finding that few people are attracted into the public service because of the ability to do things to or for society, but rather more often are attracted by social conditions or monetary rewards.
12. Friedrich, "Public Policy."
13. See Nils Herlitz, "Publicity of Documents in Sweden," *Public Law* 17 (1958): 54–59.
14. Ibid.

15. Roger Choate, "The Public's Right to Know," *Current Sweden,* no. 93 (Stockholm: Swedish Institute, 1975), p. 4.
16. Ibid.
17. See *Departmental Committee of Section 2 of the Official Secrets Act of 1911, Cmnd. 5104* (London: HMSO, 1972). Jonathan Aiken, *Officially Secret* (London: Routledge & Kegan Paul, 1971).
18. This "facelessness" and anonymity is also quite closely related to the important constitutional principle of ministerial—as opposed to civil service—responsibility for *all* public acts of the ministry.
19. Downs, *Inside Bureaucracy,* pp. 88, 92–97.
20. Germany has the most extensive arrangements of this sort through the disciplinary courts. See K. E. von Turegg, *Lehrbuch des Verwaltungsrecht* (4th ed.; Berlin: De Gruyter, 1962), pp. 339 ff.
21. One interesting account is Richard N. Billings and John Grierga, *Power to the Public Worker* (New York: Luce, 1974); Danik H. Kruger and Charles T. Schmidt, eds., *Collective Bargaining in the Public Sector* (New York: Praeger, 1969).
22. See chapters 6 and 7.
23. This can occur even for prestigious and usually successful agencies such as defense or foreign intelligence when scandals of mismanagement are disclosed.
24. Peter M. Blau, *The Dynamics of Bureaucracy* (2nd ed.; Chicago: University of Chicago Press, 1963), pp. 137–93.
25. See, for example, William M. Evan, "The Inspector General in the U.S. Army," in *The Ombudsman,* ed. D. C. Rowat (London: Allen & Unwin, 1965), pp. 147–52.
26. See chapter 6.
27. Mark V. Nadel, *The Politics of Consumer Protection* (Indianapolis: Bobbs-Merrill, 1972).
28. See Ruth Link, "Consumers Take the Initiative," *Current Sweden,* no. 78 (June 1975). Richard C. Leone, "Public Interest Advocacy and the Regulatory Process," *Annals of the American Academy of Political and Social Science* 400 (March 1972): 46–58.
29. This concept has been subject to much unfavorable analysis, especially in Daniel Patrick Moynihan's *Maximum Feasible Misunderstanding* (New York: Free Press, 1969).
30. James L. Sundquist, "Coordinating the War on Poverty," *Annals of the American Academy of Political and Social Sciences* 385 (1969): 46–48.
31. See a series of articles in the *Times* (London), 9–13 February 1976. Also, "Shaky Start to Participation," *The Economist* 258 (13 March 1976): 128. Norman Dennis, *Public Participation and Planner's Blight* (London: Faber & Faber, 1973).
32. W. Tordoff, "Regional Administration in Tanzania," *Journal of Modern African Studies* 3 (1965): 63–89. The *panchayati raj* system in India performs much the same function.
33. See Michael Lipsky and Margaret Levi, "Community of Organizations as a Political Resource," *Urban Affairs Annual* 6 (1972): 177–95.
34. See chapter 7.
35. A discussion of the problem is provided by Geoffrey Marshall, "The Techniques of Maladministration," *Political Studies* 23 (1975): 305–18.
36. For a discussion of the relative budgetary powers of a number of parliamentary regimes, see David Coombes et al., *The Power of the Purse* (London: Allen & Unwin, 1976).

37. An important counter trend is the development of the Congressional Budget Office in the United States as an independent source of economic and budgetary analysis. This office is especially significant when the Presidency and Congress are controlled by different political parties. See Allen Schick, "The Battle of the Budget," in Harvey C. Mansfield, Sr., *Congress Against the President* (New York: Praeger, 1975), pp. 64–69.

38. The best general source, although now somewhat dated, is Joseph Harris, *Congressional Control of Administration* (Washington, D.C.: Brookings Institution, 1964).

39. Winfried Steffani, "Amerikanischer Kongress und deutscher Bundestag— ein Vergleich," in *Parlamentarismus*, ed. Kurt Kluxen (Köln: Kiepenheim & Witsch, 1967), pp. 230–46.

40. Kenneth Labick and Bernard Krischer, "Lockeed Shokhuwaves," *Newsweek*, 15 March 1976, pp. 20–21.

41. There has been however, a committee formed since entry into the European Economic Community to scrutinize the directives.

42. See chapter 6.

43. Two general works on this office are Walter Gellhorn, *Ombudsmen and Others* (Cambridge, Mass.: Harvard University Press, 1967); Donald C. Rowat, ed., *The Ombudsman: Citizen's Defender* (London: Allen & Unwin, 1965).

44. The Finnish and New Zealand ombudsman is clearly given this power, while the Danish and Swedish have gained the power largely through accretion and custom. See, for example, I. M. Pedersen, "The Danish Parliamentary Commissioner in Action," *Public Law* 115 (1959): 116–20; G. Langrod, "Le controle parlementaire de l'administration dans le pays nordiques: le rôle de Ombudsman en Suede, en Finlande et au Danemark," *Revue administrative* 12 (1959): 664–73.

45. Gellhorn, *Ombudsmen*.

46. Stanley V. Anderson, *Ombudsman Papers* (Berkeley: Institute of Government Studies, 1969).

47. Frank Stacey, *The British Ombudsman* (Oxford: Clarendon Press, 1971), pp. 307–10.

48. Paavo Kastavi, "Finland's Guardians of the Law," in Rowat, *Ombudsman*, pp. 58–74.

49. West Germany has only an ombudsman for military affairs, while Sweden and Norway have a separate military ombudsman. The Danish and Finnish ombudsmen receive complaints on military affairs. The New Zealand ombudsman and the procurators in the communist countries generally do not handle military affairs. The ombudsmen in virtually all these systems have the right to receive complaints from prisoners, although few are received except in the Scandinavian countries. The Soviet procurator also is involved in prison inspection.

50. This has been especially important in dealing with prisoners and military conscripts, who tend to be generally wary of governmental authority figures.

51. Gellhorn, *Ombudsmen*, pp. 45–46, 65–66, 215–17.

52. Ibid., pp. 420–39.

53. See Donald R. Matthews, *U.S. Senators and Their World* (Chapel Hill, N.C.: University of North Carolina Press, 1960), p. 225. Charles L. Clapp, *The Congressman: His Work as He Sees It* (Washington, D.C.: Public Affairs Press, 1963), pp. 75–84.

54. Basil Chubb, "Going Around Persecuting Civil Servants: The Role of the Irish Parliament Representative," *Political Studies* 11 (1963): 272–86.

55. E. L. Normanton, *The Accountability and Audit of Governments* (Manchester: Manchester University Press, 1966); "Public Accountability and Audit: A Reconnaissance," in B. L. R. Smith and D. C. Hague, *The Dilemma of Accountability in Modern Government* (London: Allen & Unwin, 1971), pp. 311–46.

56. Harris, *Congressional Control,* pp. 135–52.

57. Normanton, *Accountability.*

58. This problem is particularly acute in Italy, where the budget merely limits the amount to be spent rather than funds a program. See articles by Valerio Onida, Vittorio Mortara, and Sabiro Cassese in Coombes, *Power of Purse.*

59. This is most notable in Germany under the Economic Stability Law of 1967. Also, the ability of the French government to put a budget into effect without approval of parliament severely reduces the "power of the purse" in that system.

60. See George A. Steiner, "Problems of Implementing Program Budgeting," in *Program Budgeting,* ed. David Novick(New York: Holt, Rinehart & Winston, 1969), pp. 328–47.

61. Steffani, "Amerikanischer Kongress."

62. Thomas E. Cronin, *The State of the Presidency* (Boston: Little, Brown, 1975), chaps. 5, 6, 7.

63. See Ezra Suleiman, *Politics, Power and Bureaucracy in France* (Princeton: Princeton University Press, 1974), pp. 137–54. Leo Monlin, "The Politicization of Administration in Belgium," in *The Mandarins of Western Europe,* ed. M. Dogan (New York: John Wiley, 1975), pp. 163–86. Lehmann, and Mayntz, *Personal im öffentlichen Dienst.*

64. F. Tannenbaum, "Política y administración publica en Latinoamericano," *Foro Internacional* 4 (1963): 243–59.

65. Jerry F. Hough, *The Soviet Prefects: The Local Party Organs in Industrial Decision-Making* (Cambridge, Mass.: Harvard University Press, 1969), pp. 149–77.

66. See, for example, Pierre Lalumiere, *L'Inspection des finances* (Paris: PUF, 1959). Also, the issues of *La Revue des deux mondes* in 1958 devoted to the *grands corps.*

67. For a discussion of the Brownlow Report and the first Hoover Commission, see Charles S. Hyneman, *Bureaucracy in a Democracy* (New York: Harper, 1950).

68. The Committee on the Civil Service (Fulton Committee), *Report, Cmnd. 3638* (London: HMSO, 1968). Committee on the Control of Public Expenditure (Plowden Committee), *Report, Cmnd 1432* (London: HMSO, 1961). John Garrett, *The Management of Government* (Harmondsworth, Middlesex: Penguin, 1972).

69. As for example in Norway following the Kings Bay coal disaster. See John Higley, Karl Erich Brofuss, and Knut Grohalt, "The Top Civil Servants and the National Budget in Norway," in Dogan, *Mandarins,* pp. 252–54.

70. See Arthur M. Schlesinger, Jr., *The Coming of the New Deal* (Boston: Houghton Mifflin, 1959), pp. 521–27.

71. See, for example, *The Reorganization of Central Government, Cmnd. 4506* (London: HMSO, 1970).

72. A summary of these problems and the reactions of the "reform movement" in the U.S. is given in York Willbern, "Administration in State Government," *The Forty-Eight States: Their Tasks as Policy Makers and Administrators* (New York: American Assembly, 1955), chap. 5.

73. Richard Neustadt, *Presidential Power* (New York: John Wiley, 1960).

74. "Who is Responsible for Caring for the Poor?" *Congressional Digest* 52 (August 1973): 195–224.
75. One recent analysis is presented by Howard S. Bloom and H. Douglas Price, "Voter Responses to Short-Run Economic Conditions: The Asymmetric Effect of Prosperity and Recession," *American Political Science Review* 69 (1975): 1240–54.
76. Perhaps the most obvious case of this conflict was between President Lyndon Johnson and William McC. Martin, chairman of the Federal Reserve Board of Governors, in 1964.
77. See, for example, Renate Mayntz and Fritz W. Scharpf, *Policy-Making in the German Federal Bureaucracy* (Amsterdam: Elsevier, 1975), pp. 42–45.
78. R. E. Wraith and P. G. Hutcheson, *Administrative Tribunals* (London: Allen & Unwin, 1973), pp. 43–70, provides a description and enumeration of tribunals in the United Kingdom.
79. F. F. Ridley and J. Blondel, *Public Administration in France* (London: Routledge & Kegan Paul, 1964), pp. 148–59.
80. Friedrich, "Public Policy."
81. Warren F. Ilchman, *Comparative Public Administration and the "Conventional Wisdom"* (Beverly Hills: Sage, 1971), pp. 35–38.
82. See chapter 3.
83. See, for example, Bernard Gournay, "Un Groupe dirigant de la Societe francaise: les grands fonctionnaires," *Revue Francaise de science politique* 14 (1964): 215–42.
84. See chapter 3. See also Howard A. Scarrow, *The Higher Public Service of Australia* (Durham, N.C.: Duke University Commonwealth Studies Centre, 1957), pp. 150–52.
85. Don K. Price, *Government and Science* (New York: Oxford University Press, 1962), pp. 95–123; Michael D. Reagan, *Science and the Federal Patron* (New York: Oxford University Press, 1969).
86. W. H. Robson, "Ministerial Control of the Nationalized Industries," *Political Quarterly* 40 (1969): 103–12, 494–96; Mario Einuadi, *Nationalization in France and Italy* (Ithaca, N.Y.: Cornell University Press, 1955).
87. Of perhaps more relevance to the readers of this volume is the "hiving off" of scientific and educational organizations such as the National Science Foundation or the University Grants Committee (UK). On attempted congressional control of the NSF see *Science* 188 (1975): 338–41.
88. In general, however, the central government is being able to extend its control over the *Länder*. See Konrad Hesse, *Der Unitarische Bundesstaat* (Karlsruhe: Miller, 1962).
89. Pierre Vinde and Tunnar Petri, *Hur Sveriges Styres* (Stockholm: Prisma, 1975), pp. 84–89.
90. See chapter 3.
91. See Graham Allison, "Conceptual Models and the Cuban Missile Crisis," *American Political Science Review* 63 (September 1969): 701–6; Jeffrey Pressman and Aaron Wildavsky, *Implementation* (Berkeley: University of California Press, 1974).

INDEX